COLLEGE
WRITING

COLLEGE WRITING

A Personal Approach to Academic Writing

Second Edition

Toby Fulwiler

Boynton/Cook
HEINEMANN
Portsmouth, NH

Boynton/Cook Publishers, Inc.
A subsidiary of Reed Elsevier Inc.
361 Hanover Street
Portsmouth, NH 03801-3912
Offices and agents throughout the world

© 1997 by Toby Fulwiler

The author and publisher thank those who generously gave permission to reprint borrowed material:

"Buffalo Bill's", copyright 1923, 1951, © 1991 by the Trustees for the E. E. Cummings Trust. Copyright © 1976 by George James Firmage, from COMPLETE POEMS: 1904-1962 by E. E. Cummings, Edited by George J. Firmage. Reprinted by permission of Liveright Publishing Corporation.

Library of Congress Cataloging-in-Publication Data

Fulwiler, Toby, 1942—
    College writing : a personal approach to academic writing / Toby
Fulwiler.—2nd ed.
        p.   cm.
    Includes index.
    ISBN 0-86709-430-3 (acid-free paper)
    1. English language—Rhetoric. 2. Academic writing—Problems.
exercises, etc. I. Title.
PE1408.F8   1997
808'.042—dc21
                                                97-27444
                                                CIP

Acquisitions Editor: Peter R. Stillman
Production Editor: Renée M. Nicholls
Cover Designer: Jenny Jensen Greenleaf
Manufacturing Coordinator: Louise Richardson

Printed in the United States of America on acid-free paper
99 98   DA   3 4 5 6

Contents

Section I

THE WRITER

Chapter One

A WRITER'S CHOICES

The reason, I think, I wait until the night before the paper is due, is that then I don't have any choice and the problem goes away. I mean, I stop thinking about all the choices I could make, about where to start and what to say, and I just start writing. Sometimes it works, sometimes it doesn't.

—Sarah

The number of choices writers must make in composing even short papers is sometimes daunting—no wonder Sarah wants to write and not choose. But in truth, I think she's fooling herself: All writing, whether started early or late, teacher-assigned or self-assigned, involves making choices—an infinite number of choices—about topics, approaches, stances, claims, evidence, order, words, sentences, paragraphs, tone, voice, style, titles, beginnings, middles, endings, what to include, what to omit, and the list goes on.

There are, however, some things you can do to simplify this choice-making process and make it less daunting, more approachable. Whenever you sit down to write, ask yourself three basic questions: Why am I writing? Under what conditions and constraints? To whom? In other words, your purpose, situation, and audience determine the tone, style, and form of your writing.

If you're ever stuck for how to approach a writing assignment, or if you're blocked about what next to do, stop and reconsider which condition seems to be the sticking point:

Is your purpose for doing the writing clear? Can you explain it in a sentence or two?

What are the circumstances in which this writing is taking place? Can you identify the social or cultural milieu in which the writing takes place?

Do you know and understand your audience? Can you articulate what your audience wants or expects?

The remainder of this chapter will examine each of these questions in more detail.

PURPOSE

Your explicit or stated reason for writing is your purpose: Why are you writing in the first place? What do you hope your words will accomplish? In college, the general purpose is usually specified by the assignment: to explain, report, analyze, argue, interpret, reflect, and so on. Most papers will include secondary purposes as well, for example, an effective argument paper may also need explaining, defining, describing, and narrating to help advance the argument. If you know *why* you are writing your writing is bound to be clearer than if you don't. This doesn't mean you need to know exactly what your paper will say, how it will be shaped, or how it will conclude, but it does mean that when you sit down to write it helps to know why you are doing so.

The rhetorical purpose of most writing is persuasive: you want to make your reader believe that what you say is true. However, different kinds of writing convey truth in different ways. If your purpose is to explain, report, define, or describe, then your language is most effective when it is clear, direct, unbiased, and neutral in tone. However, if your intention is to argue or interpret, then your language may need to be different. If you know your purpose but are not sure which form, style, or tone best suits it, study the published writing of professionals and examine how they choose language to create one or another effects.

College writing is usually done in response to specific instructor assignments—which implies that your instructor has a purpose in asking you to write. If you want your writing to be strong and effective, you need to find a valid purpose of your own for writing. In other words, you need to make it worth your while to invest a portion of your life in thinking about, researching, and writing this particular paper. So, within the limits of the assignment, select the aspect which most genuinely interests you, the aspect that will make you grow and change in directions you want to change in. For example, if you are asked to select an author to review or critique, select one you care about; if asked to research an issue, select one about which you have concerns, not necessarily the first that comes to mind. If neither author nor research issue comes to mind, do enough preliminary reading and research to allow you to choose well, or to allow your interest to kick in and let the topic choose you. Go with your interest and curiosity. Avoid selecting a topic just because it's easy, handy, or comfortable. Once you purposefully select a topic, you begin to take over and own the assignment and increase your chances of writing well about it.

As I've just implied, part of purpose includes the subject and topic. The subject is the general area that you're interested in learning more about. For example, all of these would be considered subjects: American literature, American literature in the 1920s, New York City authors, the Harlem Renaissance, Jean Toomer, *Cane.* Even though the subject *Cane* (the title of a collection of short stories by Jean Toomer) is far more specific than American literature, it's still only a subject until you decide what about *Cane* you want to explore and write about—until you decide upon your topic in relation to *Cane:* perhaps a difficulty in one particular story in the collection, a theme running through several stories, or its relationship to other Harlem Renaissance works.

The general subject of a college paper could be a concept, event, text, experiment, period, place, or person that you need to identify, define, explain, illustrate, and perhaps reference—in a logical order, conventionally and correctly (usually—see Chapter Fifteen *Writing Alternate Style* for exceptions). Many college papers ask that you treat the assigned subject as thoroughly as possible, privileging facts, citing sources, and downplaying your writer's presence.

Learn your subject well before you write about it; if you can't, learn it while you write. In either case, learn it. To my own students I say plan to become the most knowledgeable person in class on this subject; know it backward and forward. Above all else, know it well beyond common knowledge, hearsay, and cliche. If it's a concept like *postmodern,* know the definition, the explanations, the rationales, the antecedents, and the references, so you explain and use the term correctly. If it's an event such as the Crimean War, know the causes, outcomes, dates, geography, and the major players. If it's a text, know author(s), title, date of publication, genre, table of contents, themes, and perhaps the historical, cultural, social, and political contexts surrounding its publication. Then write about a specific topic within this subject area that you are now somewhat of an expert on. The following suggestions will help you think about your purpose for writing:

1. Attend closely to the *subject words* of your assignments. If limited to The Harlem Renaissance, make sure you know what that literary period is, who belonged to it, and the titles of their books.
2. Attend closely to the *direction words* of all your assignments. Be

aware that being asked to argue or interpret is different from being asked to define or explain—though, to argue or interpret well may also require some defining or explaining along the way.

3. Notice the subjects to which your mind turns when jogging, driving, biking, working out, walking, or just relaxing. Will any of your assignments let you explore one of them further?

SITUATION

The subjects of college papers don't exist in isolation. The environment, setting, or circumstance in which you write influences your approach to each writing task. The general setting that dictates college writing is educational and academic, though more particular circumstances will surround each specific assignment. For example, each assignment will be affected to some extent by the specific disciplinary expectations of a given college, course, and grade level, so that if you want to write a given paper successfully, it's your job to identify these. Are the expectations at a college of Arts and Sciences any different from those at the colleges of Business, Engineering, Agriculture, or Education? What conventions govern the writing in English courses and how are they different from those that govern sociology, art, or nursing? What assumptions can you make if enrolled in an advanced class versus an introductory class?

You already know that writing in college, like writing in secondary school, will be evaluated, which puts additional constraints on every act of writing you perform. Consequently, your writing, while displaying appropriately referenced disciplinary knowledge, must be clear, correct, typed, and completed on time. Be aware that in your physical absence, your writing speaks for you, allowing others to judge not only your *knowledge,* but other intellectual habits, such as your general level of *literacy* (how critically you read, how articulately you make an argument), your personal *discipline* (the level of precision with which the paper meets all requirements), your *smarts* (does your approach demonstrate intelligence, thoughtfulness?), and possibly your *creativity* (is your approach original, imaginative?). In other words, every piece of writing conveys tacit, between-the-lines information about the writer, as well as the explicit information the assignment calls for. (For more information on the academic community, see Chapter Five.) Therefore, as you are writing consider the following:

1. Know who you are. Be aware that your writing may reflect your gender, race, ethnic identity, political or religious affiliation, social class, educational background, and regional upbringing. Read your writing and notice where these personal biases emerge; noticing

them gives you more control, and allows you to change, delete, or strengthen them—depending upon your purpose.

2. Know where you are. Be aware of the ideas and expectations that characterize your college, discipline, department, course, instructor, and grade level. If you know this context, you can better shape your writing to meet or question it.

3. Negotiate. In each act of writing, attempt to figure out how much of you and your beliefs to present versus how many institutional constraints to consider. Know that every time you write you must mediate between the world you bring to the writing and the world in which the writing will be read.

AUDIENCE

Most of us would agree that talking is easier than writing. For one thing, most of us talk more often than we write—usually many times in the course of a single day—and so get more practice. For another, we get more help from people to whom we speak face to face than from those to whom we write. We see by their facial expressions whether or not listeners understand us, need more or less information, or are pleased with our words. Our own facial and body expressions help us communicate as well. Finally, our listening audiences tend to be more tolerant of the way we talk than our reading audiences are of the way we write: nobody sees my spelling or punctuation when I talk, and nobody calls me on the carpet when, in casual conversation, I miss an occasional noun-verb agreement or mis-use the subjunctive (whatever that is).

However, writing does certain things better than speaking. If you miswrite, you can always rewrite and catch your mistake before someone else notices it. If you need to develop a complex argument, writing affords you the time and space to do so. If you want your words to have the force of law, you can make a permanent (written) record to be reread and studied in your absence. And if you want to maintain a certain tone or coolness of demeanor, this can be accomplished more easily in writing than in face-to-face confrontations.

Perhaps the greatest problem for writers, at least on the conscious level, concerns the *audience* who will read their writing: What do they already know? What will they be looking for? What are their biases, values, and assumptions? How can I make sure they understand me as I intend for them to? College instructors are the most common audience for college writing; they make the assignments and read and evaluate the results. Instructors make especially difficult audiences because they are experts in their subject and commonly know more about it than you do. Though you may also write for other audiences such as yourself or classmates, your primary audience remains the instructor who made the assignment. The remainder of this chapter will examine the nature of the audiences for whom you most commonly write in academic settings.

Writing for Teachers

When you are a student in high school, college, or graduate school, your most common audiences are teachers who have requested written assignments and who will read and grade what you produce. But teachers are an especially tough audience for most of us.

First, teachers often make writing assignments with the specific intention to measure and grade you on the basis of what you write. Second, teachers often think it their civic duty to correct every language mistake you make, no matter how small. Third, teachers often ask you to write about subjects you have no particular interest in—or worse, to write about *their* favorite topics! Finally, your teachers usually know more about the subject of your paper than you do because they are the experts in the field, which puts you in a difficult spot: You end up writing to prove how much you know more than to share something new with them.

You can't do much about the fact that teachers will use your writing to evaluate you in one way or another—they view it as part of their job, just as they do when making assignments *for your own good* (but not necessarily interest). However, as an individual writer, you can make choices that will influence this difficult audience positively—especially if you understand that most of your instructors are fundamentally caring people.

In the best circumstances, instructors will make writing assignments that give you a good start. They do this when they make clear their expectations for each assignment, when they provide sufficient time for you to accomplish the assignment, when they give you positive and pointed feedback while you are writing, when they create a climate in which it's clear that the subject belongs to *you,* not to them, the text, or the school, and when they evaluate your papers according to criteria you both understand and agree with.

But regardless of how helpful you find your teacher, at some point you have to plan and write the paper using the best resources *you* can muster. Even before you begin to write—or as you think about the assignment through writing about it—you can make some important mental decisions that will make your actual drafting of most assignments easier:

1. Read the assignment directions carefully before you begin to write. Pay particular attention to instruction words such as *explain, define,* or *evaluate*—terms that mean something quite

different from one another. (See Chapter Eight for more information on instruction words.) Most of the time when teachers develop their assignments, they are looking to see not only that you can demonstrate what you know, think logically, and write clearly, they also want to see if you can follow directions.

2. Convince yourself that you are interested in writing this assignment. It's better, of course, if you really *are* interested in writing about *Moby Dick,* the War of 1812, or photosynthesis, but sometimes this isn't the case. If not, you've got to practice some psychology on yourself because it's difficult to write well when you are bored. Use whatever strategies usually work for you, but if those fail, try this: locate the most popular treatment of the subject you can find, perhaps in a current newsstand, the *Reader's Guide to Periodical Literature,* or the World Wide Web. Find out what has made this subject newsworthy. Tell a friend about it (Did you know that . . . ?). Write in your journal about it, and see what kind of questions you can generate. There is a good chance that this forced engagement will lead to the real thing.

3. Make the assignment your own. This can be done by any of the following methods: recasting the paper topic in your own words; reducing the size/scope of the topic to something manageable; or relating it to an issue with which you are already familiar. Modifying a writing task into something both interesting and manageable dramatically increases your chances of making the writing less superficial because you're not biting off more than you can chew and because the reader will read caring and commitment between the lines.

4. Try to teach your readers something. At the least, try to communicate with them. Seeing your task as instructional puts you in the driver's seat and gets you out of the passive mode of writing to fulfill somebody else's expectations. In truth, teachers are delighted when a student paper teaches them something they didn't already know; it breaks the boredom of reading papers that are simple regurgitations of course information.

5. Look for a different slant. Teachers get tired of the same approach to every assignment, so, if you are able, approach your topic from an unpredictable angle. Be sure you cover all the necessary territory that you would if you wrote a more predictable paper, but hold your reader's attention by viewing the terrain somehow differently: locating the thesis in *Moby Dick* from the whale's point of view; explaining the War of 1812 through a series of dispatches to the London *Times* from a British war correspondent;

describing photosynthesis through a series of simulated field notebooks. (I provide these examples only to allude to what may be possible; teacher, subject, and context will give you safer guidelines.)

6. Consider your paper as a problem in need of solution, or a question in need of an answer. The best way to start may be to try to write out in one sentence what the problem or question actually is, and to continue with this method as more information begins to reshape your initial formulation. For example, the question behind this section is: What is the role of audience in writing? The section itself is an attempt to answer this. (The advice my high school math teacher gave to help solve equations may be helpful here: What am I given? What do I need to know?) Approaching it this way may help you limit the topic, keep your focus as you both research and write, and find both a thesis and a conclusion.

7. View the paper topic from your teacher's perspective. Ask yourself how completing this paper helps further course goals. Is it strictly an extra-credit project in which anything goes? Or does the paper's completion also complete your understanding of the course?

Each of these ideas suggests that you can do certain things psychologically to set up and gain control of your writing from the outset. Sometimes none of these suggestions will work, and the whole process will simply be a struggle; it happens to me in my writing more often than I care to recount. But often one or two of these ideas will help you get started in the right direction. In addition, it helps to consult the teacher with some of your emerging ideas. Because the teacher made the assignment, he or she can best comment on the appropriateness of your choices.

Writing for Classmates

Next to the teacher, your most probable school audience is your peers. More and more teachers are finding value in asking students to read each other's writing, both in draft stages and in final form. You will probably be asked to share your writing with other students in a writing class, where both composing and critiquing papers are everybody's business. Don't be surprised if your history or biology teacher asks you to do the same thing. But equally important to remember is that you could initiate such sharing yourself, regardless of whether your teacher suggests it. The benefits will be worth it.

Writing to other students and reading their work is distinctly different from simply talking to each other; written communication demands a precision and clarity that oral communication does not. When you share your writing with a peer, you will be most aware of where your language is pretentious or your argument stretched too thin. If you ask for feedback, an honest classmate will give it to you—before your teacher has to. I think that students see pomp and padding as readily as teachers do and are equally put off by it. What's the point in writing pretentiously to a classmate?

The following are some of the possible ways to make sharing drafts profitable:

1. Choose people you trust and respect to read your draft. Offer to read theirs in return. Set aside enough time (over coffee in the snack bar?) to return drafts and explain your responses thoroughly to each other.

2. When possible, *you* decide when your draft is ready to share. I don't want someone to see a draft too early because I already know how I am going to continue to fix it; other times, when I am far along in the process, I don't want a response that suggests that I start all over. There's a balance here: it's better that I seek help on the draft before I become too fond of it, when I tend to get defensive and to resist good ideas that might otherwise help me.

3. Ask for specific responses on early drafts. Do you want an overall reaction? Do you have a question about a specific section of your paper? Do you want help with a particularly intricate argument? Do you want simple editing or proofreading help? When you share a draft and specify the help you want, you stay in control of the process and lessen the risk that your readers will say something about your text that could make you defensive. (I'm very thin-skinned about my writing—I could lose confidence fast if I shared my writing with nonsupportive people who said anything they felt like about my work.)

4. When you comment on someone else's paper, use a pencil and be gentle. Remember how you feel about red ink (bad associations offset the advantages of the contrasting color), and remember that ink is permanent. Most writers can't help but see their writing as an extension of themselves. Writing in erasable pencil *suggests* rather than *commands* that changes *might* rather than *must* be made. The choice to do so remains where it should, with the writer rather than the reader.

5. Ask a friend with good language skills to proofread your paper before submission. Most readers can identify problems in

correctness, clarity, and meaning more easily in another person's work than in their own. When students read and respond to (or critique) each other's writing, they learn to identify problems in style, punctuation, and evidence that also may occur in their own writing.

Writing for Publication

Writing for publication is something you may not have to do while you're still in school. Conversely, you may have already done so in letters to the newspaper editor or articles for a school paper. However, you may have a teacher who wants you to experience writing for an audience that doesn't know who you are. When you write for an absent audience, there are a few things to keep in mind:

1. Assume ignorance unless you know otherwise. If you assume your audience knows little or nothing about what you are writing, you will be more likely to give full explanations of terms, concepts, and acronyms. Because you will never know exactly into whose hands your published piece will fall, it's always better to over- than to under-explain. (This suggestion, of course, is also a good one to use for known academic audiences. The cost of elaborating is your time. The cost of assuming too much will be a lower grade.)
2. Provide a full context that makes it clear why you are writing. This is true in books, articles, reviews, and letters to the editor. You can often do this in a few sentences early in your piece, or you can provide a footnote or endnote. Again, no harm is done if you provide a little extra information, but there is a real loss to your reader if you provide too little information.
3. Examine the tone, style, and format of the publisher before you send your manuscript. You can learn a lot about the voice to assume—or avoid—by looking at the nature of other pieces printed in a publication.
4. Use the clearest and simplest language you can. I want to be careful here not to prescribe too much, because the level of language you choose is dependent on your analysis of the situation in which you're writing. However, I would not try overly hard to sound erudite, urbane, or worldly; too often the result is pretension, pomposity, or confusion. Instead, let your most comfortable voice work for you, and you'll increase your chances of genuinely communicating with your reader.
5. If you are worried about having your manuscript accepted, send

a letter of inquiry to see what kind of encouragement the editor gives you. This gives you a better indication of what the editor wants; it also familiarizes him or her with your name, increasing your chances of a good reading.

Writing for Yourself

When you write strictly for yourself, your focus is primarily on ideas—you don't need to follow any guideline or rules at all, except those that you choose to impose. In shopping lists, journals, diaries, appointment books, class notebooks, text margin notes, and so on, you are your own audience, and you don't need to be especially careful, organized, neat, correct, or clear, so long as you understand it yourself.

However, keep in mind your own intended purpose here: a shopping list only needs to be clear until the groceries are in, probably the same day; however, many of these other personal forms may have future uses that warrant a certain amount of clarity when your memory no longer serves. When checking your appointment book, it helps if planning notes include names, times, and places you can clearly find six days later. When reviewing class notebooks, it's nice to be able to make sense of class notes taken six weeks ago; when reading a diary or journal written six years ago, you will be glad you included clarifying details.

Even when writing for the other audiences described in this chapter, audiences carefully hypothesized or imagined in your head, you will write better if you are pleased with your text. Your first audience, at least for important writing, must always be yourself. If the tone strikes you as just the right blend of serious and comic, if the rhythms please your ear when read aloud, and if the arguments strike you as elegant and the title as clever, then your audience will more than likely feel the same.

APPENDIX

SUGGESTIONS FOR JOURNAL WRITING

1. Think about the last paper you wrote. Describe any problems you remember having to solve about *purpose, situation,* and *audience.*

2. For whom do you write most often, a friend? a parent? a teacher? yourself? How do you write differently to this person than to somebody else?

3. Who was the toughest audience for whom you have ever had to write? What made him or her so difficult? Would that still be true today?

SUGGESTIONS FOR ESSAY WRITING

1. Write a short paper or letter that you shape to three distinctly different audiences. (Make these *real* so that you actually keep an individual in mind as you write.) Sandwich these three papers in between an *introduction* and a *conclusion* in which you explain something interesting that you notice about writing to these different people.

2. Choose one assignment that you have already written a paper for in one of your classes. Reshape it as a short article for your school newspaper. Before you do this, make observations in your journal about what changes you intended to make and, after completing it, what changes you actually did make.

SUGGESTIONS FOR RESEARCH PROJECTS

1. INDIVIDUAL: Interview an instructor or other published writer in your community and ask questions about how he or she solves composing problems. Transcribe this interview and share with classmates.

2. COLLABORATIVE: As a class, select a topic about which you would like to know something more. Locate one or two sources of information (from the library or other people) and take good notes. As a class, identify as many different possible audiences as you can think of until the number of audiences equals the number of students in class. Write one per slip of paper and place in a hat and let each student draw an audience out of a hat. Each now write a paragraph to the audience drawn making the information relevant to that particular audience. (Results could be read and evaluated by playing the same game in reverse, with different students role-playing these different audiences for each other.)

Chapter Two

THE COMPOSING PROCESS

I start by writing down anything that comes to mind. I write the paper as one big mass, kind of like freewriting. Then I rewrite it into sentences. I keep rewriting it until it finally takes some form.

—Brady

If I have the time before I begin to write (which I usually don't) I make an outline so I have something to follow. An outline kind of gives me a guide to fall back on in case I get stuck.

—Jennifer

Then I start in the middle because it's easier than trying to figure out where to start. The ending is easy because all you do is repeat what you just said. After the middle and the end, I try to write the beginning.

—Pat

Everybody writes a little differently from everybody else. Brad starts fast, Jennifer outlines (when she has time), and Pat starts in the middle because the beginning needs to be written last. Whose way is best? Trick question. Whatever works best is the best way. However, experienced writers can teach us all a few tricks and perhaps make our best ways even better. The next few pages outline a composing process that roughly describes the way many writers work on their way to completing a piece of writing. This process includes several distinct phases, from exploring and researching ideas to drafting, revising, and editing them—and perhaps publishing them to the world.

While writing is never effortless, I believe that if you understand this messy, unpredictable, and amazing process, you will be a little less hard on yourself when it doesn't come out just right the first time. This discussion includes strategies used by many experienced writers for working through each phase of the composing process with the most efficiency and least pain. After nearly thirty years of trying to help people write better, I am convinced that some ways of writing seem to work for more people on more occasions than others. Yes, writing is a complex, variable, multifaceted process that refuses foolproof formulations. Still, people have been writing since the dawn of recorded history (the invention of writing IS the beginning of recorded history!), some 3000 years, and during that time some habits and strategies have proved more helpful than others. Learning what these are may save some time, grief, energy, or perhaps all three.

EXPLORING

The earliest phases of writing are often explorations. In fact, writing is the thinker's way of exploring the world, inside and out. If you want to write something—an assigned paper, a story for yourself—and you turn on your computer or pick up a pen, you really can have it both ways, since writing starts from ideas, and ideas start from writing. When you write, you explore your memory, texts, neighborhoods, the news, and the library. We could call this first phase of the composing process by many different names, such as planning, inventing, discovering, or trying out, but for our purposes here, exploring will work: you'll know what I mean.

Writers explore topics and approaches to topics when they make notes, start lists, generate outlines, write journal entries, and compose rough drafts. They also discuss, E-mail, telephone, visit, and consult with others. And they also explore less deliberately when they walk, jog, eat, read, browse in libraries and bookstores, converse with friends, and wake up in the middle of the night thinking. The following sections treat, in detail, different ideas about exploring.

Write to Yourself

Forget about publishing your ideas to the world; publish them to yourself. Tell yourself what you're thinking. Write out what's on your mind. Write it down and you'll identify it, understand it better, and leave behind a memory of what it was. Any writing task can be accomplished in more than one way, but the greatest gain will occur if you articulate *in writing* these possibilities, looking and sorting, trying some while discarding others. Starting also involves limiting your options, locating the best strategy for the occasion at hand, and focusing energy in the most productive direction. It doesn't matter if you make outlines or lists, freewrite or draw maps, or do these activities freehand or with a computer. What does seem to matter is getting the ideas out of your head in a tangible way so you can look at them, see what they are and where else they could go. My own most common way of finding and exploring an idea is writing in a rambling sort of voice in my journal (see Chapter Three).

Plan to Plan

If you plan to explore a little before you actually start writing, the odds are that in the long run, your writing will go better, be more directed, purposeful, and efficient. Finding ideas is a back-and-forth process—it starts in one place, ends up in another, and goes on all the time—so long as you keep writing. This whole messy process can be both wonderful and exhausting. Remember that when you are in the planning stages of any writing task, finding and exploring ideas counts more than making them neat or correct. Most commonly, I plan to plan by sitting down with my journal or at my computer for some small period of time almost every day. I make planning a habit.

Move Back and Forth

While exploration comes first, it also comes second, third, and so on, for as long as you keep working. No matter how carefully considered your first ideas, the act of writing usually generates even better ones, all the way through the writing process, as you think about why you are writing, about what, and for whom. For example, when the purpose for writing is vague, as it may be when someone else requests a report or makes an assignment, you may write to discover or clarify your purpose. (What is this assignment really about, anyway?) When you want to communicate to someone else, but aren't sure how you'll be received, try several different versions and figure out for yourself which works best. When I return to revise a chapter draft, I always explore and test the whole draft all over again, no matter how finished I thought it was the last time I wrote.

DRAFTING

When I draft a piece of writing, I try to establish direction, the main form of the argument or story, and some sense of beginning, middle, and end. When I revise, I pay attention to getting the whole paper just right:

organizing the material, supporting my arguments, getting down essentially what I want to say. When I edit, I pay attention to the smaller details of writing, to getting the particular sentences and words just right, working on matters of style, precision, diction, and correct documentation. First, let's look at some ideas about starting a first draft.

Start Writing to Start Writing

Write your way to motivation, knowledge, and thesis. No matter what your subject, use language to find out more about it. What do you already know about it? What do you believe? Why do you care? (Or why don't you?) Where could you find more information? This writing will help in two ways: First, it will cause you to think connected thoughts about the subject for a sustained period of time, a far more powerful, positive, and predictable process than staring at the ceiling or falling asleep worrying about it. Second, it will create a written record from which to conduct further digs into your subject and to prompt your memory and help you continue a thought. (I keep such records in my journal, others keep them on index cards. It doesn't matter where; what matters is keeping them.)

Make an Outline and Promise Yourself Not to Stick to It

In other words, outlines are helpful as starters and prompters, but they are harmful if they prevent further growth or new directions in your draft. I don't always use outlines when I write, especially on short projects (fewer than ten pages), trusting instead that I can hold my focus by a combination of private incubation and constant rereading of the text before me. When I do outline on shorter papers, what proves most helpful is often the very process of generating the outline in the first place. If it's a good outline I quickly internalize its main features and go from there. On longer projects, I am more likely to outline at some point in my writing, but not necessarily before I start. I seldom stick religiously to the formal method of outlining taught me in seventh grade, but like Jennifer (above), I find an outline useful to fall back on when I get stuck. When I do make a detailed outline, I find it easier to see coordinate and subordinate relationships in my project, although I almost always discover these after I've been writing a while and not in my initial outline. The alternation of writing/outlining/writing/outlining often works well because both the outlining and the writing are acts of discovery for me.

Plan to Throw Your First Page Away

Once you actually begin to compose a draft on lined pads of paper or, as I do now, on a computer monitor, don't lock yourself into keeping the first words you produce. In fact, I find it quite helpful to deliberately view each first paragraph or page as a throwaway. The absolutely worst part of writing for me is starting, staring at a blank page or monitor. If I can just get some words down, the task looks started, and I relax a bit. I've learned that once I start, my words come a lot easier. I shift from the slow first gear into progressively higher gears as my thoughts begin to accelerate. When this happens, my writing not only comes more easily, it's better writing. In this sense, I agree with Brad (above), who started out fast to create an initial mess to refine later.

Learn to Write with a Word Processor

Word processors make writing easier, primarily by allowing you to write words electronically on a screen before you print them out in ink on paper. The advantage is that you can move language around as you see fit, until it is just right. Because I rewrite virtually everything, (except notes and journal entries), word processors allow my writing to be more careful, organized, and precise than on lined pads of paper. Having my text on a disk also allows me to use an automatic computer spelling-check program to help me proofread as well as design finished papers with an attractive array of fonts and graphics. If you use a word processor, try to get in the habit of composing first drafts on the screen; that will save you a lot of time in the long run and help you to see your first draft as primarily experimental.

RESEARCHING

When you write, you need content as well as direction. Unless you are writing completely from memory, you need to locate ideas and information from which to start and, later on, with which to support and convince. Remember, you essentially do research whenever you pose questions and then go looking for answers. It's virtually impossible to write a decent critical, analytical, or argumentative paper without doing some research and reporting it accurately. Even personal and reflective essays can benefit by finding additional factual information (journal entries, photographs, interviews) to substantiate and intensify what you remember. In other words, research is a natural part of most people's writing process—and like exploration it happens at all stages of the process, from first to last.

Newspaper and television reporters conduct research when they investigate background sources for a story on political, economic, or social issues. Historians, philosophers, and lawyers research in libraries to locate past records, data, and precedents. Scientists, engineers, physicians, and psychologists research in laboratories to find new answers to puzzling questions. Sociologists, anthropologists, political scientists, educators, and social workers research in communities, neighborhoods, and schools to find practical answers to difficult questions. In every case, these researchers report their findings in writing. It may be time for you to begin to think this way, too.

Research Texts

You do a form of research every time you write analyses or interpretations of texts—reading and rereading is the research. You also do research when you compare one text to another or track down the dates of this or that historical event in encyclopedias, dictionaries, and reference works. And you do text-based research when you scan a CD-ROM disk or log onto the Internet—your textual and graphical printouts become useful, hard data. When you use text-based research carefully (and here I don't mean stringing together a bunch of quotes because they're handy) you add a whole extra dimension of credibility to whatever you are writing about. When you add strong quotations from named sources, you also add life and energy to your writing.

Research Sites

You can do observational and experimental research at sites other than libraries, such as in chemistry and physics laboratories, and on geology and biology field trips. Any place that you visit is a potential research site, capable of providing information and evidence to use in your writing: museums, galleries, concert halls, stadiums, college offices, professional buildings, corporate headquarters, industrial plants, lakefront developments, junkyards, local malls—the list is endless. In writing a paper on lake pollution, go to the lake, describe the water, the shoreline, the activities you see there; in writing about your summer experience working at Dunkin Donuts, go to the nearest store and take notes on details you may have forgotten. (For more information on research techniques, see Chapters Nine–Twelve.)

REVISING

Plan to rewrite everything, more than once, if you can. Good writing is rewriting, reseeing your first words and determining whether or not they do the job you want them to do. The more drafts you are able to manage, the better your final piece is likely to be. If you've got a week to do a given assignment, start something in writing the first night and see where it goes; plan to reread and return to it as often as time allows. If you compose in longhand, write in pencil, double space, on only one side of lined paper—this lets you add and subtract from your initial draft with a minimum of recopying, and allows you to cut out and move around whole portions of your text.

Attend First to the Larger Problems

Thesis, organization, and support should be rethought first; edit later to solve sentence-level problems. It's simply more efficient to spend time getting your whole paper in order first, before you turn your attention to the somewhat smaller matters of style—getting just the right turn of phrase, deleting unnecessary words, changing repetitions, and the like. It's more efficient because you don't want to perfect sentences and paragraphs that you would prefer to delete in a later revision. The last stage of editing is proofreading, in which you check for spelling, punctuation, and typing errors.

Write Your Introduction List

Here I agree with Pat (above), who plans to start in the middle. Of course, if you are able to introduce your piece before you write it, do so. But if you have been outlining and reoutlining, freewriting and journal writing, and finding new ideas and combinations of ideas as you've been going along, it's unlikely that any introduction written first will still do the job. I often try to write introductions first, to point me in a certain direction, but by the time I'm finished, I always need to write a new one.

Seek a Response to Your Writing

Once you have written a passable draft, one you feel is on the right track but far from finished, ask a classmate or friend to read and respond to it. When I do this, I usually specify the kind of feedback that would be most helpful. Does my argument hold up throughout the whole paper? Do I use too many examples? Which ones should I cut? Does my conclusion make sense? Sometimes, when I am quite pleased with my draft, I simply ask a friend to proofread it for me, not wanting at that point to be told about holes in my argument or redundancy in my text.

EDITING

To finish well, you edit. You edit in the later stages of writing to recheck your whole text, to make sure it reads as you intend it to read. You want to see that everything works, from the clarity of ideas to the logic of the paragraphs, the vitality of sentences, the precision of words, and the correctness and accuracy of everything, from facts and references to spelling and punctuation. Whether you have written three, five, or ten drafts, it's the last one you want to be perfect—or as near perfect as possible. Many writers edit first to please themselves; at the same time, they edit for readers—for some imagined but distant audience—hoping to please them as well.

While it makes more rational sense to edit after you have composed and revised and dealt with larger conceptual issues, in my own composing I often violate that step in the process and edit as I go, working a sentence or paragraph over and over until I get it just right, sometimes feeling as if I can't move on until I articulate a thought a certain way. I think computers, especially, allow that easy blurring of the composing, revising, and editing processes. Though I treat editing here as a later stage in writing, it matters less *when* you do it than *that* you do it. The real point is to care enough about your writing to make it your finest possible expression.

Edit for Yourself

Make sure the voice, the beliefs, and the language are yours. Make sure, first, that you sound right to you, so that you represent yourself honestly and accurately. Then think about your intended readers, those that you imagine will ask questions, frown, smile, read carefully, and understand. When I write well, I can tell it before my audience lets me know.

Read Aloud

Ask of your phrases, sentences, and paragraphs, does this *sound right, natural, conversational?* Does it sound like my voice? When I read aloud this sentence or passage, is the rhythm pleasing to my ear? If not, what word or words are out of tune? More than anything, I think I edit for rhythm so my language sounds good to my ear.

Attend to Sentences

Ask of your sentence, is this the best way to state this idea, to ask this question? Would another term or phrase be more appropriate or powerful or accurate? Have I said what I mean as directly—or evasively—as I want to? Do my sentences end emphatically, with the strongest point at the end? Do I want them to? Can I replace abstract nouns with concrete nouns? Can I replace passive verbs with active verbs? Do all my words contribute toward my meaning? Answering these questions is editing.

Write with Titles and Subtitles

Good titles help you view your writing as a whole, and good titles catch readers' attention, pique their curiosity, and describe what your writing is about. Subtitles (subordinate titles, or subheadings) are words or phrases that stand for a set of ideas or a section of a paper; write them in the margins and let them help you structure your paper for both you and the reader. Subtitles do two things at once: they serve as categorizers for concepts, and they operate as transitions from one concept to the next. I try to do this as early as I can, but I find both the main title and the smaller subsections most clearly when I revise. (You see that I use many subtitles in this book. Are they helpful to you?)

Proofread

At the very end, just before your manuscript is handed in or mailed, *proofread* the revised and edited pages to make sure there are no errors in spelling, punctuation (especially commas), noun/verb agreement, paragraphing, typing, formatting, and the like. Use your computer spellchecker, read each line using a ruler, and share the writing with a trusted friend. In addition, check to see that the writing is laid out well on the page, has a title, author, and a date. Make the small changes in pencil. Reprint if the changes make your text look messy.

Communicate

Keep in mind at all times that the goal of editing is to improve the communication, to make it as sharp and pointed and persuasive as possible, to share your ideas so that both the ideas and you, the writer, are well received. It would be a shame for good ideas to be dismissed by the reader because the whole of the writing does not seem careful or serious—which can happen for a variety of reasons, including vague, undefined or inappropriate terminology, misspellings, and typos.

APPENDIX

SUGGESTIONS FOR JOURNAL WRITING

1. How do you compose? See if you can reconstruct the process by which you wrote your last paper: What did you do first? second? In what ways does your composing process resemble that described in this chapter? in what ways differ?

2. Select any paragraph from this chapter and see if some editing could improve it. (I've come to believe almost any text—certainly my own—can be made tighter, stronger, more effective by careful editing.)

3. Keep your journal on a word processor for a week. Do you think it

makes any difference in the thoughts you write? In the way you put your thoughts?

SUGGESTIONS FOR ESSAY WRITING

1. Write an essay on writing an essay. Use yourself as a model and see if you can explain some of the process of writing that, for most of us, remains a constant mystery.

2. Attach to the next essay you write a record of how it was written: Where did the idea come from? How many drafts did you write? at what time of day? Would you identify discrete stages in the process of its composition? (You could do this best if you kept a log documenting each time you did anything related to completing this essay.)

SUGGESTIONS FOR RESEARCH PROJECTS

1. INDIVIDUAL: Investigate the composing process of one of your favorite writers. Check the library to find out whether he or she has ever been interviewed or written an essay or letters on how he or she writes. (See, for example, the *Paris Review* anthologies, in which writers talk about their writing.) Then look closely at some of this writer's work and see if you can find any examples of this process in action. Write a Composing Profile of this writer, supporting your findings with examples from the writer's publications.

2. COLLABORATIVE: Locate teachers in your school who are serious writers and interview them. Do they write only after they have all of their data? Do they keep journals or logs of the process? How would they identify the steps or stages or phases of their own processes? Share interview data and write, individually or as small-group teams, a Resource Guide to Composing documented with the interview data collected.

Chapter Three

THINKING WITH WRITING

Writing feels very personal to me. I usually write when I'm under pressure or really bothered by something. Writing down these thoughts takes them out of my mind and puts them in a concrete form that I can look at. Once on paper, most of my thoughts make more sense & I can be more objective about them. Puts things into their true perspective.

—Joan

A few years ago, I asked my first-year college students to write about their attitudes toward writing. Did they write often? Did they like to write? When did they do it? Why did they do it? For whom? When I read their responses, I was a bit disappointed because all of my students but one said something to the effect that writing was hard for them, that they didn't do it very well, that they didn't like to do it, and that they only wrote in school when they had to for teachers, who graded them. (This last statement seemed to explain a lot about the earlier ones.)

The only exception to this discouraging testimony was Joan, who had stayed out of school for two years and entered my class a little older than her classmates. Joan wrote the paragraph that opens this chapter and, as you can see, valued writing in a different way than the other first-year students. She did not write only to please her teachers. Writing helped her to reflect, to figure things out, and to gain some perspective on thoughts and feelings. This is a valuable way to approach your writing.

USING LANGUAGE

We use language all the time for many reasons. We use it to meet, greet, and persuade people; to ask and answer questions; to pose and solve problems; to argue, explain, explore, and discover; to assert, proclaim, profess, and defend; to express anger, frustration, doubt, and uncertainty; and to find friendship and declare love. In other words, we use language to conduct much of the business of daily life.

When we think of the uses of language, we think primarily of speaking, not writing. We think about speaking first because we do it more often and because it is somehow easier, more available, less studied, more natural. Without being taught, and long before we went to school, we learned to speak. By the time we completed first or second grade, we had also learned both to read and to write. It was in school that we memorized spelling lists, learned to tell nouns from verbs, and diagrammed sentences—none of which we did when we learned to talk. It was in school that we also wrote stories, poems, themes, reports, and examinations, with varying degrees of success. In fact, many of our early associations with writing include school in one way or another.

The farther we advanced in school, the more we were required to write, and the more our writing was criticized and corrected. We wrote more often for grades than for sharing our ideas, for the fun of it, or just for ourselves. For many of us, writing became associated almost exclusively with what we did in school, which was quite different from what we did on weekends, on vacations, for ourselves, or to have a good time.

The purpose of this chapter is to convince you that written language, like spoken, can do many things all the time for various reasons—for ourselves. In fact, the degree to which you understand how writing works *for you* may be the degree to which you succeed in college. To be more specific, let me describe three generally distinctive uses to which you can put your writing: to communicate, to imagine, and to explore.

WRITING TO COMMUNICATE

It is easiest to describe writing as communication because this is the use to which school writing is most obviously put. For years, teachers in elementary, middle, and high school classes admonished you to write clearly, correctly, concisely, and objectively about topics they hoped would interest you. In school they put most of their emphasis on writing; to write clear, correct, concise, objective prose they taught you to use thesis statements, topic sentences, outlines, footnotes, transitions, and titles, but to avoid cliches, digressions, redundancy, and split infinitives. Later, they said, the same principles would be emphasized in your workplace.

In writing to communicate, you probably produced, at one time or another, essays, book reports, lab reports, term papers, five-paragraph themes, and essay answers. You most likely spent many hours in school practicing how to use written language to communicate effectively with other people. Of course, much communicative writing is also imaginative and exploratory, for writing's functions frequently overlap.

WRITING TO IMAGINE

You also spent some time studying, usually in English class, another kind of highly structured language often called *imaginative* or *creative*. Poetry, fiction, drama, essay, and song are the genres usually associated with imaginative language. This kind of language tries to do something different from strictly communicative language—something to do with art, beauty, play, emotion, and personal expression—something difficult to define or measure, but often easy to recognize. We sometimes know something is a poem or a play simply by the way it looks on a page, while with a story or essay, we may not.

For example, I could write some language here that you'll read as poetry, largely because of how I make it look:

> Writing to imagine
> Is different from
> Imagining to write
> Isn't it?

But if I simply wrote the sentence, "Writing to imagine is different from imagining to write, isn't it?" you would pay it less attention. Ultimately, it is difficult to describe exactly what makes some writing quite imaginative (a poem by e.e. cummings) and some less so (my lines above).

Poems, novels, and plays are often governed by alternative conventions of language use. Some poets use rhyme (Robert Frost) and some don't (Robert Frost); some fiction writers use conventional sentences and paragraphs (Ernest Hemingway), while others run single sentences through several pages (William Faulkner); most authors capitalize and punctuate conventionally, but some don't (e.e. cummings). One glance at this untitled poem by cummings demonstrates an imaginative writer's freedom to violate certain language conventions:

> VIII
>
> Buffalo Bill's
> defunct
>   who used to
>   ride a watersmooth-silver
>   stallion

and break onetwothreefourfive pigeonsjustlikethat
                                             Jesus
he was a handsome man
                         and what i want to know is
how do you like your blueeyed boy
Mister Death

In other words, imaginative uses of language often gain effect not only from the ideas about which the authors are writing, but also from the form and style in which those ideas are expressed. In fact, some of the most important elements of imaginative writing may be formal and stylistic; if the author wanted simply to convey an idea clearly and logically, he or she would probably resort to more conventional prose.

WRITING TO EXPLORE

A third kind of writing is that which you do for yourself, which is not directed at any distant audience, and which may not be meant to make any particular impression at all, neither sharply clear nor cleverly aesthetic. This kind of writing might be called *personal, expressive,* or *exploratory.* It helps you think and express yourself on paper. You've written this way if you have kept a diary or journal, jotted notes to yourself or to a close friend, or begun a paper with rough drafts that you want to show nobody else. Here is an example of such personal/exploratory writing from one of my composition classes, in which Missy reflects on her experience writing high school papers:

> I was never convinced that it wasn't somehow possibly a
> fluke—like I got lucky & produced a few good papers—that
> it wasn't consistent and that it wasn't a true reflection of
> my writing skills. I felt like this because I didn't know *how*
> I wrote those damn papers. I had no preset method or for-
> mula like you are required to have in science. That is why
> I wasn't convinced. I just sat down and wrote those papers
> and w/ a little rework they worked! Presto—now that re-
> ally baffled me & that is why I thought it was pure chance
> I turned them out.

This piece of writing is remarkable only in its honesty, but that, of course, is the key feature of writing to yourself—there is no point in pretending. Missy writes in a voice with which she is completely comfortable. In fact, the rhythms of her writing sound as if she is talking to herself on paper: she uses frequent contractions, first-person pronouns (I), shortcuts for words (& and w/), and colloquial language (damn and Presto) as if talking to a good friend.

The key feature of this kind of language, spoken or written, is the focus on subject matter as opposed to style or form. When you write to yourself, you concentrate on thoughts, feelings, problems, whatever—and not on an audience. When you write to yourself to figure things out, you use your most available, most comfortable language, which is talky, casual, fragmented, and honest.

This doesn't mean that journals like Missy's need be entirely private, like personal diaries. Actually, Missy wrote this entry in a journal that I asked my students to keep, so she wrote it knowing I might look at it, but knowing also that she could show me only those entries she chose to and that the journal would not be graded. (Class journals will be discussed more specifically in Chapters Four and Five.)

As an example of a piece of writing written strictly for the writer, I'll share with you a passage from my personal journal in which I wrote about my daughter, when she was twelve:

11/6 Annie is running for student council in her 7th grade class—she's written a speech, a good one, with a platform and all (more options for lunch, etc.). She's rehearsed it over and over—has planned to talk slow and look at just one or two people in her audience to avoid laughing. I'm proud of her—I don't know where she got the idea or guts to do this—but I'm proud of her! She takes it quite seriously—and seems to trust my observations on what she has planned.

I wrote this entry some time ago. As I reread it now, I remember that Annie did not get elected and my heart went out to her. It had been brave of her to run for student council in the first place, and to lose didn't help her fragile twelve-year-old self-confidence. I also remember thinking at the time that it was a harder loss for me, her father, because I realized so clearly the limits of my help and protection: she was really on her own.

So what is the value of having this personal recollection from my journal? At the time I wrote it, while I wrote it, I gave my undivided attention to thinking about my daughter's growing up, something I need to do more of. Now, later, that single recorded thought triggers still more Annie memories: since that time she's begun speaking up more in French class, and she's just had her first boy-girl birthday party (seventeen kids!). And I'm thinking her confidence is in pretty good shape. Quite simply, personal writing such as this increases your awareness of whatever it is you write about.

Another form of personal writing occurs in letters to close friends or people you trust. Such letters reveal your candid, sometimes uncertain, reactions to things; your errant thoughts; and your casual speculations, dreams, and plans. In other words, there are people emotionally close enough to you that writing to them is very much like writing to yourself. In fact, teachers might even turn up in this trusted category. A sixth-grade teacher (Mr. K.) shared with me the following letter written by one of his students after he had talked with his class about alcoholism. He had also given her a magazine article to read.

> Dear Mr. K,
> Thank you for the discussion [of drinking] in class. I needed it. I have had a lot of it [alcohol abuse] in my life-time. The article you gave me "When your child Drinks" I think should be read in front of the class. But it is up to you.
>
> Your friend,
Marianne
>
> P.S. Your a lifesaver.

I would call this letter a sample of exploratory writing, also, because it is an honest expression of concern to an audience the writer trusts thoroughly. You will notice that neither you nor I was ever intended to read this letter: I had to explain the context of this letter to you (as it was explained to me) so that you would understand the references in it. This is another characteristic of exploratory writing: it isn't intended to go very far away from the writer and thus includes few introductory remarks. The writer (Marianne, an eleven-year-old student) doesn't bother to explain context or elaborate on details to her audience, Mr. K.: They were in class together the previous day and both knew exactly what "the discussion" was about and what "it" refers to.

We have just looked at some samples of exploratory writing in different forms—a class journal, a personal journal, a private letter—and noticed that such writing has common characteristics: it is centered on ideas important to the writer; honest in judgment; tentative in nature; informal in tone; loose in structure; and not entirely clear to an audience outside the context in which the writing took place. We might note that this writing is bound by few rules. Perhaps it should be legible to the writer, but even that is not important in all cases. It simply does not matter what exploratory writing looks like, because its primary audience is the writer (or someone very close to the writer who shares his or her context).

RELATIONSHIPS

Each of the three uses of language we have just explored has a distinct function: to communicate, to create art, and to speculate. In reality, of course, any single piece of writing may have features of the other modes: for example, a piece of writing may be primarily informative but also have aesthetic and personal features. Of the three forms, the most useful for you as a student and learner is the exploratory writing you do to think with. In fact, we could say it is the very matrix from which the communicative and imaginative modes of writing emerge, as we work through possible meanings toward those that we would be willing to share with others.

If, for example, you are assigned a term paper in some course, a good way to begin would be to write to yourself about what you *could* write about. Do some writing to help you think about doing more writing; but the kind you do first, for yourself, need not be shown to anybody else or graded. In the following example from one of my American Literature classes, Robin works out her impressions and questions about the Edgar Allan Poe story "Descent into the Maelstrom" in her journal before she begins the first draft of a critical review paper:

9/13 I have to admit, after reading this story over for the second time, I am still not sure what Poe is trying to tell us. The only thing that even crossed my mind about the whirlpool was, what a fool Poe's companion was not to try some means of escape. Certainly by hanging on continuously to the "ring bolt" he was headed for inevitable death.
     Maybe that was one part of what Poe was trying to say, that as life goes on day after day, you can sink into the same routine causing your life to become stagnant and boring. . . . In the story, for example, Poe took the chance of jumping off the boat and hanging onto the barrel—so what could trying something else hurt? Perhaps Poe is also trying to show how fear of death can paralyze a person.
     . . .

I reproduce Robin's journal entry here because it shows so clearly how a writer must start wherever he or she can to make sense of new information—in this case a story—before being able to write about it for someone else. By admitting her initial confusion, and then going on to speculate about possible interpretations, Robin begins to make sense of the story. The informal writing helps the thinking, which, in turn, helps the formal writing.

What all this means in practical terms is simply this: thinking takes place in language, sometimes language that is mathematical, visual, musical, and so on, but most often in everyday words of our native tongue. The degree to which we become fluent, efficient, and comfortable with language as a mode of thinking is, to a large extent, the degree to which we advance as learners.

By writing to ourselves in our own casual voices, we let the writing help us think and even lead our thinking to places we would not have gone had we merely mulled things over in our heads. When you write out your thought, it becomes language with which you can interact, manipulate, extend, critique, or edit. Above all, the discipline of actually writing guarantees that you will push your thought systematically in one direction or another.

THINKING WITH WRITING

Writing helps us figure things out in at least two ways. On the one hand it makes our thoughts visible, allowing us to expand, contract, modify, or discard them. We can hold only so many thoughts in our heads at one time; when we talk out loud and have dialogues with friends, or with ourselves, we lose much of what we say because it isn't written down. More importantly, we can't extend, expand, or develop our ideas fully because we can't see them. When we can witness our thoughts, we can do something with them.

On the other hand, the act of writing itself generates entirely new thoughts that we can then further manipulate. Writing one word, one sentence, or one paragraph suggests still other words, sentences, and paragraphs. Writing progresses as an act of discovery; no other thinking process helps us so completely develop a line of inquiry or a mode of thought. Scientists, artists, mathematicians, lawyers, and engineers all *think* with pen to paper, chalk to blackboard, hands on terminal keys. Extended thought about complex matters is seldom possible, for most of us, any other way.

Asking and Answering Questions

A colleague of mine teaches chemistry to classes of two hundred students. Because this large class doesn't easily allow students to raise their hands to ask questions, the instructor has asked the students to write out their questions during the lecture and deposit them in a cardboard box labeled QUESTIONS that sits just inside the doorway to the classroom. At the beginning of the next class period, the instructor answers selected questions before moving on to new material. A few of the questions from the chemistry question box are reproduced here exactly as they were found,

Figure 3-1

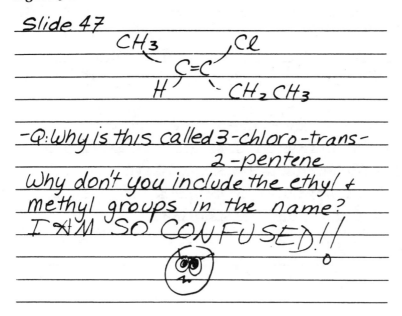

demonstrating how sometimes writing out the question can actually lead to the answer.

A fairly typical question from a fairly confused student is given in Figure 3-1. In this example, there is no evidence that in writing out this question the student is one whit closer to finding an answer than when he or she started, which, of course, will often be the case. But consider the next question, Figure 3-2. In this example, the student writes out a question that he or she takes a stab at answering at the same time: "Is sulfur an exception?" The instructor read this question to the class and simply answered *yes* as the student was actually ahead of the lectures at this point.

Now look at the next example, Figure 3-3. Here the student began to ask a question during lecture, and in the process of writing out the question, figured out the answer. (We have this sample only because other unanswered questions were written on the same scrap of paper.)

In the last example, Figure 3-4, a similar process is at work. This student not only realizes that "the peptide bond" is the answer to the question, but decides to share the discovery with the instructor to thank him, apparently, for the opportunity of asking questions in the questions box in the first place.

The principle at work in the last two examples is a powerful one: the act of saying how and where one is stuck or confused is itself a

Figure 3-2

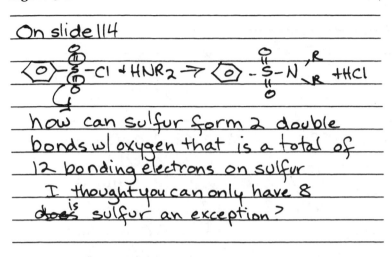

On slide 114

how can sulfur form 2 double
bonds w/ oxygen that is a total of
12 bonding electrons on sulfur
I thought you can only have 8
~~does~~ is sulfur an exception?

Figure 3-3

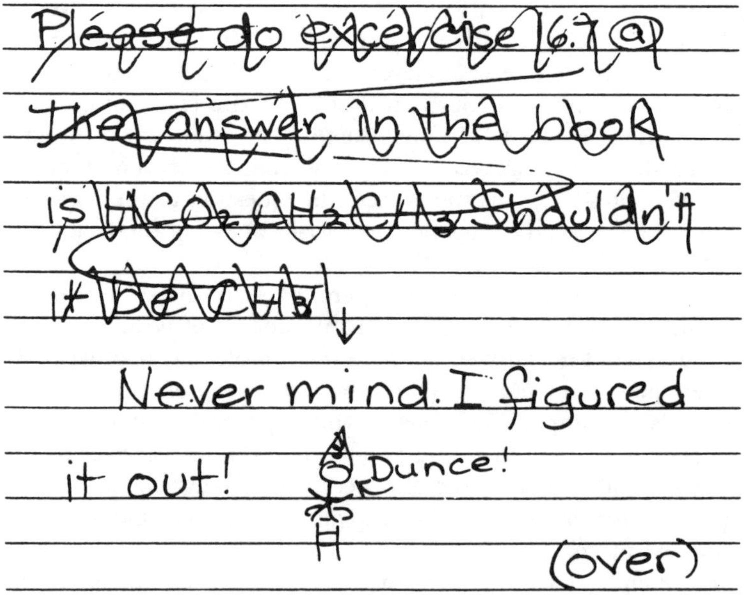

Please do exercise 16.7 @
The answer in the book
is HCO₂CH₂CH₃ Shouldn't
it be CH₃↓

Never mind. I figured
it out! Dunce!

(over)

Figure 3-4

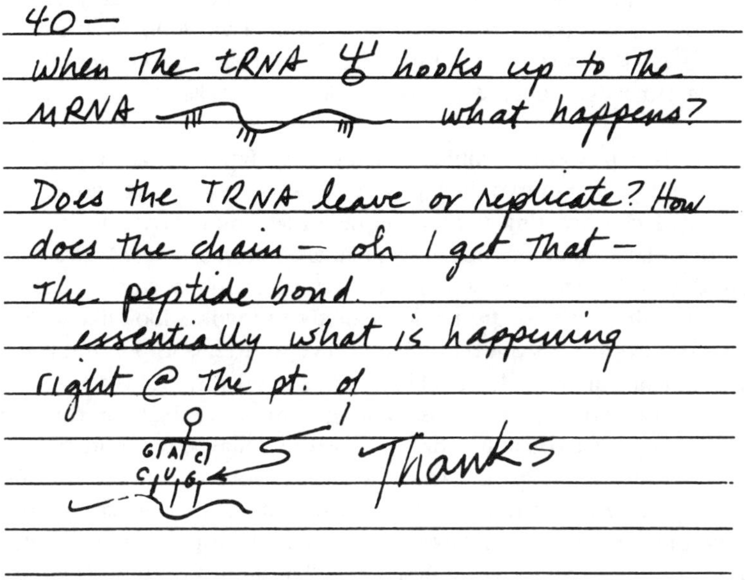

liberating process. It is unclear exactly why this happens or how to guarantee that it will continue to occur, but I suspect that we've all had similar experiences, both in speech and in writing.

The next time you are confused about a math problem or the lines of a difficult poem, try to write out the precise nature of the confusion. It is possible that in articulating your question you will find your answer, but if not, at least you will have a clear statement of the question from which to begin a more methodical quest for an answer.

Freewriting

Freewriting is fast writing—likethis—about anything that comes to mind—as fast as you can do it & without worrying about what it looks like at all—just trying desperately to write as fast as you can think—as I am now—not worrying at all about what the words look like, trying rather to catch the flow of thought on my mind—which right now IS freewriting & so I write here as fast as I can for a fixed period of time (for me I usually write from 5 to 10 minutes at a crack, then back off & look at what I've wrought—writ—whatever). I don't freewrite well on the typewrite because I make so many typing mistakes—wihch distravct me—and so I usually freewrite by hand either in my journal or on a scratch pad. In this sample I've gone back and fixed most of the typing mistakes—otherwise you'd spend more time deciphering it than I did writing it.

Freewriting is a powerful problem-solving tool. Ignore it at your peril! Writing fast helps you in two distinct ways. First, freewriting is a good way to start any piece of writing; the technique forces you to write on, instead of stare at, a blank piece of paper (or a blank computer screen). You stop trying to decide *how* to start; when you freewrite, you just start and don't worry about where it's going or what, exactly, the words look like at this particular time. If it turns out that what you've written is important, you'll go back later and make it look nice; if it has been a stimulus to one or two good ideas, you'll copy those and go on from there; if nothing interesting happened, you'll just throw it away and maybe try another one.

Freewriting also helps because it turns off your internal editor and insists that you write out the very first word/thought that occurs to you, much like the exercise of free association, where in response to a prompt (*black,* for example) you say the first word that comes to mind (*white?*). The benefits to a thinker, problem solver, or writer—at least during initial stages of writing—are substantial, because if you can avoid editing your thought before it comes out, you have more to look at, play with, modify, and expand. During these initial phases of problem solving, it's more important to see variety and quantity than development and quality. Freewriting helps spread out the problem for examination.

It doesn't matter whether you use freewriting as a technique to find out what's on your mind, to address a specific issue that puzzles you, or to start composing a formal paper. It's an all-purpose generative activity and, as such, is transportable to many different situations.

The directions for freewriting are quite simple: write fast; keep your pen moving; use whatever shortcuts you like (& for and) and don't worry about spelling, punctuation, and the like; let the words chart your thinking path (which means digressing is just fine); write for a fixed period of time (ten minutes works well); if you can't think of anything to write, write "I can't think of anything to write" until you do.

Techniques such as freewriting do not work for everyone. One of my students, Sean, wrote the following passage in his journal:

> I'm not sure that this rapid fire methodology helps me. I need to look over my work. Scratch it out. Curse at it. Scream. Cry. And all those other things that make me a writer.

I tried to convince Sean that he could write fast sometimes and go back and do the more careful stuff later, but he was never comfortable with freewriting, and I didn't push it. Different techniques work for different people.

Conceptual Mapping

Writing doesn't always look like writing as the examples from chemistry class demonstrate. I find that many times when I'm trying to figure something out, I'll write single words or short phrases on a sheet of paper, circle or put boxes around them, then connect these to one another with lines or arrows. In fact, I use this shorthand *visual writing* more than any other kind when I'm trying to delimit a problem or think about a freewriting topic. Sometimes I do this on empty journal pages, other times on restaurant place mats—whatever is handy.

Here is one concrete example: If for any reason you need to break a problem or question down into manageable size—say to make a presentation about the Vietnam War or locate the best marketing strategy for a hypothetical business venture—consider making a quick visual map to see what the problem territory looks like. Start by writing out your general topic area (for example, the Vietnam War) in the center of a sheet of paper and put a circle around it. Then you see how many possibilities you can think of and cluster them around your central idea in smaller circles, as in Figure 3-5.

Figure 3-5

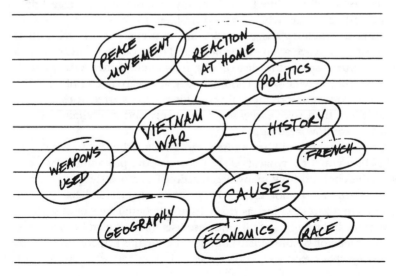

At this point you may have already found the issue you want to investigate, in which case you can continue using this technique to refine your topic, your next circled word being *Causes of the Vietnam War,* and so forth.

If you want to discuss a number of the issues you have just diagrammed, you might put priority numbers next to the various circled terms. In the Vietnam War example, we might enumerate these subtopics to explore further: (1) history, (2) politics, (3) reaction at home. This list then becomes the beginning of an outline into which to add still more detail, or it becomes an order of investigation on your part. The point is that the visual spread of ideas helps you both to see relationships and to discover new possibilities, and it does so even more rapidly than freewriting.

List Making

People make lists every day to remind them of projects to do, things to buy, errands to run. Most obviously, when you make a list of grocery items, you have a record to consult in the store. Equally important, however, in starting the list is the power of the list itself to generate useful associations and new thoughts: you write *eggs* and think also about bacon; you write *milk* and remind yourself of other products in the dairy case. The same thing works with the lists I make in my journal or appointment book to remind myself of what I need to do today, this week, before vacation, etc. By writing the list I remind, remember, and create a visual display of ideas to mull over and modify.

I make lists all the time both to jog my memory and to suggest new possibilities. I make lists when I have a problem to think about, a project to develop, an article to write, or a lecture to prepare. Moreover, I often revise those lists to see what else is possible. For instance, to create a class syllabus, I often start with a list of authors—Twain, James, Crane, Frost, Eliot, Dickinson, Melville—then add, subtract, and rearrange until I like the logic of the course before me. To write this book, I started with a list of three chapters, then later expanded it to twenty, and finally cut it to the sixteen you are now reading.

After I have an idea I like, I often start with another list to see where else that idea could go, what its dimensions are, the pro arguments I can think of, the con, and how many organizational sections the paper might have. Even *this* list is not exhaustive. I arbitrarily decided to find five examples—the list could just as easily have numbered four or twelve.

Writers and thinkers of all kinds use lists to initiate and continue to develop a piece of writing. Instead of settling for the first idea that pops into mind for that narrative English paper or history research report, write it down and see what other possibilities exist. In this sense, list making is like an abbreviated freewriting exercise or a conceptual map; the same principles are at work.

Outlining

Outlines are organized lists. After you have decided what to write about (what problem to solve), an outline can give you a clear direction, a goal toward which to write. To make an outline, you list ideas according to their relative weight: some ideas are equal to others (coordinate), and other ideas are supportive of larger ideas (subordinate). In formal outlines, broad coordinate ideas are designated with Roman numerals, and related supportive ideas are clustered beneath larger ideas, with progressive indenting from there. Here, for example, is an outline of part of this chapter:

> I. Asking and Answering Questions
> A. Chemistry Example #1
> B. Chem #2
> C. Chem #3
> D. Chem #4
> II. Freewriting
> A. Directions for Doing
> B. How It Helps
> 　1. Starting
> 　2. Continuing
> 　　a. free association
> 　　b. focusing
> III. Conceptual Mapping (etc.)

For me, outlines are always generative; that is, I use them in the formative stages of determining what to write and where to direct my writing. And while I do use Roman numerals and capital letters on occasion, on other occasions my outline is a series of words or phrases arranged and rearranged to show relationship and direction. Outlines are important in that they let me think through a project roughly before actually beginning it, but I never hold a writing project to the outline that helped originate it because I see outlines—like freewrites, maps, and lists—as planning, not governing, activities.

Where outlines prove especially useful is in bigger projects such as long papers, books, reports, and grant proposals, in which it is important that readers receive a map, or a table of contents, to help them through the long written document; in essence, a table of contents is an outline of the work, allowing both writer and reader to find their way.

Writing to Learn

What all this means in practical terms is simply this: all thinking takes place in language, sometimes mathematical language, visual, musical, and so on, but most often in the everyday words of our native tongue. The degree to which we become fluent, efficient, and comfortable with language as a mode of thinking is, to a large extent, the degree to which we advance as learners.

When we write to ourselves in our own easy, talky voices, we let the writing help us think and even lead our thinking to places we would not have gone had we never written, but only mulled things over in our heads. Thought written out becomes language you can interact with; your own thought objectified on paper or computer screen becomes thought you can manipulate, extend, critique, or edit. Above all, the discipline of doing the writing in the first place guarantees that you will push your thought systematically in one direction or another.

APPENDIX

SUGGESTIONS FOR JOURNAL WRITING

1. Make a list of all the writing you do in the course of a normal week: document when you make shopping lists, write checks, doodle, take notes, whatever. At the end of the week, divide your list into the three categories we discussed in this chapter—communicative, imaginative, and personal—and determine how much of each kind of writing you did. On the basis of these figures, make a case for altering the teaching of writing in the elementary and secondary schools.

2. Describe one time when you were stuck trying to figure something out and you had that "Ahah!" experience like the chemistry student in this chapter. What circumstances helped create this insight?

3. Think about one problem, personal or academic, you are currently trying to solve, and explore it using at least two of the modes—freewriting, mapping, listing, etc.—discussed in this chapter.

SUGGESTIONS FOR ESSAY WRITING

1. Describe the greatest problem in life or school that you remember solving. Explain the role language played in identifying or solving the problem. (To begin this assignment, use one or more of the problem-solving strategies described in this chapter; append a sample of this to your completed paper.)

2. Think about one thing you are especially good at (sports, hobbies, etc.). Describe the kind of problems you face, and explain how you go about solving those problems. (Begin this assignment as an exploratory journal entry and append this entry to your finished essay to show how you helped solve this writing problem.)

SUGGESTIONS FOR RESEARCH PROJECTS

1. INDIVIDUAL: Conduct a library search on the literature of problem solving and create a bibliography of what you found. Write a report in which you describe the use of problem solving strategies in a field that especially interests you.

2. COLLABORATIVE: In addition to (or instead of) searching the library, conduct interviews with people who work in a particular field or discipline and ask them about how they identify and solve problems. Divide up the interview tasks, but share the results and write (or orally report) about the problem solving strategies in the field you investigated.

Chapter Four

KEEPING A JOURNAL

9/7 Perhaps this journal will teach me as much about myself
as it will about English. You know, I've never kept a journal or such before. I never knew what a pleasure it is to
write. It is a type of cleansing almost a washing of the
mind . . . a concrete look at the workings of my own
head. That is the idea I like most. The journal allows me
to watch my thoughts develop yet, at the same time, it
allows me a certain degree of hindsight.

—Peter

In this passage, Peter describes journals well when he calls them places
"to watch [his] thoughts develop" and to allow him a "certain degree of
hindsight." Journals are collections of thoughts, impressions, musings,
meditations, notes, doubts, plans, and intentions caught chronologically on
paper. You write them for yourself in your most comfortable language.

JOURNALS, LOGS, NOTEBOOKS, AND DIARIES

The informal notebooks that collect your personal thoughts have a long
and respected history. Documents like journals, diaries, or notebooks have
existed ever since people discovered that writing things down helped
people remember them better. For travelers and explorers, the journal was
the place to document where they had been and what they had seen.
Some of these journals, such as those by William Byrd and William Bradford
in the seventeenth-century, are especially useful for modern historians in

reconstructing a portrait of the settlement of colonial America—as are *The Journals of Lewis and Clark* about the settlement of the west in the early nineteenth century.

Some writers, like James Boswell, wrote journals full of information about other famous people—in Boswell's case, Samuel Johnson. Other writers, such as Ralph Waldo Emerson and Virginia Woolf, kept journals that contained nearly all the germinal ideas and language for their later published manuscripts. And the notebooks of Dostoyevsky and Kafka provide crucial insights into the troubled personalities of these disturbing writers.

Many famous literary figures, of course, kept journals; some became more widely read than anything else they wrote. For example, Samuel Pepys' *Diary* remains one of the liveliest accounts of everyday life in seventeenth-century London, and Anaïs Nin's *Diaries* (all four volumes), which describe life in mid-twentieth-century Paris, have contributed more to her fame than have any of her other works.

Other creative people have depended on journals to locate, explore, and capture their ideas. In the journal of Leonardo da Vinci, we find a wonderful mix of artistic and scientific explorations, including both sketches and words. Painter Edgar Degas' notebooks of visual thoughts acted as his journal. Photographer Edward Weston's "daybooks" explored all manner of his personal and aesthetic life in Carmel, California, in the 1920s and 1930s. Le Corbusier's *Sketchbooks* document in detail the emergence of his architectural ideas.

We gain numerous insights through the published journals of noteworthy people. In Charles Darwin's diaries, written aboard the HMS Beagle, we witness the evolution of the theory of evolution. In B. F. Skinner's journals, we locate the rational mind of the father of behaviorism. And in the diaries of Arthur Bremer and Lee Harvey Oswald, we witness the twisted minds of political assassins.

If you want to explore the many possibilities of journal writing, you might investigate one of these published journals in an area that interests you. It would certainly give you some ideas about keeping one yourself.

Academic Journals

When you keep a journal for a college or university class, it's a good idea to avoid the extremes: the personal diary and the impersonal notebook. At the one extreme you find diaries, which are private accounts of a writer's thoughts and feelings and which may include more writing about emotion than intellect. At the other extreme are documents such as class notebooks, which are usually meant to be impersonal recordings of information and other people's ideas. I diagram the differences this way:

Diary _____ Journal _____ Class Notebook
[I-centered]   [I/subject]   [subject-centered]

But even the opposite ends of the spectrum are related: both are regular, often daily, records of people writing primarily to themselves about things that concern them. For academic purposes, I suggest a judicious blend of both diary and class notebook, taking from the diary the crucial first-person pronoun *I* (as in *I think* and *I wonder*) and taking from the notebook the focus on a given subject matter (English, history, political science).

Observing

In a small loose-leaf notebook, Mary describes the ideas she finds in reading the essay "The American Scholar" by Ralph Waldo Emerson:

9/25 In the first few paragraphs of this address, Emerson seems
discouraged at the way society is run, that there are no
"whole men" left. . . . He seems to feel that scholars
should learn from books, but he says beware that you
don't become a "bookworm." Use the books to inspire your
own thoughts, *not* to copy the thoughts of others.

Mary is a first-year student enrolled in a literature class, and she is using her journal to *observe* more carefully what she reads by writing about it. Notice that she copies direct quotations from what she reads, key phrases that she will remember better because she has written them out. These observations become particularly useful to her the next day when these essays are discussed in class; they are also useful later when she studies for her final examinations.

In a spiral notebook, Alice, a biology major, describes what she sees happening in the petri dishes containing fern spores:

9/5 Well, first day of checking the spores. From random observation it seems that the Christmas Fern is much less dense
than the Braun's Holly Fern.

Alice makes the following notations amidst other data describing what she sees in each of the twenty petri dishes she is monitoring as part of her senior thesis project:

1a nothing
2a an alive creature swimming around a pile of junk
3a looks like one spore has a rhizoid
4a one spore has a large protrusion (rhizoid beginning?)

In a science class, students commonly keep something like a lab or field notebook in which they both collect and speculate about data. This, too, is a kind of journal—a daily record of observations, speculations, questions, and doubts. Whether you are observing the words in books or the spores in petri dishes, the journal helps you look, remember, and understand.

Defining

Journals are good places to ask yourself questions about what you are doing with specific assignments, in specific courses, and in your major. In the following entries, we see students in several different disciplines trying to define or explain to themselves what, exactly, their fields of study are really about:

4/24 What makes politics scientific? How is it related to other disciplines? What tools do political scientists depend on most? Is it really a discipline by itself or does it need to be combined with other disciplines (i.e., the social sciences)? This is a hard subject to write about.

—Oscar

5/2 Sociologists study groups for various reasons. They teach us to recognize how a group functions, how to seek out and influence the leaders, how to direct and control the masses. There are questions of ethics raised. It is taught as a process. The process is all-important. . . . Taking apart a jigsaw puzzle, sociologists learn to unravel and identify distinct parts of the process.

—Marc

3/7 Unlike math, where you must learn how to add and subtract before you can multiply and divide, philosophy is a smattering of different things with no exact and precise starting place. In philosophy we could start anywhere and end up anywhere without ever having gone anywhere, but we would have uncovered many rocks along the way. Ah Hah! This is our task: uncovering rocks along the way.

—Doug

On one level, it simply helps to put any concept or term into your own words to try to make sense of it in language you understand. Each of the writers here writes his own definition and so increases the chances of truly understanding the concept.

In addition, as we become immersed in our own disciplines, we begin to take too much for granted. Sometimes your instructors stop questioning, at least in public, the basic assumptions around which their disciplines are actually built—assumptions that need periodic reexamining if the disciplines are to remain healthy. Journals are good places in which to ask yourself why you are studying what.

Wondering

One of the best uses for a journal is speculating on the meaning of what you are studying and thinking about. Speculating is essentially making attempts at answers that you are not yet sure of. Speculating on exams or papers is dangerous; doing it in journals is natural. In the following entry, one of my literature students speculates on the meaning of a well-known passage in Henry David Thoreau's *Walden:*

10/24 What really caught my attention was the specific description of the fight between the black and red ants. In this chapter is Thoreau trying to put his friends (the wild animals) on the same line as those people in the village?

Bill's question, which poses an answer, is a good one. The more he speculates on the meaning of the various passages in *Walden,* or any other book in any other subject, the more ideas he will have to discuss in class and the more material about which to write further papers or exams. The speculation in his journal could lead to further investigation into other places where Thoreau makes similar comparisons.

When Missy was working on a report for my composition class the semester before she was to graduate, she wrote this passage:

3/12 (after class) Look, we botanists don't ask "Does that plant exist?" and we don't ask about the aesthetic value of a flower. We ask "What is the economic value of this plant?" But that is not the primary interest of a true botanist.

We want to know why it grows there (ecologists), why a plant has the structure it does (evolutionist), how it does its stuff (physiologist), etc. The discipline of botany has *excluded* lots of other questions and that is why I'm having some problems with it. . . . Yikes! I think it's all coming together!

Missy doesn't explain for us exactly what she sees coming together, but then she isn't writing for us either. She is using the journal to think through some important issues that concern her now that she's about to become a professional botanist; in fact, she was using a lot of her composition journal to wrestle with matters closer to botany than English. This is exactly what a journal is for: talking with yourself about the issues that concern you most deeply. Sometimes it even seems to answer back.

Connecting

Use your journal to find connections deliberately. Make as many as you can in any direction that works. Connect to your personal life, connect to other courses, and connect one part of your course to another. In the following entries Kevin works on connections in a course on macroeconomics:

2/16 One of the things about this course seems to be the fact that many theories can be proved algebraically. For example, the teacher said that a possible exam question might be to trace through a Keynesian model. In order to trace it one has to use a lot of algebra, substituting variables inside certain functions to prove equations . . . by explaining it this way you get a better grasp of things . . . economics becomes less ambiguous. Theories backed up by mathematical, algebraic, or statistical evidence always seem much more concrete.

2/26 It [economics] is beginning to pull together. After reading the chapters for the second time, I'm beginning to see a sequence or passage of ideas from chapter to chapter.

If you read the material twice, review your notes, and keep a journal, connections are bound to happen. In Kevin's case, he is pulling it together, and the journal is a helpful part of this process.

RESPONSES TO READING

A colleague of mine who teaches the History of Science asks his students questions about their reading that are to be answered in their journals. He enjoys it when students write entries such as the following:

#17 What did Darwin find on the Galapagos Islands? Lions & tigers & bears? Oh no. Turtles & lizards & seals! That's what he found. Different from species found anywhere else in the world. Tame and unafraid of humans. Adapted to a harsh isolated environment. The birds, such as the wood-pecker thrush, had learned to use tools. No other species, except man and baboons, I think, had learned to use tools. Some birds had no more use for flight so their wings atrophied.

When I teach my literature classes, I tell students "Write about everything you read in here, even if just for five minutes. Whenever you complete a chapter, a poem, an essay, write something, anything, about it in your journal. Date your entry and try to identify something specific in what you are reacting to." By making this assignment I am hoping to make writing about reading a habit. If you write about what you read, you increase your chances of remembering it, understanding it, and asking intelligent, specific questions about it. A first-year literature student wrote the following entries while reading *Moby Dick.*

11/30 The thought of running into that squid makes me sick. Don't these men get scared of these strange creatures? Nobody can be that strong all the time.

12/1 What I thought was funny is that Stubbs calls the ship they meet the Rosebud and it is giving off a gross odor because of all the sick and dying whales it carries. What's even more humorous is that the ambergris (yellow substance) is used in perfume—it comes from the bowels of dying whales!

The more personal Sarah's reaction, the more I believe that she is engaged in the book; the more she discovers that she finds funny or notable, the more likely she could use that entry as a seed from which to start an analytic essay or research project.

Reacting

Journals are not the place for class notes, which are frequently mere copies of teacher's thoughts, but they are good places in which to examine what took place in class, to record your opinion of the worth of the lecture or points made by classmates during a discussion. In the following entry, Caroline, a senior English major, comments on her Shakespeare class:

2/9 In Shakespeare class today I was aware of my fellow students and wondered what each one of us was thinking—

about the class in general, about the professor, about each
other's comments, about Shakespeare. I could sense and
see that some students were there only in body. Some of
them obviously hadn't read *Hamlet,* many hadn't even
brought their books to class. I felt they had closed themselves to literature—What, in contrast, makes me care
about these plays?

Caroline's candid reaction to class will inevitably help her remember both
the form and substance of that particular class meeting better than if she
had not written about it. Repeated entries such as this would be likely to
sharpen her powers of observation and depth of understanding as well.

After a few weeks of keeping a journal in his first-year writing class,
Kurt wrote:

9/28 I am really amazed at myself! I don't ever recall writing
this much in my life—especially in a journal. I write down
a lot of ideas I get, I write in it when a class is boring
(usually chemistry lecture) and I write in it because I
want to. It helps me get things off my chest that are bothering me.

Kurt's reaction is fairly typical of students who are starting to get serious
about some elements of college (not necessarily chemistry) and are finding the journal a useful companion in advancing their thought—sometimes to their own surprise.

Starting a Dialogue

If your teacher asks to collect and read your journal, then you have a good
chance to initiate some dialogue in writing about things that concern you
both. Journals used this way take on many of the qualities of letters, with
correspondents keeping in touch through the writing. As a writing teacher,
I have learned a great deal about my own teaching from written conversations with my students.

Remember Alice, the biology major studying the fern spores in the
petri dishes? Her professor responded to nearly every one of her observations, briefly, to let her know if she was on the right track. At midpoint
in her project, her professor wrote the following:

10/15 Here are some questions designed to organize your
thoughts in groups: (1) What interspecific interactions
are promoted? (2) What intraspecific interactions are

promoted? (3) What about the experimental design casts
doubt on your inferences about interactions?

I don't understand these questions, and you probably don't either, but in
the context of Alice's project journal, they made complete sense. In journals you can carry on virtually private, closed, tutorial-like conversations
with your instructor, even if he or she never asked you to keep one.
Sharing journal entries is more like sharing letters than any other kind of
writing you are likely to do in college.

Assessing

Your journal may also prove to be a good place in which to reflect on the
value of journals themselves. I no longer believe journals work for everyone—some people just don't like to be reflective in language—but as
course assignments go, they are fairly painless. Let me conclude with some
of Jim's observations. He started keeping a journal in my first-year writing
class with some reluctance; later he wrote the following on page 192 of
his journal:

11/11 As I scan through my journal, I found a lot of memories. I
wrote consistently on my classes and found grades to be
one of my big hang-ups. . . . The entries which helped me
the most were those about myself and my immediate sur-
roundings. They helped me to realize who I am. Maybe I
should say what I am. I have a little bit of everyone inside of me. . . .
I really enjoyed looking back to see what I wrote.
Some entries were stupid. . . . Many times I wrote what I
really felt. A journal wouldn't be worth keeping if it
didn't. Who wants to read about what others think?
Never once did I feel it a burden to write. If you would
have told us to write in it everyday, I would have told
you where to go. My roommate says I write too much,
but I think I write too little.

I have presented these examples from college student journals in a variety
of grades and disciplines to make the case that journal writing can be
among the most important writing you do in the academic world. It *is* the
language of thought written down. In the next chapter, I will describe
some of the particular strategies that will make journals work in easily
among your other college assignments.
If you are asked to keep a journal for a class, the chances are that

your teacher wants it to focus on his or her course. Like me, other teachers assign journals, hoping to increase your understanding of the goals, readings, lectures, and discussions that compose this class in composition or literature or history or biology. Such a journal will be useful to the extent that you maintain the focus on the course content and, at the same time, write honestly and personally about that content.

If you elect to keep a journal on your own and not because a teacher asked you to, bear in mind that it will be useful to you only if you write in it regularly and candidly about problems and insights that really concern you. Assigning yourself a journal—for one class in particular or your whole academic term in general—is a good idea because it is the one writing assignment that works for you more than for someone else.

WRITING A RESEARCH LOG

10/14 I reread John's comments about my paper. He's right, I need to add more about the 1930's and 40's. He also mentioned a letter from Einstein to the President which I never heard of. I'll have to find out about that. I think I need chronological order instead of subject order—and I need a better opening. Also I want to put more of my voice into it.

—Lisa

The above entry is taken from the log Lisa used to keep track of her research project for her college English class. This entry was written after she had shared her first three-page paper draft with a classmate and received back his written critique. In this section, we will look at a special kind of journal called a research log, which documents your daily journey from class to the card catalogue to the library stacks to the pile of notes on your desk. From the time you begin a research project through the final draft of your completed typed manuscript, this log collects your starts and stops, questions and answers, notes, speculations, and doubts—just like any journal, except here, you maintain a single focus on one project. Of course, an easy way to keep a research log is to partition off the back section of your journal or class notebook, keeping all of your course records together.

If you write daily in the log, you improve your chances of both finding and catching insights, which you will need to write insightful papers. Most serious writers use something like a log to help them start and then monitor the development of major writing and research projects. Broadly interpreted, research logs can be about any thoughts you have while doing your research. Here are some initial questions to start a research log:

1. On what subject do I want to spend time reading and researching?
2. What do I already know about this subject?
3. What question or questions do I want to answer?
4. Can I break my general question into a series of more specific questions?
5. Who can I talk to who knows something about this?

Lisa's initial interest in writing about Albert Einstein came from reading an article by Banesh Hoffman, entitled "My Friend Albert Einstein," in the anthology assigned for the course. The article altered Lisa's initial impression of Einstein as a mythical twentieth-century scientist to that of a human being who married (twice), raised children, and mowed the lawn. Her first reaction to Hoffman's ideas recorded on the first day of October begins as follows:

> I had a preconceived image of him being so scientific and mechanical. Uptight and bookwormish. However Banesh Hoffman showed Albert Einstein in a completely different light. That interests me, because it's a side we don't normally see in historical figures—especially scientists & Nobel Prize winners. We see only their contributions & none of their personalities or the reasons behind their contributions. He is someone I'd love to get to know now.

Establishing Assumptions

Whenever you tackle a new job or assignment, you start out with certain beliefs and assumptions, which may be reinforced, modified or abandoned as your work progresses. Log writing can be helpful, because as you write out your assumptions, you become aware of what they are, increasing the chances of doing something productive with them. Lisa's next log entry, two days later (10/3), reveals her uncertainty about herself as a student of history:

> I don't know anything about history—it's my worst subject & it puts me to great disadvantage when it comes to writing or thinking about people in the past—it's out of context. . . . Anyway, I assume both wars went on during his life. The Nazis and Hitler & holocaust, Hitler torturing the Jews

& later in his life maybe the WW II w/ Japanese bombing Pearl Harbor.

In this entry, Lisa reveals some confusion about the two World Wars that dominated the first half of the twentieth century. Although she realizes that Einstein was involved with both of them, she seems to believe that the war with Germany was a different one from the war with Japan. Lisa's uncertainties will lead to her first questions because she must check out her own preconceptions.

Asking Questions

Curiosity is the necessary precondition to writing well about anything: The more questions you have, the more likely you are to pursue answers; the more answers you have, the more you have to write about. In the log, especially, there is no penalty for not knowing something, as there may be in a formal paper or examination. The log is also a place to keep a record of the questions you are pursuing, and to witness how writing one question down often inspires yet another.

On 10/7, about a week after her initial investigation of Einstein, Lisa writes about what else she wants and needs to know about him:

I need to know more of the things which influenced him. His personal life, when he was younger, his young adult-hood, his family, etc.

Also the events going on in Germany & Europe in general. I believe this has an influence on his ideas & personality. I'd like to be able to fit him into history & see him in his time.

I'd like to see what people of his time thought of him & how he related to them. I'm interested in the image given by Banesh Hoffman because it makes Einstein seem like such a real person—I'd like to know if other people saw him in the same way or if he was "untouchable" because of his fame & brilliance.

I guess my question continues to be what he was like as a person, & how his early life was influenced to make him such a genius.

Focusing Questions

As Lisa pursued her questions, she recorded what she found in her research log and asked more focused questions. This jotting activity can be an important kind of entry, as lists of questions allow the writer to see the range of possible topics to pursue further. Below, on 10/10, Lisa recorded the following fragments and questions:

—used the library today, need more on what influenced him
—need to read his essay in book to hear his voice
—more on personality
—check dates & places (schools, jobs)
—find out what religion and beliefs
—family
—try to focus my paper more, maybe not just life and young adulthood, but how it affected his future, fame, genius
—relate personality to how he became brilliant or known
—did he relate as well to others as he did to science?

Researching

Before Lisa ever started a draft of her actual research paper, she worked out what she knew and what she didn't. We find this entry for 10/13:

I know little about the beginning of WW I [or] what was going on before. I do know that he's very against WW II & outspoken w/ his beliefs. He's a pacifist.

It's difficult to tell if she has discovered the differences between the two World Wars yet, but she's clearly attending to Einstein's involvement in World War II. Although she doesn't reveal a lot here, it's important for the log writer simply to keep going, recording even little bits and pieces to keep the research momentum alive. The incessant presence of the log (perhaps coupled with some insistence from the instructor) ensures that the research project is not dropped until the day the paper is due.

Planning

Lisa's teacher asked her to write a discovery draft before actually beginning a formal draft of the paper. The purpose, of course, was to discover how the information was coming together and whether some controlling ideas were emerging that could actually structure her paper. (At this point, students exchanged papers and critiqued them for each other, resulting in the entry of 10/14 reprinted at the head of this chapter.)

On 10/15, Lisa records in her log how she moved from discovery to first draft:

I merely changed the order & reworded sentences & paragraphs. Everything was moved around. I tried to fill in left out information, but when I reread, I realize a lot is still missing. I like this order much better & now I can fill in things easier & in a more organized fashion.

Evaluating

On 10/16, Lisa, apparently pleased with the organization but not with the tone of her language, has further thoughts about this initial draft:

I'm not happy w/ the way the paper sounds. It doesn't seem to flow right. It's almost as if it has more than one voice—many voices. . . . I'm not working on the first draft today however.

She's right. In looking at her first draft, we find a tone more typical of an encyclopedia than that of an eager research writer. Here are a few sentences from her opening paragraph:

Albert Einstein was born on March 14, 1879 in Ulm, Germany, as the first child of Pauline and Hermann Einstein. Shortly after, he and his parents moved to Munich. Einstein never liked school or did well in it. He disliked the rigidity of the Catholic school he attended.

Revising

On 10/18, Lisa has again visited the library and also begun to revise her first draft:

I found another book that gives me a little more insight to his life. I reworded a lot because it made no sense & sounded childish & dry—no voice, just facts. I still need a better intro and conclusion.

It is now two and a half weeks into the Einstein project, and Lisa's log shows entries nearly every day. Here, she mentions again her dissatisfaction with the voice in the paper, but because she's talking more to herself than to her instructor, she doesn't fill us in on what, exactly, she found childish. This is a good time for Lisa to have a one-to-one conference with her writing teacher.

More Reading

On 10/20, Lisa writes:

> I wouldn't say I felt like a historian, but I found the best
> book today, *Einstein: Profile of the Man.* The author inter-
> views Einstein's son & wrote the most personal account of
> his life. . . . I'm used to essays that go over my head or
> dry encyclopedia articles—packed w/ facts w/ no personal-
> ity. Just by flipping through the book & reading a page
> here & there, I found a goldmine of information.

She is aware here that she still isn't behaving as a historian would; however,
to make that observation, she obviously knows something about what
historians do. In fact, I'd guess that she *is* beginning to feel like a historian,
despite her disclaimer—an especially important development when compared to her attitude on 10/3, where she professed, "I don't know anything
about history."

Finishing

It's now about three weeks since Lisa began to work on the research
project for her writing class. During that time, she not only wrote several
drafts of the paper itself, but fifteen separate log entries documenting her
thinking about it. On 10/20, she writes:

> Today I copied 1st draft over including notes added on the
> side. It's getting much longer & I'm quite happy with it. It
> seems like one whole thing now, instead of facts. *Profile of
> the Man* helped a lot getting my mind and the paper in the
> right order. I can relate the facts to each other much better
> now. I still have no conclusion—I didn't like the other one.

At this point Lisa's research log stops. The rest of her energy on this project
went into finishing the paper she had now worked on for three weeks.
Her log had been a tool to work through the process of writing the paper;
once the paper was finished, the log itself became a historical document.
Her final paper opens with some of the same material, but in a voice that
seems more confidently Lisa's own:

> As a boy, Einstein never really liked school nor did very
> well in it. He disliked the rigidity of the Catholic school and

was bored with the study of language and history. But he loved science.

FROM JOURNAL WRITING TO DRAFTING

Journal writing is an essential part of my own composing process. In fact, most of the articles, chapters, and books that I write in my publish-or-perish life as a college professor start out as ideas discovered and explored in my journal. I even keep a separate journal when, during summers, I travel around the country on my motorcycle, and even *this* journal has led me to writing articles. Here, for instance, is a note from my nonacademic travel journal kept while attending a one-day motorcycle riding school in New Hampshire:

> 3:40 last riding session just over—I came in two laps early—very much afraid of my own tiredness at this time of day—several people had just passed me, the FZR and a K75—tempting me to overreach and pass them back. But I've I really learned to trust my tires, maybe more than myself—especially coming out of the hairpin (turn 3) and entering the bowl (turn 4).

This entry is typical of my fast road writing, with little attention to the formalities of language, but much to the details and insights that I can record in a few minutes. Remember, it's seldom the journal, as it is written at the time, that will be published, but more likely the careful thoughts it inspires.

I so enjoyed my day at the New Hampshire track that I wrote an article about it for a motorcycle magazine that published rider stories. In "Trusting My Tires, Trusting Myself" (*BMW Owners News,* April, 1994) here's a passage that reveals what became of the hasty journal entry:

> Twice in the afternoon I leave the track a few minutes early, so tired I scare myself, aware now among Stirling Moss fantasies, the draining concentration it takes to drive for even thirty minutes with total, absolute, one hundred percent attention—anything less and you're off the track, into the barricades, into the grandstand wall, embarrassed or maybe dead.

The only things left from the original journal entry are the time of day, the references to leaving the track early, and the seed of my final title. These details helped make my story, but when I recorded them in the journal, I didn't know that.

This entry also helped in another, more abstract way, by reminding me of what I knew but had not recorded. In other words, long after the event, the journal prompts your long-term memory to produce further thoughts and insights.

GUIDELINES FOR KEEPING A JOURNAL

I usually do my journal writing with pen and ink in lined paper notebooks. In fact, I keep several different journals, each in a different notebook: my personal/professional journal in a small (7 × 10) leather loose leaf; my teaching journal in an equally small cardboard loose leaf; my travel journal in an even smaller (5 × 7) spiral bound (carried in a tank bag on cross-country motorcycle trips). I always have the personal journal with me, in my book bag, to catch thoughts related to my everyday life or, in the back section, to think about professional projects now underway or in need of doing. It's the ease and portability I enjoy, always having with me a favorite fountain pen, preferring to do my journal writing in especially comfortable places—on a couch, under an apple tree, on my front porch.

However, I also do journal writing with my portable and desk top computers for more specific research projects that lead to writing projects. In these instances, I keep related files in a single folder/directory on my hard drive along with other notes about that project (and a backup copy on disk). By using the computer for deliberate acts of journal writing, I already have typed copy started that sometimes I import into documents I'm writing.

My own habits may serve as a preface to the following suggestions for keeping a journal. It really doesn't matter whether you use pen and paper or a computer, so long as you are able to write when you need to. The only real limitation of keeping a journal on a computer is that you may not have it when you need it—journal writing in class, for instance. What remains important is that you write as a way to reason. The following suggestions may help you keep your journal active:

1. If required to keep a journal for class, buy a loose-leaf notebook. Removable paper is an advantage if teachers want to see selected entries: you can hand some in without surrendering your whole notebook, or you can delete sensitive or trashy entries if the whole notebook is collected.

2. Divide your notebook into sections: one for class, another for more personal thoughts, and maybe another for a specific research project or even another class.

3. Date each entry. The dates of journal entries allow you (or instructors) to witness the evolution of your thoughts over time. I

also add day of week, time of day, and weather—just to complete my record keeping. With a computer, if you open a new file for each entry, date and time are automatic.

4. Start each entry on a fresh page. Blank pages ask to be filled, and the more you write, the more you think. (The inevitable white spaces on half-filled pages also invite the taping in of clippings, notes, news items, and photos—making your journal something of a scrapbook as well.)

5. Write in your natural voice. Use the voice that's most comfortable; first person, contractions, and other easy language shortcuts. A journal is a place for capturing ideas in their rough and ready stages; worry about more careful language when you write to audiences other than yourself.

6. Experiment with writing at different times of day; notice how early-morning thought differs from late-evening thought.

7. Experiment with writing in different places; notice how in-class writing differs from library writing, and how both differ from writing at home or on the beach.

8. If asked to hand in your journal at the end of a semester, prepare it for public reading: delete unimportant entries; add titles for each entry; add page numbers; make a table of contents; star important entries; and write an introduction alerting a stranger to themes or ideas to look for. Preparing your journal in this way not only helps an instructor read it, it helps you remember what you wrote when.

APPENDIX

SUGGESTIONS FOR JOURNAL WRITING

1. Think of five good questions to do journal entries about for this class you are now taking. Share these with your teacher and classmates.

2. For one week, focus on one dimension of journal writing that you normally ignore (e.g., observation of evaluations) and write as many entries that do this as you can. (And, of course, write a journal entry about the results.)

3. Keep a research log (separate from your normal class journal in some way) for three or four weeks about whatever subject interests you. Note there all of your preconceptions, hunches, theories, tentative conclusions, good leads, and false starts.

SUGGESTIONS FOR ESSAY WRITING

1. For two weeks, keep a journal in another class you are taking (use the back part of the class notebook). During this time, try to make as many entries as you can of an exploratory or questioning nature, about both the class and the readings. After two weeks, write the story of your journal keeping experiment, using evidence from your actual journal, reflecting on the results.

2. Keep a reading journal about one book you are currently reading. When you have finished, examine the pros and cons of writing while reading, including in your essay any passages from your actual journal that may support your case. (Append a sample of your journal to the end of this paper.)

3. Keep a journal for the duration of one research project or paper you are doing in another class. When the project or paper is finished, edit and write an introduction to this journal in which you explain its role in finishing the product. (Append the finished paper to the journal for reference.)

SUGGESTIONS FOR RESEARCH PROJECTS

1. INDIVIDUAL: Locate in the library the published journal of somebody who interests you or was mentioned in this chapter. Write a report in which you explain how this person used the journal and speculate how it might have related to his or her work.

2. INDIVIDUAL: Keep a research log about a topic you are investigating, noting your initial hunches and speculations, the useful resources you locate, and all the false starts, dead ends, and missing resources you find as you pursue your research. Complete your project, write an imaginative paper about it, and append to it this log.

3. COLLABORATIVE: Interview some of your teachers or other working people in your community who keep a record or something like a journal. Find out why they keep it, how they use it, and how often they write in it. Put together a report for this class on the current use of this informal mode of writing in your community. Write about one suggestion here that strikes you as new and why you think it will be useful to you.

Section II

COLLEGE WRITING

Chapter Five

WRITING IN THE ACADEMIC COMMUNITY

> I hate to write. My writing never says what I mean. I can see the idea in my head, but I can't seem to express it in a way that others understand, so I don't get good grades. Is there some secret I don't know about?
>
> —David

With great clarity, David expresses his frustration as a writer. In fact, his expression is so clear that I'm tempted not to believe him: How could it be that he doesn't know the secret? However, as a writer myself, I know exactly what David means. He is honest, and what he says is true.

Do you ever find yourself thinking like David, that everyone else finds writing easier than you do? I don't always think that, but sometimes I do. The truth is, everyone doesn't, and there is no secret. In fact, most writers, experienced and inexperienced alike, find writing difficult, demanding, ornery, often frustrating work. Experienced writers, however, have learned that difficulty comes with the territory, that with patience, persistence, and grit, even the most difficult writing task will, in the end, work itself out. And experienced writers will also tell you that, while there is no secret, there is often excitement, great satisfaction, even joy from writing well.

There are, of course, conditions: To write well, you need a good reason to be doing it, a reason you believe in. When you've elected to write on your own, good reasons are no problem—you have something you want or need to say, and the writing is the saying. But sometimes, in both school and work settings, the reasons are given to you. They're not yours at the outset, and that's trouble. In school, instructors assign writing tasks to fulfill their teaching agendas. In the workplace, employers commission reports, clients seek answers, newspaper editors assign stories. Regardless of the initial motivation, once committed or assigned, it's your job to figure out the why, what, where, when, and how of the writing task, and to ask: What do I need to do? Where am I in relation to this assignment? What are the conditions that shape and determine my writing?

This book assumes that you are a college student, that the general conditions that determine your writing are academic, and that the better you understand these general conditions, the better you'll write. This chapter outlines some of those conditions and suggests a few strategies for coping with them. Knowing what academic communities expect will simplify and clarify your writing tasks, but it won't *guarantee* speedy and successful results. Even for the patient and persistent, there are no guarantees, just better odds. Each time you put pen to paper or fingers to keyboard the whole mystifying process of composing begins anew.

As for the specific conditions that determine your writing—which college, which major, which year, which course, which instructor, which assignment, not to mention which student (you and what you bring to the writing)—well, those I won't know about, but in the last part of this chapter, I'll provide some guidelines for you to examine them more carefully yourself.

THE ACADEMIC COMMUNITY

If you are reading this book while enrolled in college, you are already a member of an academic community. What, you may ask, is the big deal? I'm in school, I'm studying, taking tests, writing papers, and getting grades—as I've done since first grade. What's the difference? Well, this time there may be a difference that could influence everything you write. Let's look at the nature of a college academic community.

College and university communities were established to study something called the truth. Each discipline pursues, investigates, and teaches some small part of it: the sciences investigate what is true in the natural world, the social sciences the social world, the humanities the individual world, the arts the aesthetic world, and so on. Of course, truth is seldom packaged in tight disciplinary units, so understanding something fully often requires the crossing of disciplinary lines. The most extreme case may be the study of literature, in which to understand what is true about a single novel by Charles Dickens or Virginia Woolf you may need to know some history, philosophy, psychology, physics, anthropology, economics, or politics. In some cases, new hybrid disciplines have been created at the juncture where one pursuit of truth meets another—for example, biochemistry, psycholinguistics, and social anthropology.

To establish truth about the physical world, scientists have developed a particular way of asking questions and looking for answers which is called "the scientific method." Finding out biological or chemical truth may require similar methods but different tools. Those who investigate the social world—sociologists, economists, political scientists, psychologists, geographers, and anthropologists—have, in many instances, adopted the scientist's methodologies. They often find that the social world is even harder to pin down for examination than even the most distant star or complex microorganism.

To establish truth in the so-called humanistic world, humanists—philosophers, literary scholars, and historians—have developed a potpourri of investigative methods, ranging from the scientific to the imaginative and intuitive. In contrast, practitioners of the arts—musicians, composers, poets, novelists, playwrights, directors, actors, painters, sculptors, and dancers—do their best to escape classification of any kind. Neat disciplinary categories become increasingly messy when you realize that historians study social behavior but are usually called humanists, and that psychologists, who study individual behavior, are usually called social scientists, as are the geographers who study the physical space of the earth.

Furthermore, the professional schools of business, law, education, agriculture, health, natural resources, and engineering have put together their own specialized programs to train people to do certain highly specialized work in the larger community. As part of the process of training, these schools require at least an introductory-level knowledge of the different disciplines.

Despite these differences, many fields of study make assumptions about teaching, learning, and knowledge that have more in common than not—which is why we can even talk about the academic community as an entity. In fact, if you look at the modes of establishing truth in disciplines as different as history and physics, you may be more surprised by the assumptions on which they agree than those on which they differ. For example, both historians and physicists depend heavily on close observation for the accumulation of facts on which to make generalizations, which they then try to disprove. Biologists and English teachers, too, may have more in common than meets the casual eye.

THE GROUND RULES

Certain beliefs operate as glue to hold together the otherwise disparate community of teachers and students that compose the academic community: You cannot write successful college-level papers without understanding these things.

Belief

As both student and writer, it helps to remember that establishing belief is the job of (1) the entire university community, (2) each general field of study within the university, and (3) each individual student writer in each particular course in that community. There is a necessary relationship among these three elements which is relevant to every single act of communication or expression you do while a member of this community. You want those who read your laboratory reports, term papers, and essay tests to believe that what you say is essentially *true*. Your job as a college writer is to persuade your readers that what you say is true, which introduces the next element.

Persuasion

Every serious act of writing is essentially an exercise in persuasion: If you describe an experiment, you want your description to *persuade* your chemistry teacher that this is what actually happened; if you analyze the major causes of the Civil War, you want to convince your history teacher that, yes, these were the causes; if you evaluate the merits of a Robert Frost poem, you want your English teacher to believe your evaluation. While this may seem obvious, you must remember that persuasion is also the goal of most advertisements and political propaganda, but something rather important sets persuasion in the academic world apart from persuasion in the world of profit and politics: the use of evidence.

Evidence

How writers create belief is largely a matter of how they marshal their *evidence* to support what they say. In the first place, there must *be* evidence to back up any assertions; otherwise, they are unsupported or weak generalizations. In the academic world, there is often a premium on evidence derived from books—preferably numerous books, each written by an expert with credentials that can be checked. Depending on your discipline, other sources of evidence might be observation, experimentation, statistics, interviews, or personal experience—each documented in some verifiable way.

Documentation

To make an assertion in the academic community as convincing as possible, you should always provide your audience with a complete account of where you got your information, ideas, or evidence (more on this in Chapters Nine-Twelve); hence, the importance of footnotes, endnotes, references, bibliographies, and literature searches. Essentially, your readers want to know *who* said *what, where,* and *when.* When you provide this information, readers believe that your student ideas are buttressed by expert ideas and are more likely to believe them. In college writing you ignore documentation at your peril.

Subjectivity

In many disciplines, your personal opinion may not be worth very much; in others it will be. In the more interpretive disciplines, such as history, philosophy, and literature, you will generally find more room for *personal interpretation* than in the more quantitative disciplines, such as chemistry, physics, and mathematics. (The social sciences fall somewhere in between.) To be safe, whenever you make an academic assertion in any discipline, use the best evidence you can find and document it. But in all disciplines, your own reasoned, and necessarily subjective judgment will at some times be necessary; if it is, just be sure to state it as such ("In my opinion. . . ." or, "It seems to me. . . .") and give the best reasons you can.

Objectivity

In the academic community, the way in which you search for truth is supposed to be *impartial* and *objective,* with some very clear exceptions within the humanities and fine arts. For many disciplines, however, when you perform experiments and do research, you attempt to remove yourself from the situation as much as possible and attempt to demonstrate that the results of your work are objectively, not subjectively, true; that is, that the results you are reporting are not a figment of your imagination and personal bias and that anybody else doing this work would find the same results. In science, the best experiments are replicable (repeatable) by other scientists; the social sciences generally try to follow suit. This point is important to you as a writer because it means that it's advisable, whenever possible, to mention how you got your results (by objective methods, of course). In some cases, it's even preferable to use a deliberately objective tone (passive constructions, no first-person pronouns) and quantitative detail (statistics, graphs) in your writing, if you want to persuade members of these more or less objective communities to believe you.

Relativity

Students of even the most objective scientific disciplines make absolute statements at their peril. In the twentieth century, especially since Einstein, *relativity* has been the watchword: there is no such thing as certainty in the physical universe, and that concept has filtered, in one way or another, into every field of study. We now believe that there is more than one possible explanation, more than one possible interpretation, more than one version of nearly everything that happens. How does this apply to your writing? Quite simply, every statement you make within the academic community will be subject to question, objection, interpretation, and cross-examination; the farther you progress in your studies, the more likely it is that your ideas will be challenged. As a result, when you make academic assertions, pay attention to the qualifying words (perhaps, maybe, possibly, actually) and tentative phrases ("Have you considered . . . ?" "It is likely. . . . " "In my judgment. . . . " and "In all probability. . . ."). These phrases signify that you recognize the tentative nature of the truth. So, though you *try* to be objective in your work or writing, you also need to acknowledge that it is ultimately impossible.

Balance

This last rule is related to the notions of objectivity and relativity. Because there are multiple interpretations for so much that happens in the natural and social worlds—multiple versions of right and wrong, good and bad, correct and incorrect—it becomes useful for writers to represent these possibilities in their discourse through assertions that give *fair* (honest, nonemotional) treatment even to positions with which the writer disagrees. Important here are balance phrases ("On one hand/on the other hand. . . ." "However, . . .") and the recognition of multiple causes ("in the first place/in the second place," "in addition," "also," "finally"). When you use these phrases in your spoken and written language, they suggest that you know the rules of the academic community.

Unfortunately, the foregoing generalizations are just that, generalizations that we don't have time to explore fully. In fact, the only thorough elaboration takes place semester by semester as you are progressively initiated into membership in the world of college or university studies. But no discussion of writing formal academic papers is useful unless you understand generally the nature and context of your academic audience. Every suggestion in this book is predicated on your understanding of this community and its ground rules and expectations. Once understood and agreed to, the many seemingly arbitrary assignments you will receive may begin to make better sense to you, and, in turn, your handling of them as a writer will make better sense to your teachers.

THE RESEARCH IMPERATIVE

The need for knowledge is the rule I didn't mention directly, yet this need is an imperative behind every college paper you write. And the primary way of coming to knowledge in the academic community is through research—conducting your own investigations of the world and reading the results of what others have found in their investigations. Research papers and papers based on research will be among your most common academic assignments.

Authentic research begins with yourself, when you ask questions and look for answers. In looking, you pose more questions, talk to people, dig in libraries, and try one method then another. It's not easy, but it's sometimes fun. And always *you* are present, the guiding curiosity and controlling intelligence, trying to find something out.

WHY RESEARCH ASSIGNMENTS?

Let's look more closely at the reasons why research papers—or term papers, or formal reports—are a major staple in the academic diet. At their best, such assignments ask you to think seriously about what interests you, to formulate questions you care about, to begin poking around in places (both familiar and arcane) for answers or solutions, to master some method for taking and organizing notes, to integrate fragments of knowledge into a meaningful conceptual framework, and to compose the whole business into a coherent report that answers the questions you originally posed—which task, itself, brings to bear all of your accumulated rhetorical skills.

Any assignment that asks you to perform the variety of activities outlined here might justly be considered central to what learning is all about. As you perform these activities for the first time, you may find them difficult. However, as you become better at them—better at investigating, conceptualizing, criticizing, and writing—research will get easier and you'll have a good time. In short, good, open-ended research assignments taken seriously make you a more agile, careful, and tough thinker, as well as give you practice communicating that agility, care, and toughness to others.

ASKING QUESTIONS

Why

Research implies finding an answer to a question or solution to a problem that puzzles you. It also implies that you care what the answer or solution is. Finally, research implies a process or method of looking that varies from field to field. In science research we call this method *scientific* and employ microscopes, computers, telescopes, and test tubes to help us find answers; in the humanities, we might call it criticism and usually confine ourselves to the study of texts. The point is that along with having a question, we also need a method for answering, one that we trust to yield useful language or numbers.

Who

Research implies a searcher, someone to pose questions, formulate hypotheses (hunches), look for and test solutions—a person who, in many science experiments, is supposed to be out of sight, but who in the humanities might well be center stage in the experiment, like Sherlock Holmes injecting his analytical intelligence into a muddle of disparate clues. In all cases, however, whether covertly or overtly, the intelligence of the researcher is the controlling force that guides the search for solution. This understanding, that the researcher must be in control as a master interrogator or detective, is crucial to giving the research project integrity, dignity, and worth.

Where and How

To find answers to research questions, you need to know where and how to look. The college library is one obvious source of knowledge; so too are textbooks, laboratories, computers, and your local community. To write effective college papers, learn where to locate diverse sources of information, how to assess its value, and how to include it in your writing.

APPENDIX

SUGGESTIONS FOR JOURNAL WRITING

1. How would you classify yourself as a writer, experienced, inexperienced or somewhere in between? What about writing do you already know? What else do you want to know?

2. Describe the differences you already perceive between your high school and college learning environments. Explain in what ways you are treated differently by your professors than you were by your high school teachers. Are your reading or writing assignments noticeably different? How so?

3. Which of this chapter's so-called ground rules (for example, that your job as a writer is to create belief) are new to you? On which ones could you elaborate further, with examples from your own experience? Can you add other rules to this list?

SUGGESTIONS FOR ESSAY WRITING

1. Describe your evolution as a writer from some fixed points in time (e.g., third grade or summer camp). Explain how you developed, and identify any milestones along the way.

2. Agree or disagree with one of the ground rules described in this chapter. Support your assertion with as many examples as you can.

3. Imagine and identify a new college discipline. Create a set of ground rules to support it—ground rules that may or may not correspond to those described here. Be imaginative, but persuade us that your new rules make sense.

SUGGESTIONS FOR RESEARCH PROJECTS

1. INDIVIDUAL: Locate two or more successful (A or B) papers you wrote for one of your high school courses. (If you're not living at home, you may need to send home for samples.) Examine these papers and ask: Is the writing believable? Does the paper have a serious persuasive intent? Are my assertions supported by evidence? Have I documented all claims? Is my voice relatively subjective or objective (or is it sometimes one, then another)? Do I make any claims that something is absolutely true? Would I call this paper's treatment of the subject balanced?

   See if you can point out words, sentences, or paragraphs where your writing specifically acknowledges or violates these different academic conventions. Write a short paper in which you analyze your own past writing in terms of whether or not it subscribes to the premises of the academic community described in this chapter, being sure to append a photocopy of your original paper(s) to the end of your paper.

2. COLLABORATIVE: Think of a discipline that you and some of your classmates are considering for a college major. Examine it as an academic community. Which ground rules seem to apply most? To find out more information, some of you look this up in the library while others interview professors in the field. Options: (a) write a collaborative paper or (b) share research but write an individual paper that describes the special ground rules of your possible major. Include full interviews and library sources as appendix material.

Chapter Six

WRITING TO REMEMBER AND REFLECT

10/19 When I write a paper, I inevitably make it personal. I put
myself into it and I write well. I'm paranoid when people
criticize it because they tell me to make it more impersonal—to take me out of it. I'm afraid I can't write unless
I am in the paper somehow. . . . I guess I feel defensive
because this paper has so much of me in it that I'm just
laying myself open to all kinds of attacks, and I'm scared
to read it to someone. I want to take it to [my teacher] tomorrow and ask him what he thinks. . . . What I want
badly is for him to say it is a really good paper—but I
won't believe him. I think it's good. But if he's looking
for an analytical paper I may as well forget it. . . . If
someone says I should rewrite it, make it less informal,
I'd die inside and give up.

—Jody

Essays of both personal experience and reflection draw more on a writer's
inner reserves than on outer resources. When you write from memory,
your problem is not so much locating material in library or laboratory and
weighing its usefulness as in retrieving what you already know and presenting it clearly and usefully to someone else.

WRITING TO REMEMBER

Writing about your personal experience is risky. You invite readers in,
show them your life, and hope that they'll like what they find. Or, if they

don't, that they'll at least tell you so gently. In the journal entry here, Jody describes this fear quite well. Later she came to talk to me about her paper. I think she went away from our talk feeling relieved, not to mention alive.

Figuratively, at least, writers find ideas to write about in one of two places: inside or outside. The inside ideas come from people's own memories, imaginations, and insights, aspects of the self uniquely one's own. The outside ideas come from books, people, objects, and events. (Never mind that what's inside was once out or that what's outside has to, at some point, come in.) To write about personal experience, writers go inside, retrieving impressions, images, and words buried somewhere in their memories; from these resources writers create personal narratives, informal essays, autobiographies, and a variety of personal manifestoes.

To write about something unfamiliar, where memory has no stock of stored information, writers must go elsewhere—to additional reading, fresh observation, or new research. From these resources stem much of the writing we call academic—term papers, critical essays, laboratory reports—as well as most of the writing in the working world.

Of course, categorizing all writing as either inside or outside is too simplistic. Many serious writers mix and match sources of information—some with greater abandon than others—so that few pieces of writing are strictly one category or the other. No one can remember *everything* that happened in even one simple experience, and others who were there will remember it differently.

Writers fill the gaps in their memories by reading newspapers, talking to other people, inventing dialogue, fabricating description, and revisiting places in which experiences occurred. Likewise, in writing research reports, authors may draw on remembered ideas, associations, events, current insights, as well as books, interviews, and observations.

To further complicate the matter, some writers also search their minds to imagine and create *what never happened or existed;* we call this kind of writing imaginative, creative, fictive, or poetic. Poets and novelists, of course, are the greatest mixers and matchers of all, having *poetic license* to move freely from memory to library to imagination in a single page, paragraph, or sentence. The reader should note that while strictly imaginary writing is outside the scope of this book, the lines between the imagined and the remembered are often blurred.

A good example of the mix of inside/outside sources in a single essay can be found in one of Annie Dillard's short personal narratives, "Living Like Weasels,"* which is based on her encounter with a weasel in the woods. Look at the mix of sources she draws on in these six short samples taken within a few pages of one another:

Teaching a Stone to Talk (New York: Harper & Row, 1982)

1. She leads with a statement and a question:

   A weasel is wild. Who knows what he thinks?

2. She explains the context of the essay:

   I have been reading about weasels because I saw one last week. I startled a weasel who startled me, and we exchanged a long glance.

3. She describes the weasel both literally and figuratively:

   Weasel! I'd never seen one wild before. He was ten inches long, thin as a curve, a muscled ribbon, brown as fruitwood, soft-furred, alert.

4. She retells a story from a book about weasels.

   And once, says Ernest Thompson Seton, once a man shot an eagle out of the sky. He examined the eagle and found the dry skull of a weasel fixed by the jaws to his throat. The supposition is that the eagle had pounced on the weasel and the weasel had swiveled and bit as instinct taught him, tooth to neck, and nearly won.

5. She questions and imagines on the basis of her reading:

   I would like to have seen that eagle from the air a few weeks or months before he was shot: was the whole weasel still attached to his feathered throat, a fur pendant? Or did the eagle eat what he could reach, gutting the living weasel with his talons before his breast, bending his beak, cleaning the beautiful airborne bones?

6. She speculates about the meaning of life:

   I think it would be well, and proper, and obedient, and pure, to grasp your one necessity and not let it go, to dangle from it limp wherever it takes you. . . . Seize it and let it seize you up aloft even, till your eyes burn out and drop; let your musky flesh fall off in shreds, and let your very bones unhinge and scatter, loosened over fields . . . from any height at all, from as high as eagles.

In rapid succession, the essay writer has wondered, explained, described, researched, questioned, imagined, and reflected about a single personal experience. In so doing, she has made that experience rich, multidimensional, and full of potential meaning about herself, the weasel, their encounter, and the world.

PERSONAL NARRATIVES

narrative: n. the general term for a story long or short; of the past, present, or future; factual or imagined; told for any purpose; and with or without much detail.

You are most likely to write personal narratives—that is, writing based on more truth than fiction—in composition courses where your awareness of yourself (where you came from, how you got here, what you believe and why) is often central to your further development as a writer. However, you may sometimes write in the personal narrative mode in another discipline that emphasizes self-knowledge, such as psychology, philosophy, religion, education, art, or nursing. Writing a personal narrative implies that you tell some story about yourself, about something that happened in your life or that you witnessed. This experience should be one that has meaning for you, or something you would be willing to explore to find meaning.

In the process of such self-exploration, writers often search their memories and reconstruct believable stories with beginnings, middles, and ends. Some personal narrative writing assumes the first-person point of view ("I"), uses simple past tense ("Last summer I worked at McDonald's"), and is organized chronologically. Other narrative may be told from an objective point of view ("Last summer *he* worked at McDonald's") or mix chronology (starting in the present and working backward). And, of course, still other narrative includes much of the writing in novels and short stories, an enormously rich, complex category we won't attempt to deal with in this book.

Narrative writing includes elements long familiar to all of us. *Description* fills in concrete detail, sets scenes, and allows readers to *see* the events narrated. *Dialogue* provides a sense of the dramatic, the present moment realized, and allows readers to witness people and situations crucial to the narrative. *Exposition* explains what's going on and helps readers keep abreast of the narrative action. In other words, writing from and about personal experience asks you to draw on many of the same writing skills useful in writing critical essays and research papers.

Subject

Inexperienced writers sometimes assume that they have to write about something dramatic or sensational to interest readers: the afternoon I scored the winning touchdown, the night I danced the Sugar Plum Fairy role in *The Nutcracker Suite,* or the morning I nearly died drag racing my father's Porsche. I'd like to suggest that some of the strongest narratives often result from taking something less significant—even disappointing— that happened to you and making it come to life for your reader. Instead of the big touchdown, how about the game you sat out on the bench? Instead of the dance performance, how about dance rehearsal? Instead of near death in the Porsche, how about your near death, one day, from boredom? What I'm suggesting, of course, is to take something fairly common and make something uncommon out of it, which sometimes focuses on the disappointing or tedious moments of life.

Recently, I asked the twenty-two freshmen in my writing class to write narratives about topics of their choice. As you might guess, they wrote about nearly everything: high school sports, the first day at college, the death of a grandfather, the divorce of parents, childhood games, record collecting, a mother-daughter relationship, and a number of work experiences.

For the moment, let's look at six papers. Five dealt with jobs, the sixth with a judo class the writer attended. Most of these students didn't write about the drama of their experience, but about the everyday nature of it. Here are their lead paragraphs:

JOAN: I was a Dunkin' Donuts girl. Just another face behind a pink hat and a grease-stained uniform. The job could have been degrading if I ever let it get under my skin. To get the job I had to be able to count out a dollar's worth of change and read . . .

JEFF: The heat from the huge multiple amplifiers drains every bit of energy out of me. The sweat from my body soaks my uniform right through, like I fell into water. It's dripping into my eyes, burning them because it's mixed with sulfuric oxide. My safety glasses are constantly slipping to the end of my nose . . . None of these precautions do any good because I'm wet with sweat in 150-degree heat, waiting like a target to be shocked . . .

SUE: Every morning when I woke up, the dull throbbing of my lower back reminded me that I worked the night before. The odor of stale cigarettes, French onion soup, and grease from the grill lingered in my room, coming from my uniform crumpled on the floor . . .

FRANK: I never really minded running around, it was just so monotonous. The life of a gopher could be summed up in a few short commands: "Hand me that! Pick up these! Help me with this!"

STEPHANY: T.G.I.T. Thank God It's Tuesday. I always look forward to Tuesdays. They mean two things: Tomorrow is my day off and today is my boss's day off, so I won't be asked to pick eggs. I really hate picking eggs—I get all covered with dust, eggs, and grain. By the end of the day I'm so tired I just want to sack out. When I was hired my boss told me I'd only have to pick eggs once in a while, but this week I had to pick three times. It really gets me, because my real job is candling eggs. . .

KATE: "Ten pushups? You've got to be kidding!" I don't think
I've ever done more than two in my life. I strain my arms
trying to touch the mat . . .

It's not the subject, of course, but the treatment that draws us in or turns us away. In these examples, Joan's bouncy opening reminds us more of a cheerleader than a coffee shop waitress, and we wonder what else lies ahead. Jeff starts fast, giving us little context, except to see him drenched in sweat on the battery assembly line waiting to be electrocuted (do we read on, in part, to see how he survives?). Sue describes her job from the morning after; Frank describes his with the words of his many bosses as he helps lay underground cables; Stephany's colloquial, talky voice carries us into her piece; Kate's present tense puts us with her on the mat doing warm-up exercises.

Some of these writers, such as Kate and Jeff, wrote their opening paragraph on the first draft and let it stand through successive revisions; others, such as Stephany, found this opening only in the last draft. And one, Joan, scrapped the strong opening printed here for a different approach in subsequent draft. In short, each writer had to work through his or her own process to find the writing that was most satisfying.

Time

One of the most difficult problems of writing narrative or autobiography is deciding how much time to spend on what. A common mistake is trying to cover some great expanse of time, often resulting in diluted generalizations: my summer job at McDonald's, all seventy-four days of it; or how I learned karate, starting with my life as a ninety-pound weakling. Instead of trying to cover such vast periods in a few pages, writers are likely to benefit when they focus sharply in time and space. Instead of trying to generalize about all summer at McDonald's, how about one hot day behind the hamburger grill? Or one afternoon? Or one hour?

Ironically, the smaller the focus in time, the more you will find to say. You really can't say much about a generic day or generic hamburger grill, but you can say something truly substantial about that humid Thursday in August when you worked the grill on your own for the first time.

Look again at the paragraphs describing the students' jobs, and you will notice how several begin quickly by putting you right there, at a specific spot on a specific day: in the battery factory, at the egg farm, on the judo mat. We reexperience these particular places with the writers and feel as if we're present, on the spot, glimpsing into a real and private world— that's what makes us read on. Strong narrative makes us relive an experience with a writer and adds to our own store of vicarious experiences.

Don't misunderstand: great narratives have been written that cover great expanses of time; others offer outrageous generalizations. Nevertheless, for most writers most of the time, specificity is the key to creating belief.

Belief

There are few rules to follow when writing narrative, but the writing that works best for me portrays a chunk of experience and makes me *believe* that this really happened, this is *true*.

Being honest as a writer and creating belief for the reader may be slightly different. Many writers of personal narrative believe that they must stick only to precisely remembered, detailed fact. ("I can't include that detail because I'm not sure of exactly what I said, and I don't remember what I was wearing.") Keep in mind, however, that writing a nonfiction narrative about something that happened in your life will not result in an exact report of what really happened; you will omit some details, select only certain facts, forget some emotions, and misremember more than you realize. No matter how hard you try to get it right, you will distort, modify, and, in effect, *lie*. It is unavoidable. Writing can represent reality; it can never replicate it.

The trick is to remember as best you can and be willing to *recreate* to fill gaps. If you don't remember exactly what you said, you might re-create dialogue that is approximate, typical of you, close to what you might have said; if you don't remember the exact shoes you wore on that hot Thursday, you might remember shoes you could have worn, and what they looked like and how they felt. If this sounds devious, consider that we do it all the time when we tell oral stories. Of course, how you create belief is often through the careful use of pertinent detail.

Detail

As a writer, you can make your narrative believable in several ways. In the following examples, our student writers convince us that they are telling the truth by providing concrete detail, precise action, appropriate language, honest emotion, and documentable facts.

1. Inside knowledge—Readers like to be let into worlds that they have seen only from the outside. Often the small details let them in. In the following passage, Sue shows us what she knows as an experienced filler of salad bars:

    > I could fill three crocks in one trip, unless it was something messy like beets or applesauce. It took time to refill those because they splashed.

In the next passage, Stephany, who worked summers on an egg farm, teaches us about a job few of us knew existed, candling eggs:

> Candling is easy. All you have to do is take four flats of somebody's eggs and spin a hundred of them in front of a bright light to look for cracks. Then I count the number of cracked eggs and write it down on my candling sheet next to the egg picker's name.

2. Action—Narrative writing includes action that convinces us the writer has been where he or she claims to have been. Here, Kate describes her judo instructor's demonstration of a hold in class:

> He grabs the student around the neck, holding the head tight with the elbow and shoulder. The extended arm is pulled in and the instructor also holds it in position. As the student struggles to get free of the hold, it only tightens.

3. Authentic language—Convincing narrative shows people talking in rhythms of speech that sound believable. In the following passage, Kathy recreates her first day working at a supermarket, and we can hear her talking:

> I can't believe it, I actually started work at Wilson's today—my first job! They hired me as a cashier, but now they tell me I'll be bagging and keeping the strawberry bin full, at least for a while. I guess they want me to become familiar with their system and working with people before they train me to run a register.

4. Emotion—Feelings are part of remembered experience. In the following passage, Bobby describes both his own and his father's emotion in a tension-filled automobile:

> "I can hardly see the road, it's raining so hard!" my father yelled. . . . Sensing the nervous frustration in my father's voice, I felt a chill that came from knowing that my cool, calm, collected father was in a state of panic.

In the next example, Joan recreates her disillusionment about her job at the donut shop through understatement; we can hear her feelings between the lines:

> The thrill of this job is gradually wearing off. I guess I still haven't gotten over the incident with Mr. Stacy. I'm on the night shift now, 6 p.m. until 2 or 3 a.m., so I don't see him much. He usually calls a few times during the night to ask how many customers are there and how much money I've made, but stays home.

5. Facts and figures—Narrative often gains in credibility the same way that more objective writing does, with believable data. Jeff has conducted research about the battery factory in which he has worked and, at one point, tells us the following:

> With sixteen manufacturing plants and 5,800 employees, Johnson Controls is the largest of five major competitors in the country.

6. Figurative language—Narrative is often strengthened when the writer makes a telling analogy, simile, or metaphor that makes us *see* the story more vividly (remember Annie Dillard's weasel "thin as a curve, a muscled ribbon"?). In the following example, Paul, who has worked on a farm, describes the first time he was shown how to butcher lambs:

> I looked up when I heard a PLOP. The warm hide had fallen to the floor like a wet towel. The lamb now glistened as the gelatinous fatty tissue reflected the bright shop lights.

These examples convince me that the writers knew what they were talking (writing) about; in each case, I'm ready to hear more.

Form

Personal narratives are often structured by chronology: first this happened, then this, which led to that. However, narratives can be told through flashbacks, mixed chronology, and even multiple points of view. Of all the short writing forms, the narrative may have the simplest organizational scheme. This probably accounts for its reputation as an easier form than essays organized by other argumentative and explanatory schemes. But don't be fooled: narrative that seems direct and straightforward may have gone through dozens of drafts to reach its final form.

Consider also that new forms and formats can bring new life to narratives. In fact, they are generative, creating new insights even if you only intended to alter the form. In the example mentioned before, Joan began to tell her story of life in the donut shop by looking backward, reflecting in the past tense, "*I was a Dunkin' Donuts girl.*" Later, however, she abandoned that perspective for the present tense created by the journal format: "October 23. *I've driven into Durham daily, but no one's hiring.*" One is not necessarily better than the other; each simply makes both writer and reader experience the event from a different perspective.

In playing with your narrative, in looking for your final point of view, focus, theme, or whatever, consider playing with the form: What would happen if I told this as an exchange of letters? Could the reader experience it differently if it resembled a drama, with lots of recreated dialogue? Could it be tailored for a column in a magazine, such as "My Turn" in *Newsweek?*

READERS AT WORK

When you include descriptions of actual events and places in your story, the accumulation of detail begins to tell your story for you. Let it. In early drafts of narrative writing, authors want to explain to the readers everything that happened, why those things were important, and exactly what the reader should get from reading this. In later drafts I recommend letting your skillful recreation of details *show* your story to the reader.

Showing works better than summarizing because concrete detail allows readers to *see* your experience and then make their own summary statements. When Kate writes, "*He grabs the student around the neck, holding the head tight with the elbow and shoulder,*" we see the mode of control; had she instead written, "He holds the student so she cannot move," the writer would skip to the net effect of the judo hold, but would deprive us of visualizing it—and in visualizing it, we become more engaged with it and, in turn, provide our own summary or judgment: "she cannot move." Specific detail actually makes a reader work harder in a positive way. When, instead, the writer does all the work, providing the summaries, judgments, and editorials, readers become passive or even withdraw: "I am about to tell you about the hardest job I ever had. . . ." The judgment has been rendered and there's less to do. What you want instead is for readers to enter into the interpretation of your story and actually to help in finding out what it means. The net result is more investment on their part as they enter your story with you and locate themselves within it and figure out what the story you tell means. Recall how Jeff put you in the battery factory or Stephany the egg farm. In these cases, the readers experience the difficulty and make their own judgments. When the reader has done that, you've created belief.

So What?

While a narrative is based on something that actually happened, keep in mind that the reason you write about it is to portray something about yourself that has some meaning or value and that makes a point. Narratives, just like reports, critical essays, and research papers, must make a point, must have a reason for having been told. As a reader, the question I commonly ask when I finish reading is "So what?" What difference has it made that I read this? Why did the author choose to tell me this? As a writer, I try to keep the same question in mind at all times: why am I bothering to tell this particular story and not some other? What do I intend my reader to take away from this reading?

However, making a point in a narrative isn't always easy. Seldom are our lives broken up into neat modules or stories with clear beginnings, middles, or ends. Our tasks as writers will be to fashion convincing lives for our readers, as if such starting and stopping points existed. In that sense, whatever you write as truth will have some element of fabrication about it. Sometimes a narrative will start with a strong directly stated thesis (in the first set of student samples, Frank's "monotony"). However, it is more likely that a narrative lead will imply, but not state, the actual thesis (Sue's "dull throbbing of my lower back" or Jeff's "target waiting to be shocked"). Many narratives make their point through the accumulation of detail, asking the reader to make meaning from a revealed slice of life.

Writing from Experience Checklist

1. What story have I told? Is it primarily about me? an event? somebody else?
2. When I finish reading the story and ask "So what?" does my story provide an answer?
3. Have I *shown* rather than *summarized* the action and details of this story? Can you see where it takes place? Can you hear my characters speak?
4. Do I make my readers do some interpretive work? Or do I provide all the judgments and explanations for them?
5. Does my form work? What effect would other forms (journal, letter, essay, drama) have on the story I want to tell?

AUTOBIOGRAPHIES

Much of what I have written about personal narratives is also true of autobiography. You usually write in the first-person mode ("I"), from re-membered experience, in more or less chronological order. As in personal narrative writing, you remember as best you can, and invent what you need to make it more credible. However, in autobiography you may have an even greater need to be selective and inventive, depending on how far back you attempt to go to make sense of your life.

Scope

What separates autobiography from other narratives is scope and focus. The scope of an autobiography is some substantial portion of your life, and so the advice about taking one small chunk of time and elaborating in great detail is less helpful. With a lifetime of experience—be it eighteen years or forty-eight—to account for, it's unlikely that an autobiographer would choose to focus on the smaller moments of his or her life. However, when small moments generate life-changing insight, they hardly classify as small moments, do they? Keep in mind that no matter how large the scope, it's the particulars that persuade.

Strategies

Two obvious strategies for writing an autobiography present themselves, one inductive, the other deductive. The *inductive* method would involve the following activities: make a list of what you would call the important events in your life: confirmation, high school graduation, reading a particular book, making a new friend, etc. Tinker with the list until it seems a reasonable representation of your life and then start writing—anywhere about any incident—and keep writing to see what themes or patterns emerge that you didn't predict. Take one of these themes or patterns and make that your controlling thesis.

If you want your life story to be strong and meaningful, you will need to discover, fabricate, or invent a controlling idea that shapes the story and somehow gives insight into who you are today and what you stand for: your passion for order or for art, your inability or your readiness to commit, etc. In short, when writing an autobiography, you deliberately select a focus and supporting detail from among the many possibilities to give an external shape and meaning to your life. Remember, your writing will never *be* your life, but only one of many representations, which explains who you are and how you got there.

To write *deductively* about your life, you reverse the process and begin as if you had something to prove: you start with an idea of a quality or theme that seems to characterize your life: your competitiveness or insecurity; your need to be in control or believe in something; your decision to become a teacher or an astronaut; your fascination with words or insects. Your writing then begins to explore this theme, as you deliberately bring to mind all those elements that seem to support this pattern, ignoring incidents that don't help develop your point about yourself. Again, your aim is to fashion a version of your life both believable to your readers and reasonably true to your own conception of things.

Every time I've begun to write about a piece of my life the inductive and deductive have gotten mixed up: I begin to write deductively, believing there is a pattern, and find many elements that are important but don't fit. Then I end up writing inductively to discover what the new pattern may be. But I accept that as one valid way to go about this difficult writing task, perhaps more realistic than either of the one-dimensional modes.

While it is unlikely that college students will be asked to write full-fledged autobiographies, they may be asked to write more sharply focused self-portraits to learn more about limited dimensions of their lives. Consider, for example, assignments I call language autobiographies and self-profiles.

Language Autobiographies

Writing a study of yourself as a user of language is a limited and focused way of looking at who you've become. A language autobiography tells the story of how you came to be the language user you are today; it focuses on those influences you perceive as most important, the ones that shape how you read, write, speak, and think. The following list offers some suggestions for constructing a language autobiography.

Write about family, friends, and teachers who taught you things about language—first words, code words, critical words. When possible, locate artifacts such as letters, diaries, and stories you wrote or letters and report cards others wrote about you.

Write about favorite books and authors, especially those that live most actively in your mind. Be specific and name titles and characters while examining why these particular stories stayed with you.

Write about the way your use of language was influenced by your neighborhood, hobbies, sports, clubs, politics, religion, and special interests of any kind. At first, it may not be obvious that these influenced your language use, but odds are they did.

Write about schools—the grades, classes, subjects, teachers, assignments, and activities that revolved around or stretched your literacy skills.

Write about your writing—remembered, retrieved, or current. What do you like to write about? How often do you write when you don't have to? What are you writing now?

Pair with a classmate and interview each other to push out ideas that you, on your own, may not recall. Practice asking each other follow-up questions: When did you read that? Why did you like it? How often were you read to? And so on.

Self-Profiles

Unlike language autobiographies, a self-profile focuses on the present: who you are now. These are among the most interesting and frustrating assignments imaginable: how do you decide who you really are? And how much do you want to share with an instructor or classmate? As an instructor, however, I find self-profiles especially rich because they are so challenging—both for first-year writers and graduating seniors, since both groups are at pivotal places in their lives, looking backward and forward at the same time. The following list offers some suggestions for profiling yourself.

Write from memory. Write fast and impressionistically, and try to capture important or defining moments that contribute to who you are today—playing high school basketball or field hockey; acting in middle school plays; moving to a new state as a child; your relationship with a brother, sister, mom, or dad, and so on. What happened in our past sometimes determines who we are in the present.

Write about artifacts. Examine your most valued possessions: posters on your wall; saved letters or journals; your favorite hat, cap, or T-shirt; what you carry in your pockets. Describe this *thing* as carefully as you can and explore possible dimensions it reveals about you.

Write what people say about you. Interview friends and family members, recall old and recent conversations, find teacher comments on papers and report cards, make stuff up. Adding other voices spices things up, adds other perspectives, and complicates your identity.

Write about how you spend your time now: describe a typical day or week. Describe current activities, sports, hobbies, passions, and places you seek out or hang out. Examine why you do these things, what they mean to you.

Write standing in front of a mirror. Describe the person you see before you—hair, height, clothes, nose, eyes, mouth, expression. What does your physical self say about your psychological self?

Write I am. . . . Compose a series of sentences, each starting with the words "I am" and continue on from there:

> I am shy and quiet on the outside, more bold and noisy inside. I am Irish, German, and Polish—a mongrel, an American. I am Peter Pan, Huckleberry Finn, and Michael Jordan (or Wendy, Anne of Green Gables, and Madonna)—at least sometimes and in my dreams.

Keep writing, trying out different characters, and see who else you might be.

REFLECTIVE ESSAYS

> **reflect:** v. 1: to bend or fold back; to make manifest or apparent; 2: to think quietly or calmly; to express a thought or opinion resulting from reflection.

Reflective writing is thoughtful writing. Reflective essays take a topic—any topic—and turn it around, up and down, forward and backward, asking us to think about in uncommon ways. Reflective writing allows both writer and reader to consider—but especially *reconsider* things thoughtfully, seriously, meditatively—but demands neither resolution nor definitive answers.

When you write to reflect, part of your motivation is to figure out something for yourself, in addition to sharing your reflections with somebody else. Such writing is commonly characterized by a slight sense of indirection, as if the writer were in the actual process of examining a subject closely for the first time.

Purpose, more than subject, distinguishes reflective writing from other types of writing. In reflective essays, writers ask *why?* Why do people live and behave the way they do? Why does society develop this way rather than that? Why does one thing happen rather than another? In asking these questions—and offering possible answers—they try to make sense of some small portion of their world.

Reflective essays are as varied as the thought processes of the people who write them, but one especially common pattern is worth extra attention. Many reflective essays describe a concrete subject or actual situation, pause for a moment, focus on a larger topic stimulated by the subject or situation, make a point, and then conclude by coming back to the subject that prompted the reflection. The subject that causes the reflection in the first place is not the actual topic of the essay.

For example, you could write a reflective essay on a subject such as electric light bulbs, in which your topic became the influence of artificial light on twentieth-century American culture. Here the topic is a clear subcategory of the subject. However, a reflective essay that started with the subject of electric light bulbs could just as easily move to personal memories of summer camp—the cabin illuminated by the light of a single electric bulb—and end up a meditation on the value of summer camp for American adolescents. In this case, the light bulb is a catalyst to deeper, more reflective thoughts. In other words, in reflective essays the nominal subject may or may not be closely connected to the actual topic of the essay.

Like personal narratives, reflective essays invite your opinion. Assignments that contain direction words such as *imagine, speculate,* or *explore* invite a kind of writing that features your ability to see a given subject from several sides and to offer tentative answers to profound questions. These assignments are common in the more speculative disciplines such as history, philosophy, and religion, as well as in writing classes. In these assignments, it may be important to include factual information; however, such information is background, not foreground material.

Reflection may also be asked for in assignments that are not literally called *reflective.* For example, in an English class you might be asked to summarize and then discuss (reflect upon what you've just summarized) Yeats' poem "Leda and the Swan." In a political science class you may be asked to summarize the results of an election, then discuss its implications.

Likewise, in a biology class you might be asked to analyze the causes of fruit fly reproduction then discuss the implications.

Reflective essays are about something that's on your mind, perhaps something that's especially intriguing, even distracting, that raises questions worth speculating upon. No matter where or with what object or idea you start, your job as a writer is to bring that object or idea into sharper focus for your readers, perhaps helping them to see it differently than they have before.

Strategies for Starting Reflective Essays

Select any or all of the following strategies for starting a reflection paper:

- *Remember*—Recall a person, place, or thing that has always interested you. Close your eyes, ransack your memory, freewrite to bring it closer for more speculative examination:

  > My paper route wound up 68th street north of State, fourteen houses on one side, a deep fenced-in gravel pit on the other—which meant fourteen fewer customers on that stretch of the route. When I returned home from college last year, the gravel pit had been transformed into a supermarket with acres of parking all around.

  A reflection on growing up, change, progress, modern supermarkets? It's up to the writer.

- *Seek Out*—Look for something or someone specific about which you've already had questions or strong opinions. Examine this person, place, or thing carefully. Look at it from many sides. Take good notes so that you could reproduce it accurately in your essay.

  > Whenever I visit the Church Street Mall, the first thing I look and listen for is the clarinet man, settled in a corner by the fountain, case open, bobbing and weaving and playing his horn with closed eyes. When he's not there, the mall seems smaller, the shopping less interesting.

  A reflection on music, malls, shopping, street people?

- *Notice*—Observe the commonplace that catches your attention. The advantage of common, over spectacular, subjects is everyone has some experience with them and is automatically curious to see what you make of them. At the same time, you need to make sure your reflection itself goes beyond the commonplace and introduces readers to new dimensions or perspectives.

  > Have you ever seen the man—or maybe it's a woman—who empties the coins out of the parking meters?

> Neither have I. Makes you wonder, doesn't it, when and how they do it? Or are all the meters connected to this central pipeline, sort of like a sewer pipe, that drains the money every day?

A reflection on the city, unusual occupations, machines, money?

- *Ask why*—Write out as many questions as you can think of, maybe a whole journal page about whatever it is you've remembered, visited, or noticed. Circle those with local or physical manifestations. See which ones you would like to try to answer.

> Why do cockroaches only live in cities? *Do* they only live in cities? Is there such a thing as a country cockroach? What makes these huge bugs so indestructable? And why do people hate them so?

A reflection on bugs, people, relationships, evolution?

Strategies for Writing Reflective Essays

- *Experiment*—Take chances in writing. Your subject alone will carry interest just so far: the rest is up to your originality, creativity, and skill as you present the topic of your essay, along with the deeper and more speculative meaning you have found.

- *Pause*—Include pauses in your writing and make your reader pause with you. Once you've established your nominal subject, say to the reader, in effect, *Wait a minute, there's something else going on here—stop and consider.* The pause is a key moment, signalling the writer that it's time to work a little harder, dig a little deeper, find connections that heretofore you've not found. It signals the reader that the essay is about to move into a new and less predictable direction.

- *Shift*—Change your voice or tone or style for emphasis. Often the pause is accompanied by a slight shift in point of view, tone, or *style.* Suddenly the writer is either a little more personal or a little more formal, slightly more biased or slightly more objective. The writer may step back and use the third-person point of view for a moment or use the first-person point of view for the first time. The exact nature of the shift will, of course, be determined by the point the writer wants to make.

- *Make a point*—Be sure to answer directly or indirectly, the reader's question, *What did I learn from reading this?* The point made in reflective writing nearly always emerges near the end, rather than the beginning of the essay. That way, readers are drawn into the act of reflecting themselves and become progressively more curious to find where the author stands. In other words, reflective writers are musing rather than arguing. In fact, reflective essays are most persuasive when least obviously instructive or assertive.

- *Leave an opening for further speculation*—Reflective essays raise issues but seldom resolve them. The tradition of essay writing is the tradition of *trying* and *attempting* rather than *resolving* or *concluding*. Ending by acknowledging that you see still other questions invites your reader to join in the search for answers.
- *Read examples of good reflective writing*—Michele de Montaigne, Henry David Thoreau, George Orwell, E.B. White, Virginia Woolf, Richard Wright, Joan Didion, Alice Walker, Lewis Thomas, Annie Dillard, Richard Rodriguez, Margaret Atwood, or bell hooks. Read the reflective newspaper columnists, such as Ellen Goodman and Russell Baker. Browse among the *New York Times* best-selling nonfiction in your bookstore, or subscribe to *The New Yorker* or *Atlantic Monthly.*

APPENDIX

SUGGESTIONS FOR JOURNAL WRITING

1. List five significant experiences that happened to you during the past year. Write a paragraph on the three that seem most interesting, memorable, or in need of further examination.

2. List five commonplace, ordinary, or daily events and consider whether or not there may be a story here of interest to somebody else. Write a paragraph about three that hold the possibility of story.

3. Make a list of insights, speculations, or reflections you remember having within the past week. Write a paragraph about each that you remember well and that seems worth exploring further.

4. Draw a line diagonally down a sheet of journal paper, putting your date of birth at one end, the current date at the other. On one side of the line, in chronological order, list all *out-of-school* events, books, or people that influenced your language development. On the other side of the line, list all *in-school* events that influenced that development. Use this time line to structure your language autobiography.

SUGGESTIONS FOR ESSAY WRITING

1. Write an essay based on personal experience that begins with or uses information from your journal entries. Write your first draft as you naturally would, in the past tense; when you write your second draft, switch to the present tense and notice the difference.

Finish the essay using the tense that best conveys the story you want to tell.

2. Write a reflective essay that begins by noticing a common object in your neighborhood or a recent local occurrence of some interest. Use this concrete beginning to lead to speculate or explore a larger or more abstract train of thought. In the first draft, present the object or occurrence carefully and with great detail. In the second and third drafts, focus on possible meanings or implications that go beyond the object or occurrence.

3. Write a language autobiography as a series of prose snapshots, drawing on items from your journal time line for the content of each snapshot. Separate each verbal picture by white space and don't worry about providing transitions. (See Chapter Fifteen for more information on snapshot writing.)

4. Compose a self-portrait by following the suggestions for profile writing in this chapter. Create one version based strictly on memories, another on artifacts, another on quotations about you, and so on. Review each of these versions and integrate them into a pattern that satisfies you and that you're willing to share with the instructor and classmates.

SUGGESTIONS FOR RESEARCH PROJECTS

1. Write a portion or chapter of your autobiography. Collect from home as many things (notes, report cards, baseball cards, old magazines or records, memorabilia, wall posters, journals or diaries, letters, school papers, hobby remnants, etc.) as you or your parents can unearth that says something about your own development as a person. Find a way to weave this story of yourself at one point in time, using some of these documents of personal research to help you.

2. Write a profile of a classmate in which you make him or her come alive. Place everyone's name in a hat, and draw out two at a time. Names drawn together are to interview each other, spend time together, maybe share a meal, visit each other's living quarters, and in general keep talking to and making notes about each other. Write these up after the fashion of "Profiles" printed in *People Magazine, The New Yorker,* your daily paper, or as Studs Terkel did when he edited the tape transcripts for *Working* (Random House, 1973). Along the way, share drafts; when all have been completed collect them and publish in a class book (see *Postscript Three*).

3. Search the library periodical holdings or your own living room for magazines well known for printing interesting nonfiction (e.g., *The New Yorker, Rolling Stone, Esquire, The Atlantic, The Village Voice, Sports Illustrated, Time, Newsweek, Reader's Digest, The New Republic, Redbook*). Browse through these magazines and make notes about whatever interests you in the narrative writing you find there. Report—orally or in writing—what you found and how it relates to your own writing.

Chapter Seven

WRITING TO EXPLAIN
AND REPORT

Above all else, I want to write so clearly and accurately
that others see things exactly the way I do.

—Terry

Explaining is the task of writers in every imaginable kind of work: business, industry, scientific, technical, academic, and professional. To explain is to make some concept, event, or process clear to your reader, to *expose* or reveal it. (Another name for explanatory writing is expository writing.) In college, you may be asked to explain chemical processes by writing a laboratory report, literary events by writing a book report, political, sociological, or historical events in papers for those disciplines.

One of the distinguishing characteristics of much—but certainly not all—explanatory writing is objectivity. While it's virtually impossible for writers to achieve complete objectivity—to separate themselves from the ways they've learned to see the world—in explanatory writing, it's useful to try. Most of the time, to explain clearly requires writers to put themselves, along with their biases, in the background and their subject in the foreground, so that readers may see and understand it, as much as possible, for what it is.

Explanatory writing is defined not so much by its subject (which can be almost anything) as by the way the subject is treated. When you write to explain, you are answering one or more of these questions:

What is it?   (define)
What happened?
What does it look like? ⟩ (describe)
Where is it?

How is it related to other things?   (compare/contrast)

How does it work?

>(analyze)

Why did it happen?

How is it held together?   (synthesize)

In writing classes, explanation often takes the form of research essays and reports that inform rather than remember, reflect, argue, or interpret. The assignment may ask you to describe how something works or to explain the causes and effects of a particular phenomenon. To explain anything successfully, you need a limited and defined topic, a clear sense of who you are writing to, information about your topic that goes beyond common knowledge, a working thesis, and organized explanatory strategies. And you need to focus on the thing being explained rather than on your feelings and opinions about it.

When I teach first-year writing classes, I commonly ask students to join together in small groups to investigate a local issue and, together, write a report to the rest of us explaining its significance. In the following example, a group of six students wrote a collaborative paper investigating the water-treatment plant in the city of Burlington, Vermont. Here, they explain the nature of the pollution that periodically closes the beaches on Lake Champlain:

> The sewage overflow usually takes place after heavy rains. The sewage and storm waters are handled by the same pipe, and the pipe can't handle both the sewage and the rain water. Then the overflow goes to the lake instead of the treatment plant. The real bummer is that the beaches are closed two to three days after.

This example is simple, clear, quite general, and effective for its intended audience. (By the way, the colloquial term *bummer* in the last line is a good indicator of the audience for whom the group is writing—other college students.)

Later in the same essay, the water-treatment group provides a more detailed explanation of the lake pollution:

> Vermont has always been a casual, back to nature, "no worries" state. During the last few years the Burlington Sewage Treatment Plant has had problems containing large quantities of effluent that are deposited during and after a rain storm. Its effluent is rich in nitrates, phosphorus and bacteria and the introduction of unnatural levels of sub-

stances by the sewage plant is one of the lake's major
sources of pollution (Miller 130).

Here, they start off casually, calling Vermont a "no worries state," but
quickly get down to business, buttressing their own explanation with a
reference (Miller 130) in case the reader wants to check sources. Notice
that in both of these examples the writers mix informal with formal
language to explain most clearly. In fact, the very best explanations usually
use the writer's simplest, most direct, comfortable language. Notice, too,
how explaining relies on defining and describing to achieve clarity.

When you write to explain, keep these three guidelines in mind:
First, explanatory writing commonly uses an objective perspective; that is,
it emphasizes the thing explained rather than the writer's beliefs and feelings. Second, explanatory writing focuses on the reader's need for information rather than the writer's desire for self-expression. Third, explanatory writing is usually systematic and orderly, having a stated thesis, clear
explanatory strategies, and a logical organizational structure.

To explain material delivered in lectures or found in textbooks, it's
a good idea to do so in your own words—which shows you have digested
and understood the ideas—but also to quote selectively from your sources
for further support. In any case, when explaining material for this or that
course, be sure to use the language and conventions of that discipline as
much as possible.

Let's look more closely at the basic strategies of explanatory (expository) discourse, including the operations of *defining, describing, compar-
ing/contrasting, analyzing* and *synthesizing,* as well as the basic formats
of *reports, summaries,* and *abstracts.*

DEFINING

to define: v. to state the precise meaning of something; to describe
the nature or basic qualities of; to specify distinctly; to serve to
distinguish.

Defining is simply a more specialized mode of explaining, in which you
must be especially precise because defining something means separating
it from other similar concepts.

You will seldom be asked only to define something. More commonly,
you will be expected to act on your definition. For example, in math you
may have to define differential equations and be able to solve problems
based on your definition; in psychology you may need to define Freud's
theories and apply your definition to a case study; in business you may
need to define supply-side economics and make a case for this policy.

At one point in the water-treatment essay, the writers provide us with a technical definition of pollution that is both more inclusive and more precise than their description of Lake Champlain pollution so far:

> In order to talk about pollution, one must define the terms involved. According to the dictionary "to pollute," means, "to defile, to soil, or to make unclean." This definition is a bit too general for our needs so we incorporate another: "Pollution is the introduction of material or effects at a harmful level" (C. R. Curds and H. A. Hawkes 20).

You will notice that this example presents two external sources for authority—a dictionary and a text on the subject of pollution (Curds and Hawkes' *Ecological Aspects of Used Water Treatment*, 1975). When writing, in the academic world and elsewhere, make your definitions clear and authoritative.

Sometimes, however, it will be necessary to do your own defining, as in the following case, where Susan defines the various strands of contemporary music in order to classify and compare it:

> "Rock Classics" can be loud, raucous, and even noisy at times, but then the band will slow down with gentle ballads. The bands which play this type of music include the following: Led Zeppelin, Jimi Hendrix, Jethro Tull, The Rolling Stones, The Kinks, Neil Young, and even the Beatles.

Susan then provides a definition of several more categories: Heavy Metal, Glitter Rock, and One Hit Wonders. Here, for example, is her definition of Glitter Rock:

> This style of music is characterized by very extravagant, peculiar, and bizarre performers. It is hard to describe, being sometimes screechy, other times quiet. This type of music got its start in the early seventies with performers such as David Bowie, Alice Cooper, Lou Reed, and Frank Zappa.

Susan's task is a difficult one, since music—especially contemporary music—does not succumb easily to definition. However, notice that she uses examples of well-known rock performers to help her clarify what she means. The use of examples typically clarifies and strengthens definitions.

When writing essays that depend heavily on defining something, keep the following principles in mind: (1) in defining a word, use synonyms and not the word itself to make your definition clear (for example, "fish are cold-blooded animals living in water and having backbones, gills, and fins."); (2) illustrate with concrete examples (as Susan did above or

as we could do about fish by describing several different species of them);
(3) go back to the basics; don't assume your reader knows even the
simplest terms; don't be afraid to state what to you is obvious (that, for
example, all fish "live in water"); (4) sometimes it's helpful to point out
what your definition does not include (the term *fish*, for example, does
not normally include whales, lobsters, or scallops).

DESCRIBING

> **to describe:** v. to give a verbal account; to transmit a mental image
> or impression with words.

To describe a person, place, or thing is to create a verbal image so that
readers can see what you see, hear what you hear, and taste, smell, and
feel what you taste, smell, and feel. Your goal is to make it real enough for
readers to experience it for themselves. Above all, descriptive details need
to be purposeful. Heed the advice of Russian writer Anton Chekhov: "If a
gun is hanging on the wall in the first chapter, it must, without fail, fire in
the second or third chapter. If it doesn't fire, it mustn't hang either."

   The ability to describe something that you witnessed or experienced
so that your reader can witness or experience it is useful in all kinds of
writing from expository to argumentative, narrative to interpretative. In
the following example, Becky describes the setting of a ballet rehearsal,
explaining at the same time, the difference between amateur and professional dancers:

> The backstage studio is alive with energy. . . . Dancers are
> scattered around the room, stretching, chatting, adjusting
> shoes and tights. Company members, the professionals who
> are joining us for this performance, wear tattered leg warm-
> ers, sweatpants which have lost their elastic, and old T-
> shirts over tights and leotards. Their hair is knotted into
> buns or, in the case of male dancers, held tight with sweat-
> bands. You can tell the students by the runless pink tights,
> dress-code leotards, and immaculate hair.

To describe how processes work is more complicated than giving a simple
physical description, for in addition to showing objects at rest, you need
to show them in sequence and motion. To describe a process, you need
to divide the process into discrete steps and present the steps in a logical
order. For some processes this is easy (making chili, giving highway
directions). For others it is more difficult, either because many steps are
all happening at once or because people really don't know which steps
come before others (manufacturing a car, writing a research paper).

In either case, show the steps in a logical sequence that will be easy for readers to understand. To orient your readers, you may also want to number the steps, using transition words such as first, second, and third. In the following example, a team of students visited Ben and Jerry's Ice Cream company to write a paper explaining its origin and operation; they included the following process description in their paper:

> We learned that their ice cream begins in the Blend Tank, a two hundred forty lb. stainless steel tank that combines Vermont milk, sweet cream, egg yolks, unrefined sugar, and the flavor of the day.
>
> From there, the mix is sent in big stainless vats to the thirty-six degree (cold!) Tank Room, where it sits for four to eight hours before it receives further flavoring.
>
> From the Tank Room, the mix moves into four, three hundred gallon Flavor Vats, so they can put in the greenish liquid peppermint extract for the Mint Oreo and the brown pungent smelling coffee extract for the Coffee Heath Bar Crunch.
>
> Finally, it moves to the Flavor Vat, where they mix in big chunks of broken Oreos or Heath Bar they need for the ice cream they are producing on that day.

The ice cream making process is clear because the writers use a four-part sequence with the cue words, *begins, from, from,* and *finally,* so there is no question of what is happening when.

To describe well, use nouns that conjure up concrete and specific images, such as the *stainless steel vats* and *Heath Bars* in the Ben and Jerry's piece. Also use action verbs wherever you can, such as *scattered* and *knotted* in the ballet paper. And use modifiers that appeal to the senses—*tattered leg warmers, greenish liquid peppermint extract*—all of which help readers visualize what you are talking about.

COMPARING OR CONTRASTING

> **to compare:** v. to examine (two or more things, ideas, people, etc.) for the purpose of noting similarities and differences; to consider or describe as similar.

We compare things all the time: this college, city, or state to that; one movie, book, or record to another; and so on. As we compare, we usually also contrast, noting the differences as well as the similarities in our comparison; thus, the act of comparing often includes the act of contrasting as well. In my nonacademic life, I read the magazine *Consumer Reports* regularly to help me choose one product over another; in my academic life, I read *College English* to help me choose one theory or interpretation over another.

Throughout your college studies you will be asked to compare and contrast in order to interpret and evaluate; you will do this as often in business, math, and engineering as in history, philosophy, and literature. However, actual comparative essays are more common in the latter, more interpretive disciplines than in the former, more quantitative ones. For purposes of essay writing, you should be aware of particular *types* of comparison as well as good *methods* for doing it.

Apples and Apples

At a basic level, we compare like things to like things: one apple to another for taste, color, size, etc. We usually compare similar kinds of things to answer questions of worth or suitability: is this the best pen (of several kinds) to write with? Is this the best stereo system (of several brands) for me to buy? Is this the best interpretation (among competing ones) of this poem? In these instances, the elements being compared are similar and do similar things, and thus can be compared point by point.

Apples and Oranges

Most often people use these terms—apples and oranges—to describe a false comparison: you can't ask which fruit tastes better because the two are different. You might prefer an apple to an orange, but it makes no sense to say that one is better than the other.

Analogy

Writers deliberately compare one concept or item to another to make clearer an aspect of one: learning to write may be compared to learning to ride a bike—an analogy that stresses the part of writing that is difficult to teach but, once learned, is difficult to forget. In like manner, it is hard to explain how the human mind works, but making an analogy to the electronic on/off switches of a computer circuit board may help explain it—at least to some people. Writers use analogies to make clear that which is not.

Figurative Language

You are probably familiar with figurative language such as metaphor, simile, and personification from discussions of poetry, fiction, or drama, but here, notice the powerful effect they have on writing that is not fiction, that attempts to show the world as the writer actually sees it, that makes comparisons stick in the mind of the reader. Writers use *metaphor* to compare something abstract to something concrete or something unknown to something known. For example, in the previous chapter Annie Dillard describes a weasel as "a muscled ribbon." Writers achieve similarly vivid results when they use *similes*—a type of metaphor that states the comparison directly by using the words *like* or *as*. Here, for example, is Dillard's whole sentence about the weasel:

> He was ten inches long, thin as a curve, a muscled ribbon, brown as fruitwood, soft-furred, alert.

To make you see this weasel in no uncertain terms—as she saw it—she includes in her definition several literal descriptions ("ten inches," "soft-furred," "alert"), one metaphor ("a muscled ribbon"), and two similes ("thin as a curve," "brown as fruitwood").

Personification is the metaphorical comparison of inanimate to animate objects—especially to human beings. Notice in the following passage from *The Immense Journey** how Loren Eiseley uses this technique to make us see a landscape as he saw it:

> Some lands are flat and grass-covered, and smile so evenly up at the sun that they seem forever youthful, untouched by man or time. Some are torn, ravaged and convulsed like the features of profane old age.

In this passage, some land is said to "smile," a comparison to a happy human state, and some land is "convulsed like the features of profane old age," a sad human state.

ANALYZING

> **to analyze:** v. to separate into parts or basic principles in order to determine the nature of the whole; examine methodically.

All academic disciplines teach analysis in one form or another. When you analyze something, you must find a logic that holds it together and use that logic to take it apart. Essentially, analysis requires that you identify what parts make up a whole and that you then look closely at what parts make up each part. Depending on your discipline, of course, you may be asked to analyze a story, an argument, a social group, the circulation system, or the universe. All require a similar mental operation.

A simple example of an analytic task could be found in something

---

*(New York: Vintage Books/Random House, 1957)

as common as a table. Depending on your purpose, a table might be analyzed according to structure (legs, braces, top); type (drop leaf, trestle, end); shape (round, oval, square); purpose (dining, coffee, work); or materials (wood, metal, plastic). Each component can be broken down further: the category of wood into oak, cherry, pine, walnut, etc.

For an example of analysis, look again at the water-treatment essay collaboratively composed for my writing class. The group handed out a survey to citizens of Burlington to find out how much they knew about pollution on Lake Champlain. In order to report the results, they had to collect, tabulate, and analyze (make sense of) the responses. Here is how they reported the results of their analysis:

> Eighty-five percent of the people realized there is a serious sewage problem in Burlington. Sixty-five percent realized Burlington's drinking water comes from Lake Champlain. Seventy percent knew that the beaches closed because of the sewage problem. Forty percent blamed the sewage problem on the city, forty percent blamed it on the treatment plant, ten percent did not think there was a problem, and ten percent did not answer. Only thirty percent of the people bought water because of the problem. . . . A surprising sixty-five percent said it is worth the estimated fifty-two million dollars to fix the problem.
>
> This survey further proves that most of the people in Burlington are aware of the serious nature of the sewage problem in Lake Champlain. However, they were not fully aware of the toxic materials being dumped in the water.

Notice that the analysis here depends upon a simple methodical tabulation of quantifiable survey answers and the consequent drawing of conclusions based on the counting. (Notice also that the writer starts sentences with numbers; convention prefers that numbers at the beginning of sentences be written out; thus eighty-five percent rather than 85%.)

SYNTHESIZING

> **to synthesize:** v. to combine parts to form a new whole; arranging and combining elements or pieces to make a pattern or structure not there before.

The most sophisticated way to report or explain is to synthesize. All academic disciplines teach synthesis. To perform this operation, you put ideas or elements or parts together—sometimes things that don't seem to belong together—to form a new whole. Synthesizing may involve different operations, depending on the discipline, but in all it means putting elements together to form a new whole. In chemistry, when you combine chemicals, you produce a chemical synthesis—a new *synthetic* material may result. In history, a synthesis may involve combining one historian's theory of historical development with that of another, and so on.

The ability to synthesize is prized in both the academic and the nonacademic world, because it implies that you know not only how to take things apart but also how to put them back together, which is the work of builders, engineers, scientists, doctors, lawyers, artists, literary critics, and teachers, among others. It might be argued, however, that the ability to synthesize is a survival skill necessary to all of us in an increasingly complex world.

An example from my discipline would be the following question, commonly asked in essay examinations: "You have read three different American writers—Emerson, Thoreau, and Whitman. Identify and explain one theme common to all three." You may need to begin by *analyzing* each work, making notes or an outline of the major points in Emerson's essays, Thoreau's *Walden,* and Whitman's *Leaves of Grass.* You find that Emerson looked to the natural world for ethical lessons, that Thoreau made a spiritual symbol of Walden Pond, and that Whitman revered the smallest as well as the greatest creature in the universe. You've now got evidence for the theme of *nature* that connects all three.

In the following student example, notice how the writers of the waste-treatment essay referred to in this chapter arrive at a synthesis at the end of their paper by making recommendations based on their research discoveries:

> The first and most important thing to do is reduce the amount of your buying. If you don't absolutely need the product then don't buy it. You don't need a chemistry degree from U.V.M. to reduce hazardous chemicals in your home. You can do the following:
>
> 1) When you're buying a product make sure that if it's hazardous there are directions on how to dispose of it. If you buy something you're responsible for disposing of it.
>
> 2) Don't buy it unless you really need it.
>
> 3) Don't buy more than you need. Getting rid of the extra can be annoying.
>
> 4) Use the safest and simplest substances that you can find.
>
> 5) Recycle whatever you can: Used motor oil, paint

thinners, battery acid (and batteries), automatic transmis-
sion fluid, diesel fluid, fuel oil, gasoline, kerosene, motor
oil, and even dry cleaning solvents can be refined and used
again just like aluminum cans. (See Appendix C.) If you're
not sure what to do see the "Household Hazardous Waste
Chart." It was adapted from the Water Pollution Control Fed-
eration pamphlet, 1987.

In this case the synthesis becomes, in the end, an argument for water
conservation. Finally, the writers also attempt to persuade their readers to
act as a result of reading this essay.

As you have probably figured out by now, people don't set out to
write pieces called synthesis essays. Most often they have been explaining
or analyzing something and find the need to make suggestions or draw
inferences based on that work.

REPORTING

to report: v. to relate or tell about; to provide an account for
publication or broadcast; to submit results for consideration.

A report describes an event or tells a story about something. You may have
written a book report (a description of what happened in the book) or a
laboratory report (the story of what happened during an experiment). If
you are assigned to write reports in a particular class, your instructor will
specify what kind of report and give you guidelines for what it should
look like.

Reports require information to be conveyed to an audience clearly,
directly, and succinctly: a progress report on a project or research paper,
a report on a lecture or film that you attended, or a report on available
resources to proceed with a project. You may often relate such information
in any order that makes sense to you (and, you hope, to your audience).
However, in some disciplines the forms for reporting information may be
highly specific, as in the sciences and social sciences, where reports
generally follow a predictable form.

Reporting News and Events

Journalists train themselves to explain events by asking reporter's questions: Who? What? Where? When? Why? and How?. The advantage of remembering a set of routine questions is obvious: writing reports for daily
papers requires fast writing with little time for revision. Reporters actually call these reports stories and commonly write them in one draft,

composing in their heads while driving back from the scene of the accident, fire, speech, or whatever they have been assigned to write about that day. (At least one reporter has told me that he sometimes begins composing the story on the way *to* the event.)

For rapid composing, nothing beats a set of second-nature questions that help sort out new information by putting it into preset categories: Who is this story about? What is the issue here? Where did it occur? When—what time of day? Why did it happen—what caused the situation to develop as it did? And how did it happen—how did the events unfold? These questions are variations of those a lab scientist or a novelist might ask, as they attempt to provide a framework for talking about the world and what happens in it—be that piece of the world one's laboratory, one's news beat, or one's *Oz* or *Wonderland.*

On those occasions when you are asked to report something that happened in a meeting, concert, or public event, using the journalists' questions will quickly organize your information.

Reporting Research

I found the following format recommended in both biology and psychology for reporting the results of experiments; forms similar to it will be used in other social science and hard science areas as well:

1. Title: a literal description of the topic of your report.
2. Abstract: a summary in two hundred fifty words or fewer of the why, how, and what of your report.
3. Introduction: a statement of your hypothesis and a review of the relevant literature.
4. Methods and materials: information that would allow another experimenter to replicate your work.
5. Results: charts, tables, and figures accompanied by a prose narrative to explain what happened.
6. Discussion: a review of your results, a comparison to other studies, and a discussion of implications.
7. References: a list of all sources actually cited in your report, using appropriate documentation format (see Chapter Eleven).
8. Appendices: work pertinent to your report, but not essential to understanding it.

In the event that you are asked to write a technical report, I would consult one of the many report-writing handbooks used in technical writing or business writing courses.

SUMMARIZING

A summary reduces a long text to a shorter one by condensing the main ideas and skipping the details. For example, an *executive summary* may be a one- or two-page document that condenses a much longer piece of information into a form readable in a few minutes. A *book report* (as opposed to a *book review*) summarizes the main plot, theme, and characters of a book. The following are a few guidelines for writing summaries.

1. Keep your primary objective in mind: to reproduce faithfully the main ideas of a longer document, skipping the details.
2. Be accurate and brief: condense paragraphs to sentences, sentences to phrases, and skip sections that you judge redundant or unnecessary. (Don't, however, reduce the piece to an outline that only you can understand.)
3. Write in your own clearest style. A summary is about information: it is more important to be clear than to be true to the style of the original document.
4. Follow the organizational pattern of the original: if the original has subheadings or numbered points, use them as guides for writing your condensation.
5. Maintain the tone of the original as best you can. If the source is witty, be witty; if the source is formal, be formal (or wittily formal or formally witty).

Abstracting

An abstract is a condensed summary. Like a summary, an abstract reduces a text to an outline of its most important points. But, whereas a summary of an article's essential points may be several pages long, an abstract will be less than a page, more likely one paragraph. Here, for example, is an abstract of the advice for writing summaries (above):

> To write a summary, 1) keep your objective in mind, 2) be accurate and brief, 3) use a clear style, 4) use the organizational pattern and 5) tone of the original document.

Abstracts may be routine, but they're not easy. They are difficult because you must *thoroughly* understand the piece you are abstracting and because you have so little freedom to use your own language. To write them, follow the general advice for writing summaries, only more rigorously. Of course, the one necessary preparation for writing abstracts is to be thoroughly familiar with the piece you are abstracting. You might consider writing a paragraph-by-paragraph topical outline first, including just the topic sentence of each paragraph. Then see if you can cluster these under more condensed headings, and so on. (It helps if the piece itself follows a predictable pattern, including thesis statement, topic sentences and the like.)

A REFLECTION ON THE NECESSITY OF THESIS STATEMENTS

An informational or argumentative thesis states the theme or central idea of your paper, usually in the first paragraph or page, alerting the reader to both the subject of your paper and what you intend to say about that subject.

In explanatory and informational papers, a thesis stated early makes good sense because it tells the reader the nature of the explanation to follow. In this chapter, however, the subject is defined and explained in an introduction to explanatory writing which lasts several pages; the actual thesis is not stated until the end of the introduction with these words: *This chapter explains the basic strategies of explanatory or expository discourse. . . .* In other words, use your judgment about where and when your paper needs a directly stated thesis.

In argumentative and interpretative papers, a good thesis statement asserts the writer's position, telling readers that what follows will support that position. In fact, a good thesis helps the writer as well as the reader by articulating a clear position to defend. For example, consider these three possible theses meant to explain a history paper:

1. The Battle of Gettysburg was one of the most interesting battles of the Civil War.
2. Geography played an important role in the Battle of Gettysburg.
3. The North got to the high ground first, and the North won the Battle of Gettysburg.

In my judgment, the first sentence is a weak thesis. To call something "interesting" may be polite, but it's not in itself interesting. The second sentence, however, announces one of the specifically interesting aspects of the battle, geography, and so invites the reader to learn more about that. It makes a decent, though unexciting, thesis. The third sentence appeals to me even more. This writer suggests that he or she knows exactly where the essay is going right from the start and promises to do so in a lively prose style.

Sometimes, however, writers of argumentative papers deliberately delay revealing their thesis—their own position on an issue—until they have laid out both sides for the reader to ponder. I will say more about this *delayed thesis* in the next chapter, but again the business of stating a thesis is a matter of writer judgment, depending on what effect he or she wants to create.

In narrative and reflective essays, such as discussed in the last chapter, an *embedded thesis* often emerges by the end of the essay, but is never actually stated in so many words. Often in such papers the writer's intention is speculative or exploratory, so that providing a clear statement of purpose actually works against the writer's intention.

Finally, keep in mind that most college instructors expect to find thesis statements in the papers they assign, so check the stated expectations of assignments carefully. If you choose to ignore this expectation, it's a good idea to make sure your central point emerges in some other unmistakable manner.

APPENDIX

SUGGESTIONS FOR JOURNAL WRITING

1. What kinds of explanatory papers do you most commonly write now? What kinds have you written in the past? In your own words, explain the procedure for writing one of these forms.

2. Is there a particular kind of explanatory strategy that you would like to learn? How do you now go about writing it? What about writing it gives you the most difficulty?

3. Composition books such as this may be considered examples of explanatory writing, trying to give certain advice to writers on all the necessary points of writing the author can think of. Examine this book by comparing it to other composition books you have had in the past. What about it strikes you as different? What's the same?

SUGGESTIONS FOR ESSAY WRITING

1. Select a paper you have already written for this or another course and write a summary or an abstract of it. Exchange with another student and help make each other's papers even tighter, shorter, and more precise. Conclude with a note about difficulty doing this type of writing.

2. Write a book report of this or another book you are currently using for this course. As a class, compare your results with the brief suggestions you find in this book. Would you modify or expand any of them? Would you add any new ones?

COLLABORATIVE

This can be done with any size group—the more the merrier. Agree on a local institution (pizza parlor, drug store, teen center, library—the smaller the better). Each of you write individually about this place, focusing on something small and concrete (conversations overheard in a booth, action at the checkout counter, etc.); share your drafts, noting the different approaches each reporter took; finally, select editors and bind the results together as a class book to share with those who own or work in this place (see *Postscript Three*).

Chapter Eight

WRITING TO ARGUE
AND INTERPRET

My teacher last year would always write in the margins of
my papers *What's your thesis? Where's your evidence?
How can you prove that?* So, now when I argue something,
I *Make* readers believe me. I give them good reasons and
lots of examples and they *Do* believe me—or at least I get
better grades.

—Eric

In the academic world, arguments are a means of creating belief, changing minds, and altering perceptions. Faculty and students alike spend a
great amount of time and energy arguing *for* one interpretation, position,
or point of view, and *against* another. In fact, people making, questioning, attacking, and defending claims throughout the arts and sciences is
one of the sure guarantees that human knowledge will continue to advance.

Arguments in the sense considered here, rational disagreements
rather than quarrels, fights, and contests, most commonly occur in areas
of genuine uncertainty about what is right, best, or most reasonable. In
disciplines leading to careers in engineering, business, journalism, environmental studies, and the social sciences, *written argument* commonly take
the forms of position papers, policy statements, and editorials. In the liberal
arts disciplines such as English, art, history, and philosophy, argument is
commonly called *interpretation,* and takes place in scholarly articles, critical reviews, and interpretative essays where the meaning or significance
of an idea is open to friendly debate.

ARGUING A POSITION

> **to argue:** v. to give reasons for or against something; to consider the pros and cons; to persuade by giving reasons.

Argumentative and interpretative writing closely mirror the academic discourse of your professors, as they engage in scholarly debates about research and method in their disciplines. They participate in professional conversations by asserting and supporting this thesis or theory while attacking competing ones. Therefore, of all the essays described in this text—personal, reflective, explanatory, reportorial—argumentative ones demand from you the tightest logic and most convincing evidence. The most common form of argumentative paper in disciplines outside the humanities may be the *position paper.*

A position paper takes a stand for or against an issue about which there is some reasonable debate. To write a successful position paper on an issue, you need to answer these basic questions:

1. How will I present the *issue?*
2. What stand will I take on this issue?
3. What claims will support my stand?
4. What *evidence* will support my claims?

Issues

An issue is essentially a problem that needs solving. In selecting an issue, remember that every argument has two sides, a pro and a con, someone for, someone against. For an issue or idea to be arguable, it has to be debatable, with two or more arguable sides. If there is no debate, disagreement, or difference in opinion, then no argument exists.

Furthermore, each side of an arguable issue needs credible supporters. In other words, to be worth bothering with, the debate needs to be real, and the resolution in doubt. For example, to write a position paper today for or against slavery, women's suffrage, or nuclear war makes little sense, since no reasonable person would argue for the other side. However, in other times, say the pre-Civil War south, the early twentieth century, or World War II, serious opposition demanded serious argument.

However, as I write this chapter, I hear real debate about major national issues such as pollution, drug abuse, crime, violence, racism, poverty, and overpopulation. I hear serious debate, daily, about specific solutions to some of these problems: legislation to balance the federal budget, limit automobile emissions, reform welfare, institute capital punishment, control handgun ownership, ban abortion, curtail affirmative action, and reduce spending for everything from education to defense. And I witness local debates on everything from urban sprawl and shopping malls to alcohol in the dormitory and salad bars in the cafeteria. In other words, if you're looking for real issues about which to have real debates, you'll find them.

Keep in mind that the larger the issue, the more difficult to solve and the more difficult to resolve in a short college paper. To my own students I suggest investigating an issue with a clear, tangible, and accessible local presence. Instead of investigating abortion, gun control, or affirmative action as general national issues, investigate a range of attitudes about one of these in your local community. The smaller the issue, the more chance for your own voice to be heard; in other words, when you investigate issues that are matters of local campus debate—whether beer bars or salad bars—your position on the matter may be heard and contribute toward a solution.

An Argumentative Thesis

As noted in the last chapter, a good thesis can work for you, the writer, and for your reader. Your thesis is the stand you take on an issue, the proposition you believe, and what you want your readers to believe too. To make the idea of a thesis less intimidating, think of it as an answer to a yes/no question: Should farming be banned from the stream banks that empty into Lake Champlain? Should the city rescind the tenants bill of rights? Should the college fund a women's center on campus? Phrasing a thesis in yes/no terms helps in two ways: first, it shows the nature of the claims and evidence needed to support it; second, it highlights the other side of the debate, the *no* to your *yes,* and the *counterclaims* and evidence that support them.

Claims

A *claim* is an assertion or proposition that supports and defends a thesis. To support the thesis that a women's center should be funded by your college, you may claim that:

1. All groups that qualify for affirmative action funds should be entitled to a center.
2. Women need a place to call their own.
3. Strong support already exists for such a center on campus.

Each of these claims supports your thesis, and now needs good evidence to back it up.

Counterclaims are simply the arguments opponents make to refute your claims. If your position is indeed debatable, you can bet the other side will also have good arguments. For example, opponents to the women's center may claim that:

1. Women are not a minority group.
2. Limited campus funds already support a women's studies program.
3. There are other more pressing needs for scarce college funds.

Each counterclaim, in turn, needs strong support. This is accomplished, in part, by including relevant *evidence*.

Evidence

Evidence is the information that supports a claim and persuades others to believe you. Just as a prosecuting attorney needs evidence to convince juries to convict a person accused of a crime—against the counterclaims of defense attorneys—you need evidence to convince audiences to believe you. Consider these four classes of evidence, each of which persuades in a different way:

1. Facts are things upon which everyone, regardless of personal experience or values, agrees. It is a fact that water boils at 212 degrees Fahrenheit at sea level, that Herman Melville wrote *Moby Dick* in 1852, and that the college budget for new programs last year was $50,000. Facts are often, though not necessarily, numerical or statistical—things that can be measured and verified by standards we all accept.
2. Inferences are the generalizations or meaning we make from an accumulation of facts. Take, for example, the following three facts:
   1. Phosphorous is a fertilizer.
   2. Farmers use phosphorous to fertilize fields on the shores of Lake Champlain.
   3. Studies of streams that empty into Lake Champlain indicate high phosphorous levels.

   Each fact taken alone means little; taken together, *because* each fact is related to the next, they support the inference that farms near Lake Champlain contribute to excessive algae growth in the lake.
3. Informed opinion is the opinion of experts in a particular field. Their testimony is good evidence because the rest of us trust their knowledge: We trust a lawyer to know more about the law, a doctor about medicine, a football coach about football, and a marine biologist about lake pollution. A good example of an

informed opinion would be that of Professor Don Meals, of the College of Natural Resources, who recommends that the best way to reduce phosphorous contamination in Lake Champlain is to create a one hundred-foot phosphorous-free buffer zone around streams that feed into the lake (1992).

4. Personal testimony is good evidence because it comes from a person with direct experience of an event or situation. The knowledge of the astronaut differs from the physicist's, the tenant's from the architect's, the fisherman's from the marine biologist's, the female's from the male's. Their testimony is experiential rather than expert, but has its own authority nevertheless. Likewise, we give more credibility to a resident on Lake Champlain who reports a severe outbreak of Eurasian milfoil in the bay in front of his cottage than to those who have only read in the newspapers about such outbreaks.

Strategies for Writing Position Papers

There are no set formulas for writing position papers, but there are accepted strategies that work especially well. Think about both *thesis-first* and *delayed-thesis* strategies, and decide which is most advantageous for your particular case.

Thesis-First Pattern   The following is an effective way to organize a thesis-first paper, but keep in mind these are guidelines, not rules:

1. Introduce the issue by providing a brief background that defines, describes, and explains it, for example: Excessive growth of water plants are clogging Lake Champlain, causing fish to die, and ruining the lake for recreational purposes.

2. State the issue as a yes/no question so that the two sides are clear, for example: Should a phosphorous-free buffer zone be created along the streams emptying into Lake Champlain to prevent excess nutrients from entering the lake?

3. Assert your thesis as the position your paper will support, for example: To reduce pollution in Lake Champlain, a phosphorus-free buffer zone should be implemented along all waterways emptying into the lake. Introducing the issue, stating it as a yes/no question, and articulating your thesis commonly take place in the first paragraph of a thesis-first position paper.

4. Summarize the counterclaims against your position, for example: A phosphorous-free zone is not a cost-effective way to reduce pollution since it will hurt many farmers and be

difficult to enforce. Do this *briefly* and *before* you state your own claims, so that your claims refute the opposition and conclude your paper. The most powerful placement position in a paper is at the end because it's the last thing a reader sees and is most likely to be remembered. You want to save this for your own claims.

5. State claims that support your thesis and refute the counterclaims, for example: A recent study of the sources of pollution in Lake Champlain indicate that seventy-five percent is the result of farm fertilizer runoff. Stating your claims and supporting each with evidence will constitute the major part of your paper.

6. Provide evidence for each claim your paper makes, for example: According to the Lake Champlain Action Community, "748 metric tons of phosphorous are deposited in the lake annually" (*Tropus Status and Phosphorous Loadings of Lake Champlain*, EPA, 1970). The stronger the evidence, the more convincing your paper. Strong evidence will only result from serious research on your part, both in the field (interviewing experts, visiting sites) and in the library (locating periodicals, local documents, books). Any argumentative paper you write will be many times stronger with substantial and varied research information to support your claims.

7. Conclude by restating your thesis, now synthesizing your claims into a brief summary of your case, for example: All the recent studies of pollution in Lake Champlain point to the same conclusion: that farm fertilizer runoff must be reduced if algae growth is to be curtailed. Only by legislating a phosphorous-free zone on waters feeding the lake will the problem be solved and the lake become clean again.

The advantages of leading with your thesis are that:

1. Your audience knows from the start where you stand.
2. Your thesis occupies the strongest parts of your paper: first and last.
3. It is the most common and conventional form of academic argument, hence the one most expected by your instructors.

Delayed-Thesis Pattern   To use the delayed-thesis strategy, reorganize your paper so that it presents and explains both sides to the reader *before* you reveal the side you support. Your organization would look roughly like this:

1. Introduce the issue.
2. State the issue as a yes/no question.
3. Summarize the claims of the opposition.
4. State your *counterclaims.*
5. Provide evidence to support your counterclaims.
6. Conclude by stating your thesis based on your counterclaims.

The advantages of delaying your thesis are that:

1. Your readers are allowed to weigh the evidence for and against, and are invited to make their own decisions before hearing yours.
2. The audience is kept in suspense, thereby increasing engagement.
3. The audience empathizes with the writer over the difficulty in making a decision.

I write with a delayed-approach when both sides of an issue seem almost equally persuasive; I want my audience to reason with me and see that this has been a difficult conclusion to reach. I use the thesis-first approach when I see the issue as more clear cut; I want my audience persuaded from the start that there's really only one reasonable choice to make.

INTERPRETING TEXTS

> **to interpret:** v. to explain the meaning of; to expound the significance of; to represent or render the meaning of.

The term *interpretative essay* covers a wide range of argumentative assignments that may also be called critical, analytical, or simply argumentative. For discussion purposes, this section will focus on writing aimed at interpreting texts of one kind or another.

Interpretative essays argue that a story, poem, essay, or other created work means one thing rather than another. At the same time, writers who interpret understand that other interpretations or meanings can be found by other readers of the same material. Certain areas of study such as literature, philosophy, and religion seem to lend themselves more obviously to interpretive writing than others, such as mathematics, chemistry, and physics. This seems so in part because literary, philosophical, and religious questions seldom have agreed-upon answers, while the more scientific disciplines do—at least at elementary levels of understanding. But at the frontiers of every scientific discipline, things are still up for grabs—that is, open to interpretation. And as soon as one asks social or political questions of scientific knowledge, one is again involved in matters of interpretation.

Interpretation implies that there may be more than one explanation with merit; your job is to point out why a particular meaning is the best possible or the most probable. As I suggested at the beginning of this section, interpretation is especially important in so-called humanistic disciplines such as history, literature, philosophy, where almost all concepts are a matter of one interpretation versus another: What was the chief historical cause of the war in Vietnam? Was it ideologic, economic, or geographic? Kant believed one thing, Hegel another: With which philosophy do you most agree? What did poet Robert Frost mean in the poem "Stopping by Woods on a Snowy Evening"? These questions should be regarded as matters of interpretation rather than as having right or wrong answers.

Don't think, however, that interpretation applies only to the arts and humanities. When political scientists conduct an opinion survey, different political scientists will interpret the results to mean different things. When the economic indicators point to inflation or recession, liberal economists will explain things one way, conservative economists another—all a matter of interpretation. Some biologists believe dinosaurs became extinct because the climate changed gradually, others because it changed rapidly when a large meteor collided with the earth; physicists differ in their explanations of the origin of the universe as chemists still argue about proper definitions of the atom—still more matters of interpretation. In each of these examples, experts make a *guess* (called an hypothesis) that such or such is the case, but cannot prove, beyond a doubt, that they are correct.

In the following example, Mary *interprets* the meaning of a painting, *Inner Energies,* by artist Tracy Leavitt, in this way:

> The artist is trying to point out that technology is running away from us.

Jason, however, interprets the same painting this way:

> Thus this portrait is the expression of the woman's drive to identify with man's accomplishments.

While Ron suggests:

> With this idea Leavitt suggests that we are not following God as we should be.

In other words, *interpreting* a work, an event, an idea may lead different writers to different conclusions. Just be sure that your interpretive statement is supported by data, analysis, and/or expert opinion. The best interpretations are those that convince others to believe you.

Another kind of more personal—and more general—interpretation occurs at the end of Steve's critique of Robert Frost's poem, "The Road Not Taken," when he sums up the poem's meaning as a lesson in life:

> There comes a time in life when people have to make a decision, and people often wonder what it would be like had they made the other choice. That is what "The Road Not Taken" is about. If you take life too seriously, you are going to miss it. You have to take it one step at a time. If something does not go your way, you must learn not to dwell on it.

In this instance, Steve says the poem means this to "you." Yet I actually see his statement as a very personal one. (Were he to work further on this interpretation, I'd suggest he change the pronouns from "you" to "I" and "me.")

The most common interpretive acts in college may center around poetry and fiction. In most cases, your teacher will want you to be more precise, to stick closer to the text than Steve has above. An especially important part of interpreting is demonstrating where you got this or that idea, which often means bringing into your text a passage from the text you are interpreting. In the following example, Katherine quotes a line from the poem, "Elegy for Jane," by Theodore Roethke:

> The poet leans over her grave and speaks his last words to her, "I with no rights in this matter/Neither father nor lover." He can do nothing now, and feels remorse that he never expressed to her his love. Love, Roethke seems to argue, must be shared when it happens or it will be lost forever.

Here, of course, we see just how much an act of *interpretation* depends on careful *analysis* in the first place.

Look at a final example of interpretive writing as William investigates the meaning in Charlotte Perkins Gillman's short story, "The Yellow Wallpaper":

> We begin to question [the narrator's] emotional state when she envisions the wallpaper lady creeping, by daylight, through the estate grounds. At night, the narrator struggles to set her imaginary friend free. At the climax of the

narrator's breakdown, she falls to the level of a child's mentality. We cannot help but pity her when she begins to gnaw at the wooden bedframe out of frustration. She becomes a child in her own world—at last, secure. The story ends with her claiming, "Here I can creep smoothly on the floor, and my shoulder just fits in that long smooch around the wall, so I cannot lose my way."

John was ludicrous in claiming that his wife was suffering from only "temporary depression." She was a full-time mother, wife, and writer. She was also a victim of a full-time mental illness which required attention if ever to escape from it. Since the woman never received the necessary help, she eventually disintegrated to the level of a child.

In this example we see the documentation of the problem in the first paragraph, then the writer's conclusion, based on it, in the essay's last paragraph. This is a good job of interpretation.

When you write interpretively, keep in mind that your interpretation is one of several that may have merit: you must support assertions with evidence—direct quotations are especially useful for interpreting the meaning of texts; you must separate fact from opinion; qualifying words *(perhaps, maybe, might)* show that you are still open to other possibilities; and you must define, explain, analyze, and evaluate carefully as you work out your interpretation.

Evaluation

to evaluate: v. to ascertain or fix the value or worth of; to examine or judge carefully.

Evaluation is often a part of interpretation. To evaluate implies judgment, finding the merits and faults of something. Like the other operations described here, evaluation should be based on some analysis or interpretation already performed in the same essay. Evaluation is crucial, at some level or other, to every academic discipline: you evaluate one theory against another; one set of facts against another; one piece of art or music against another; or you evaluate against criteria.

In other words, you can evaluate in several ways, just as your teachers do when they must arrive at student grades. In one case, evaluation is against an absolute standard—each student in a class could theoretically get an *A* or an *F.* In another case, you evaluate by comparison/contrast—the best students get high marks, the weakest fail, regardless of absolute

standards. Some evaluation is carefully quantitative—points for everything are totaled; other evaluation is highly subjective—impressions determine all.

Evaluation necessarily draws on many other activities such as analysis, definition, explanation, etc. In writing evaluations of colleagues,
schools, proposals, book manuscripts, and students, I usually lead off with
the most objective statements first, both pro and con, and work up to an
overall evaluation that makes a recommendation in one direction or
another. This procedure allows those reading my evaluations to see the
criteria on which I made my recommendation and answers in advance
many possible questions—a good suggestion for student writers.

It should be obvious by now that categories described here often
overlap: William's interpretation of "The Yellow Wallpaper" is also a tacit
evaluation about the profundity of the story he has read. Let's look at other
occasions where deliberate acts of evaluation are called for.

Here are two concluding paragraphs from essays my students wrote
reviewing a collection of essays entitled *Models for Writers* by Eschholz
and Rosa. Kyle writes:

> If you pick up this book and read just one story you will
> see for yourself why this collection of essays is so good. It
> may be used for pleasure or as a text. This not only makes
> for enjoyable reading, but also provides a learning experi-
> ence for the reader. By combining these two types of read-
> ing in one book, the editors produced a book that can be en-
> joyed by all.

Kyle's statement comes at the end of an essay where he has looked at
specific contents of the book in some detail. Nevertheless, he takes greater
liberties than I'd recommend with his closing generalization that "the
editors produced a book that can be enjoyed by all." Obviously enough,
few experiences can be enjoyed by all. Here is a useful suggestion for
college writers: Avoid ending with a meaningless little flourish. Quit a line
early instead.

Betsy writes a summary evaluation of the same book this way:

> I feel the editors have put this book together well by pick-
> ing authors and essays that will appeal to college students.
> Who would ever think that Steve Martin would have an es-
> say in an English book as a model of good writing? I think
> by having such authors the student will be more willing
> to turn to this book for help. I find this book has many

enjoyable essays and would recommend it to anyone who has to write papers.

I prefer Betsy's conclusion because she works in at least one concrete reference (Steve Martin) and also raises an amusing question. There's a liveliness here. She too, however, tacks on an unlikely last line, recommending the anthology "to anyone who has to write papers."

Evaluation is often in order when you find these direction words: *compare, contrast, choose, evaluate, rank, measure, judge, justify, agree, disagree, argue, prove,* or *make a case for* in the assignment. In writing an evaluative essay, it's a good idea to establish what exactly you are evaluating, describe it thoroughly, assess its strengths and its weaknesses, and be fair in the language of your final recommendation, avoiding obviously emotional or biased terms as much as possible.

Book Reviews

Book reviews are a likely academic assignment in a variety of subjects. In writing a review, there are some things to keep in mind:

1. Provide all necessary factual information about the subject being reviewed, for example, book title, author, date, publisher, and price. Do this early in your review, in your first paragraph or as an inset before your first paragraph.
2. Provide background information, if you can, about the writer and his or her previously published books.
3. Follow a clear organizational logic (comparison/contrast, general to specific, etc.).
4. Support all assertions and generalizations with illustrative, specific examples from the book being reviewed.
5. Evaluate fairly, keeping your obvious personal biases in the background.
6. Write to the knowledge and ability of your particular audience. Modify your language according to the degree of familiarity your audience has with the subject (reviews imply that you are doing a service for someone).

There are no fixed rules about length or format when writing reviews. However, if you're in doubt, here are some safe guidelines to follow if no others are provided: allocate approximately one-fifth of your review to factual information and background, one-fifth to explaining the book's subject matter, two-fifths to an evaluation of the strengths and weaknesses of the book, and one-fifth to a recommendation of the overall worth of the book.

Better than an arbitrary formula would be to look at published book reviews. The best place to find examples of critical reviews of books (and movies, plays, records, and products) would be in popular periodicals such as *The New York Times Book Review, The Atlantic, Harper's, Esquire, Rolling Stone, Time, Newsweek,* and *Consumer Reports.* Refer also to the professional journals in your field of study—in my case I'd look at reviews of English books, specifically in *College English* and *Modern Fiction Studies,* and more generally in *The Chronicle of Higher Education.*

Critical Reviews

A critical review is essentially an assessment of something, usually pointing out both strengths and weaknesses, such as we have come to expect in book or movie reviews. Furthermore, we often expect some kind of a recommendation about whether to read the book or see the film. Another name for a critical review would be *critique.* Note that to do such a critical review essay well would usually require skillful incorporation of the other intellectual tasks we talked about in the last two chapters: exposition, definition, comparison, analysis, synthesis, interpretation, and evaluation.

Voice

When you write interpretive or argumentative essays, use a comfortable voice, not so relaxed as in a journal, not so objective as in a laboratory report—unless you have a good reason to diverge from this middle point. For more formal situations, avoid contractions, first-person pronouns, colloquial diction, split infinitives, and the like—but don't use language you are uncomfortable with or try through pretentious words to impress. For informal situations, use conversational language, keeping in mind that readers look especially closely at your organizational scheme and use of evidence in analytic essays. If your essay is solid in these respects, you have some license with your voice.

APPENDIX

SUGGESTIONS FOR JOURNAL WRITING

1. Describe your experience writing interpretive and argumentative essays. What do you consider the most difficult aspect of interpretative or argumentative assignments?

2. On the basis of your experience writing interpretative essays, what

would you say are the most important things for the writer of such essays to keep in mind?

3. List three texts that you have already read that you would be interested in interpreting or evaluating. What interests you about each text? Why?

4. List three local and three national issues about which you might write a position paper. About which are you most concerned right now? Write a paragraph on the topic of most current interest.

SUGGESTIONS FOR ESSAY WRITING

1. Select a text from this or another course you are currently taking and locate within it something that interests or puzzles you, or that you disagree with. Write an interpretive or evaluative essay about the text using your specific interest as a point of departure. Plan to end this essay with still another question that your readers themselves might pursue or puzzle over. In other words, end with an admission that more needs to be looked at; the writer herself or himself still has uncertainties.

2. Attend a play, concert, lecture, or other public event and write an interpretive or evaluative essay about your experience. Contact your local or school newspaper and see if they'll publish it.

3. Do assignment (1) collaboratively, as a member of a writing group, selecting the same text or event, and jointly draft an essay to which you each contribute. Share your group essay with another group, they theirs with you, and act as editorial review boards for each other. Plan to publish the results in a collection to leave for next year's students to read and respond to. (Your instructor will need to be the agent of transmittal if you choose this option.)

SUGGESTIONS FOR RESEARCH PROJECTS

1. INDIVIDUAL: Select any topic about which you are curious or have an opinion (informed or otherwise). Visit the library or a local museum and locate information which both supports and rejects your own ideas, or arguments about this topic. Take good notes and write an essay that synthesizes, interprets, or evaluates the information you found there. (You might reflect on whether this additional information in any way changed your mind or if it simply made you find more evidence to back up your initial opinion; write this reflection in your journal.)

2. COLLABORATIVE: Agree to disagree. In a small group, identify an issue, idea, or place about which you each have only a little information. Divide yourselves into research teams, go get some information, write it up, and share it with the group. Then, each of you take a deliberately different approach or slant on the topic and write a series of essays meant to be read in a colloquium, together, to air all sides of the issue. In class, present a series of such colloquia to entertain each other. Publish the results in a class book (see *Postscript Three*).

Section III

COLLEGE RESEARCH

Chapter Nine

RESEARCHING PEOPLE AND PLACES

In 9th grade we had to write research papers to learn them for 10th grade, and in 10th we had to write them for 11th, and then in 12th, again, to learn them for college. So what I keep learning, over and over, is to sit in the library and copy quotes out of books and into my paper and connect them up. What's the deal?

—Lucas

The hallmark of college writing is learning to write with research. Sometimes you'll be asked to write a research paper or report; other times you'll simply be asked to write persuasively or critically. In either case, your papers will profit from using expert testimony and documentable information. Sometimes assignments requesting outside sources need to be written objectively, in the third-person, with a minimum of writer value judgments; other times outside sources may be integrated with first-person pronouns and experience to create a more personal research-based paper—be sure to ask your instructors which approach they prefer. This chapter provides some suggestions for writing with a variety of research sources.

PEOPLE

Start with people. When you need to find something out, start asking around and see who knows what. People are living, current resources that talk back, smile, and surprise you. People can tell you who else to see, where to go, what books to read (and why); people can offer you shortcuts. They can also ask you questions: Why do you want to do this? What do you expect to find? Have you talked to Professor Smith yet? How far back do you want to go? Where do you plan to start?

Wherever you live, there are people who know more than you do about all kinds of things. It's your job as a researcher to discover these people and find out what they know. When you talk to people, you are in much the same situation as a newspaper reporter interviewing people to complete a story. In fact, you can learn a lot about interviewing people from investigative reporters. Here are some ideas that might help you collect information directly from people.

Expect Something

Good interviewers aren't blank slates. They talk to people to find out more about something about which they already have some ideas and hunches. In other words, they start with preconceptions, and then go on to prove or disprove them. When they talk to people, they are actively looking for answers, and they have some idea of the shape those answers will take. Acknowledging this, being aware of what you expect and why, will help you to form pointed questions and to change, modify, or adapt your expectations when something unexpected comes along.

Hang Around

I can't improve on the advice of Bill Blundel, columnist for the *Wall Street Journal,* who said, "To my way of thinking there's no such thing as a cowboy expert. The only cowboy expert is the cowboy. And the only way you can find out and appreciate what his life is like is to work with him, and to go out with him and to be there, just hanging around. I am a tremendous believer in just hanging around."

Know Something

Before you talk to knowledgeable people, become knowledgeable yourself. Even before you "start with people," check in a dictionary, encyclopedia, or the Internet to learn the terms that will help you ask good questions. Sometimes this means asking people about other people to talk to. For those other people, of whom you expect something particular, it may mean familiarizing yourself with their writing, their achievements, and their expertise in general. Keep in mind that you'll get one kind of information if you present yourself as a novice and another kind when you appear already knowledgeable. The second kind will be deeper and more useful.

Plan Questions

Prepare a few key questions in advance. This doesn't mean you should interview from a study sheet, although some people do. Writing out the questions helps you both find and remember them. Think about the nature and sequence of questions you ask. One approach is to start with a general question: "How did you get involved with the problem of homeless people in the first place?" Then ask a narrowing question: "What services do you currently provide for the homeless?" And follow-up with questions as the occasion provides: "How long have you been doing that?" Sometimes a provocative leading question will provide interesting information: "According to the Mayor, your homeless shelter is not providing the services promised." And sometimes an imaginative approach will help: "If you were the Mayor, what's the first thing you'd do to deal with the problem of the homeless?" In other words, I try to rehearse in my head what will happen if I lead with one question rather than another, try to predict what I'll get for an answer, and then see if that's the direction I want to go. I do all of this on paper, to myself, imagining, before I go into the actual interview.

Ad Lib Questions

No matter what my plans, in my best interviews, I never follow them. Good interviews move around considerably, include digressions (often loaded with information that circles back and becomes useful), and are refreshingly predictable. So I also plan for both new and follow-up questions as part of my interview. By planning to ad lib I'm not tied to my script and can follow a new lead wherever it seems most fruitful: "What exactly do you mean by that?" "Could you expand on that just a bit more?" "What else should I know?" Remember, it's the prepared questions that help you identify when it's time for the other kind!

Ask Leading Questions

If you have expectations, theories, and ideas, sometimes you might lead off with them and see what your interviewee thinks. It depends on who you are talking to. For example, if you are investigating overcrowded conditions at your local airport, the parking lot attendant will have a different stake in the matter than a cab driver, and the airport manager will have a view quite different from the resident across the street. To whom do you ask what leading question? With whom do you wait to see if the subject of overcrowding comes up? Play your hunches and see what happens.

Use Silence

This may be difficult, but it's profitable. Silence is awkward, and many of us have a natural tendency to fill it. But silence means different things at different times: sometimes ignorance, confusion, or hostility; other times thinking, feeling, or remembering. Wherever you can, allow the person some silence and see what happens. If it's hostile silence, you'll soon know it. But it is more likely that the person is doing some mental collecting and will fill the silences directly. Often, such silence can draw out rich information you never expected.

Repeat Assertions

In scanning your notes at the end of an interview, it's a good idea to repeat some of the points you find most useful and plan to use in your paper. Repeating what you believe to have heard can save you later embarrassment. You can both double-check your notes for accuracy, which is crucial if you're asking someone about a sensitive issue, and often get additional insights that have been incubating as you talked.

Tape Recording

Sometimes you want to record exactly what someone says to you, so you ask if you can tape the conversation. Sounds easy. But the trade-off for accuracy is sometimes extra nervousness for both of you and a lot of time spent playing and transcribing what you've recorded. Many good reporters, even when they have a tape recorder as backup, take quick but careful notes in a steno-pad (small, flips fast, easy to write on your lap). It helps to devise a few shorthand tricks—abbreviations for common terms, initials where clear, and standard symbols like "w/" and "&." The notes taken right there also serve to remind you about what was said both during the interview and later; having the pen in your hand helps you jot out further questions as your subject is speaking. Even if you tape, make your pen and paper work for you.

PLACES

Physical settings may play an important part in your research project. When you visit actual places where events happen or information is located, you experience your information in a way that's different than if you only read about it. Interviews, for instance, are often enhanced by reporting on the physical place where it takes place: What does the person's office look like? What's on the walls? What books are on the shelves?

Stop

Go to places and observe what is there. Investigate local issues and institutions to find out what investigative research is like. Stop and look inside the church, sit in the pews, and note what you feel. Go stand on the Brooklyn Bridge, a hundred feet above the cold, black water of the East River, and look at the city skyline, the ocean horizon. Visit the neighborhood in which the most welfare mothers are said to live and cross its streets and sit in a diner booth and drink a cup of coffee. Stop, pause, get a sense of what this place is like. Sociological reports won't generate that kind of thick information.

In the following example, Ken, a student in my first-year college class, describes his visit to a local dentist to investigate preventive dentistry:

> On entering his office I did not find the long wait, the screaming kids, and the general coldness of so many dentists' offices. Instead I found a small warm waiting room with carpeted floors, soft chairs, and classical music, with copies of *Atlantic Monthly* along with *Sports Illustrated* on the coffee table.

Look

Careful description is part of good research. The writer who is able to observe people, events, and places, and to convey that observation accurately contributes factual information to the research process. Such careful description of place establishes living, colorful, memorable contexts for all sorts of other inquiries. Look closely at the obvious and see what else is there. Go for the size, scale, color, light, texture, angle, order, disorder, smell, and taste of the place. Use your senses to find out what's there, and use your language to convey it to others. Go to the places close at hand, the library, bookstore, or student union; practice recording what you find there. Try first to record in neutral language, suppressing as much as possible your own bias; next add—or delete—your bias and give what you see as some personal color. Which seems more effective? Why?

When you interview people—on the street, in a coffee shop, in their home or office—look for clues that tell you something about the individuals. In what office, what company, what neighborhood does each one work? Researchers train themselves to look closely and take good notes so they have a context for their information. Looking and recording are the essence of research.

In the following example, Susan describes her visit to the student newspaper office:

> My eyes wander around the room as we talk. . . . One
> thing arouses my curiosity: on the pegboards between the
> large desks hang rolls of tape. All kinds, shapes and sizes
> of tape: big rolls, small rolls, thick rolls, thin rolls, full
> rolls, nearly empty rolls. Rows of electrical tape, duct tape,
> masking tape, and Scotch tape.

What does the tape say about a newspaper office? That a lot of patching
goes on? Does the tape symbolize the endless need to connect and put
together that is the essence of newspaper production? Making the note
enables her later to use it or not, depending on the slant of her story. If
she didn't have the note, neither would she have the option of using it.
Take copious notes.

Listen

Wherever you go as an observer, you are also a listener: keep your ears
open when drinking that cup of coffee; listen to the small talk in the
airport lobby; record what you hear whenever you can. A writer sometimes
finds the lead vignette for a story in some overheard snatch of conversation. Remember that research papers are essentially stories.

One of my students started her report on Evangel Baptist Church by
visiting the church, which was located across the street from the university. The following is her lead paragraph:

> The people around me were wearing everything from three
> piece suits to flannel shirts, jeans, and tennis shoes. I was
> surprised how loud everyone was talking, laughing, and jok-
> ing before the sermon. "What *happened* last night?" "*Noth-
> ing* I can tell you *here.*"

Experiment

Design situations that will help you discover new information. Some of
my students have conducted simple experiments that provide them with
original data and firsthand knowledge. For example, in an early draft, one
of my students stated that all biology majors are really "premed students"
because her two roommates happened to be biology majors with such a
focus. I challenged her on this point, so she conducted a formal survey of
a large introductory biology class—and found out that many students were
premed, but thirty-nine percent were not! She then had information to
back up whatever point she wanted to make in her paper.

In a similar vein, instead of saying that automobiles never stop at the
stop sign at the foot of Beacon Street, sit there for a morning and record

full stops, rolling stops, and no stops for a period of two hours; then you can say something based on direct knowledge.

Even simple experiments can yield useful data when you determine that such data might make you more of an authority once you understand how to collect it. There is a vast literature on designing surveys and questionnaires, but a professor in the social or educational sciences might be able to show you some shortcuts or information aimed at lay researchers.

Write

Don't spend too long visiting, interviewing, describing, and collecting without writing. Your collected information will make little sense until you force it to do so, and writing does that. Try not to spend forever making still more notes on 3 × 5 cards, shuffling and reshuffling to find the best order. All that stuff is useful, but remember that one of the best ways to see how your material is or isn't fitting together is to start writing about it. All your book notes, recordings, site descriptions, statistics, quotations, and theories only begin to make sense when you can see them in some kind of relationship with one another and watch the pattern they take.

Finally, whatever the subject of your investigation, the actual report you write can take many possible shapes, depending on how you formulate your questions about it. Consider, for example, the following lead paragraphs of three different writers who jointly investigated the minimum security Chittenden Community Correctional Center in Burlington, Vermont. Although they shared information throughout the project and visited the jail together, each wrote a distinctly different report.

> Walking up to the door of the Chittenden Community Correctional Center made me feel a bit on edge. The inmates were staring at us; I just wanted to leave. As Debbie put it, "Six girls in a Correctional Center at 8:00 p.m., I must be nuts."
>
> —Lydia

> Do you ever wonder what goes on behind the doors of a correctional center? What does it offer its inmates to improve their lives? Have you wondered what types of programs the centers provide?
>
> —Jennifer

> The Chittenden Community Correctional Center is found on Farrell Street, just off Swift Street, not five minutes from the University of Vermont campus. Within its boundaries

criminals are serving time for drunk driving, petty theft, and assault and battery.

—Debby

Each student investigated the same institution and each had a different idea for a lead and, ultimately, a different story to tell. At the same time, each lead proves interesting and invites further reading.

This chapter has opened the possibilities of college-level research to include places and issues in the local community. The next chapter investigates the research possibilities of the central institution of all colleges and universities, the library, as well as sources available on the Internet.

APPENDIX

SUGGESTIONS FOR JOURNAL WRITING

1. Describe your past experiences interviewing people. What made them go smoothly? What was difficult? How does this chapter give you help for future interviews?

2. Describe your classroom in careful detail from memory. Then, the next time you are in the classroom, notice how much detail you missed. What does this tell you about remembering versus being there in person?

3. Make a list of ten local places that it would be interesting to visit. Which one is most interesting to you? Why?

4. Make a list of ten social issues that have (or could have) local consequences. Which one is most consequential to you? Why?

5. Make a list of local people to whom you could talk about the issues listed in number four.

SUGGESTIONS FOR WRITING RESEARCH ESSAYS

1. INDIVIDUAL: Select a site listed in your journal and visit it. Describe it, interview somebody there, and find out if there is an issue to pursue further. If there is, pursue it, keeping a research log to document your way. (Possible places to investigate: public transportation centers, local businesses, government facilities, campus institutions, social agencies, parks, concert halls, malls, museums, schools, and prisons.)

2. INDIVIDUAL: Write a profile of a person in your community. Interview this person as well as people who know him or her; describe

his or her living environment; let the person speak for himself or herself in your final paper. (For profile models consult *The New Yorker, Playboy, Reader's Digest,* or *Rolling Stone.*)

3. COLLABORATIVE: Select one of the same sites as above, but tackle the project as a group (3–5 members). Divide up who visits where, interviews whom, and looks up what. Agree to share all resources by typing them up and duplicating them for group members. Finally, write either individual papers, sharing the collective research (and citing each other where appropriate), or one collaborative paper, longer, sharing the writing and editing in some equitable way among you.

4. COLLABORATIVE: Select a community of people (e.g., sports team, business associates, academic department, agency workers and clients) and develop a collective profile (use techniques as in number two above).

5. OPEN: Do any of the projects above and invent an interesting form in which to report your results: a TV script, a feature newspaper story, an exchange of letters, a short book with chapters, a drama, a technical report, a magazine article, or a multimedia event.

Chapter Ten

RESEARCHING LIBRARIES: LOCAL AND ON-LINE

My instructor wants me to use at least ten citations from at least five different sources, including books, periodicals, and the Internet. On top of that, she wants me to make the paper interesting.

—Sonya

The best writing teaches readers things they didn't already know, conveying knowledge that isn't everyday and commonplace. You are bound to do this when you write from personal experience, as nobody else anywhere has lived your life exactly. However, when you write about topics outside yourself, out there in the world of issues and ideas, you almost always need more information than you carry around loosely in your head. This is, of course, where research comes into play.

Until recently, the primary repository of worldly information was the library and its vast holdings of books, periodicals, indexes, and special collections. While the library remains the central research tool of serious writers, the library itself is less a fixed geographical entity and more an intersection of information channels. Some routes lead to paperbound books and periodicals, others to billion bit CD-ROMs, and others to virtually every other library in the world. Still, a library starts with a building, something you can see, enter, stroll through, and where you can borrow books. To the local, physically present library, we must now add the global, ethereal Internet and its vast and current resources available through any networked computer. The campus library and the global Internet are twin tickets to writing knowledgeable papers worth reading. This chapter outlines the basic routes through these powerful resources.

YOUR OWN LIBRARY

When you need information, remember the abundance of resources close at hand. Books, magazines, newspapers, and photocopies are everywhere. You and your friends have collected, informally, dozens of reference works that serve wonderfully as research starters: encyclopedias, dictionaries, handbooks, histories, atlases, anthologies, maps, tour guides, and telephone directories. At the least, these at-hand resources can help you define terms, narrow and compare topics, and provide overview information to get a research project off the ground. In short, collect and become familiar with your own reference resources.

In my own library, which has developed haphazardly over the years since high school and college, I find *Bartlett's Familiar Quotations, Roget's Pocket Thesaurus, Dictionary of the Bible, The Reader's Encyclopedia of Literature,* two *Time-Life* series (one on photography and the other on animals), the *Rand McNally World Atlas, The Hammond Road Atlas, The World Almanac for 1990, The Book of Lists,* cookbooks, home improvement books, and hundreds of paperbacks on literary, historical, social, scientific, and athletic matters, including golf, fishing, photography, and philosophy. My bookshelves are my first and most readily available library.

In addition, I have several dictionaries, including various editions of *Webster's New World, Webster's Collegiate, The American Heritage,* and *The Random House.* My own encyclopedia is the one-volume *Columbia*—quite dated (1947) but still full of useful information about historical and geographic subjects. Because it was written over fifty years ago, it isn't useful for political and current events, except as background. For more current references, I go to the library and consult a more recent edition of any of the good encyclopedias on the market: *Collier's Columbia,* the *Britannica,* or *Americana.*

BOOKS IN THE LIBRARY

In the modern university library you have access to most of the thoughts generated by humans since the invention of the printing press. Libraries provide awesome access to human ideas, knowledge, and culture—usually through the books and periodicals contained therein. Books, while more comprehensive than periodicals, will be at least a year or two out of date when you read them because of the time it takes from complete manuscript to final, edited, bound copy. So when you think of the library for research purposes, think of both books and periodicals. In addition, your university may have special collections of documents stored on tape or film: movies, audio and video tapes, photographs, paintings, and the like. The following is an overview of what the library has in store for you.

Book Catalogues

Computerized cataloguing systems identify library holdings four different ways: by author, title, subject, and keyword. In addition, many of these integrated computer systems also allow you to search the contents of periodical holdings at the same time. In some libraries, you may still find a set of file cabinets containing author, title, and subject cards. And in still other libraries the whole catalogue system may be miniaturized on film called *microfiche*. Check at the circulation or reference desk if you are uncertain how your library catalogues its holdings.

Computerized catalogue systems may vary slightly from library to library, though all systems follow the same general principles. Specific instructions for conducting a search in your own library will be posted next to the terminals. If you know the author's name or the title of the book you are looking for, follow the on-screen directions for searching by author or title. In either subject or keyword searches, the words you select to look for make the difference between success and failure. Be prepared to experiment with different words to see what gets you closest to what you want; sometimes the computer will suggest an alternate term to look under. You may gain additional help for both searches by consulting the *Library of Congress Subject Headings (LCHS)* guide which lists the exact words used to catalogue resources.

Bibliographies and Book Indexes

A bibliography is a list of works pertinent to a particular subject area. Many books include a bibliography of the various works consulted by the author in researching and writing the book. You may often find such bibliographies more helpful than a catalogue search, particularly if the book focuses on the area of your research. Check for bibliographies in any books you find through your catalogue search. In addition, you may find it useful to consult the *Bibliographic Index: A Cumulative Bibliography of Bibliographies* (New York: Wilson, 1938–date), which lists the bibliographies in books that cover a wide variety of subjects and will provide readers with lists of related sources already compiled by other authors on subjects similar to their own.

The following comprehensive book indexes list every title currently in print (still being published). These can help you discover, for example, whether a particular author has published other books that you might want to look at.

1. *Books in Print* The latest edition of this index provides a list of authors and titles currently in print and thus available at libraries,

bookstores, or by direct order from a publisher. Dated volumes are useful for author, title, and edition information.

2. *Paperbound Books in Print* The latest edition of this index lists paperback books currently in print; these are most likely to be available at local bookstores. Dated volumes are useful for author, title, and edition information.

Keep in mind that you will have to consult the catalogue to determine whether or not your library owns any of the books discovered through bibliographic and book index searches. If it does not, you may be able to order the book through interlibrary loan (from another library, usually at a nominal fee) or purchase the book yourself from the publisher.

Call Numbers

Once you have determined through the catalogue that your library owns a book you want to consult, you will use that book's call number to locate it in the stacks. For example, the book *Learning the Library* by A. K. Beaubueb, S.A. Hogan, and M.W. George, published in New York by Bowker Press in 1982, is catalogued this way:

```
Z Letters = general subject area
710 Numbers = specific division within subject
B37 Letter/number preceded by decimal point =
    placement within the division
1982 Date indicates a later edition or multiple volumes
```

Periodicals

Among the most current and specific research resources in any library are the magazines, newspapers, and bulletins that are published periodically—daily, weekly, monthly, quarterly. Periodicals are focused on particular areas of interest and, since they are published at regular intervals throughout the year, their information is usually more current than that found in books which take a longer time to be published. So many periodicals are published in each academic field, that few libraries are able to subscribe to them all. To use periodicals effectively, you need to first find the articles that interest you, then to find out if your library subscribes to it. Periodicals do not circulate; plan to read them and take notes in the library or to photocopy relevant articles to read at home.

Periodical Indexes

Periodical indexes allow you to find articles in specific journals and magazines, listing them by author and within subject categories. These indexes,
like the catalogue system, can be either in book form or computerized,
depending upon your library. Most libraries now carry these indexes on
compact discs (CD-ROMs) that will automatically conduct and print out
key word searches, generally at a nominal charge to the user (see Databases below).

The most familiar, general, and popular of the indexes is *The Readers
Guide to Periodical Literature* (1900–date). This guide lists articles of
general interest in over two hundred popular magazines, including *Time,
Newsweek, Business Week, Consumer Reports, Sports Illustrated, Science
Digest, Popular Science, The New Yorker, Esquire, Health, People,* and
Rolling Stone. Entries are arranged by author and subject, and cross-refer-
enced. (Now available on CD-ROM from 1983.)

For the more specialized and in-depth research required for most
academic assignments, the library contains specialized indexes. Listed below are some of the most useful for undergraduates:

Art Index (1929–date). Lists periodicals focusing on visual arts, including painting, sculpture, and multimedia (CD-ROM, On-Line).

Applied Science and Technology Index (1958–date). Lists periodicals
in chemistry, engineering, computer science, electronics, geology,
mathematics, photography, physics, and related fields (CD-ROM, On-
Line).

Business Periodicals Index (1958–date). Lists the contents of both
popular and specialized journals devoted to the study of business.
Prior to 1957 it was combined with the *Applied Science and Technology Index* (CD-ROM, On-line).

Education Index (1929–date). Lists all journals from the fields of
education and physical education, and related fields (CD-ROM, On-
line).

General Science Index (1978–date). Lists articles in the fields of
astronomy, botany, genetics, mathematics, physics, and oceanography
(CD-ROM, On-line).

Humanities Index (1974–date). Catalogues over two hundred sixty
periodicals in the fields of archaeology, classics, language and literature, area studies, folklore, history, performing arts, philosophy, religion, and theology. For sources prior to 1974 see *International Index,*

(1907–1965) or *Social Sciences and Humanities Index,* (1965–1974) (CD-ROM, On-line).

Social Sciences Index (1974–date). This index catalogues over two hundred sixty periodicals in the fields of anthropology, economics, environmental science, geography, law, medicine, political science, psychology, and sociology. For sources prior to 1974, see the *International Index* (1907–1965) and *Social Sciences and Humanities Index* (1965–1974) (CD-ROM, On-line)

Newspaper Indexes

Newspaper indexes list articles and stories published in newspapers. Most libraries include indexes for the two newspapers that are considered to be sources of national news, *The New York Times* and *The Wall Street Journal.* In addition, many libraries now contain the integrated newspaper/periodical index, *Infotrac.* Finally, your library may have an index of the major local paper in your area. Listed below are descriptions of these indexes.

The New York Times Index (1913–date). The index to this major paper is usually stored on microfilm and would provide a record of daily news coverage for virtually all important national events since 1913 (NEXUS, 1980–date).

Wall Street Journal Index. This is another national newspaper which specializes in business and economic information (NEXUS, 1980–date).

Infotrac. This integrated computer index, updated monthly, integrates three separate indexes: the *Academic Index,* which lists nearly one thousand commonly used scholarly publications; the *General Periodical Index,* including *The New York Times* and *Wall Street Journal;* and the *National Newspaper Index,* which adds additional large circulation newspapers to the data collection. Many entries include summaries; short articles are often included in full. Infotrac is one of several comprehensive databases which now make integrated library research both simpler and more powerful at the same time.

Databases

In most college libraries you also have access to the services of computer-conducted searches through specialized *databases* on CD-ROM (Compact

Disc—Read Only Memory, which means they convey information but cannot be added to) that are read by lasers like CDs on your home stereo system; as many as two hundred thousand pages of text can be stored on a single CD-ROM disc. This electronically-stored information is read on a computer monitor and refers you to documents, both unpublished and published. *Infotrac,* described above, is such an electronic *database* common to public as well as academic libraries.

The other giant database most commonly found in college libraries is called *DIALOGUE,* which keeps track of more than a million sources of information. *DIALOGUE* is divided into smaller, more specialized *databases,* some nine hundred eighty-seven of which are listed in the current manual, *DIALOGUE Blue Sheets,* which is available at the Reference Desk. Several of the commonly used *DIALOGUE* files include the following:

> *Arts and Humanities Search* (1980–date). A listing of over one thousand journals and abstracts of their contents.

> *ERIC* (Educational Resources Information Center) (1965–date). An index of published and unpublished papers in the field of education, including abstracts of their contents.

> *PsychINFO* (1967–date). An index of over one thousand journals in the field of psychology, including abstracts of their contents.

> *Scisearch* (1974–date). An index of a variety of journals in scientific and technological areas, including abstracts of their contents.

> *Social Scisearch* (1972–date). An index of over fifteen hundred journals, including abstracts of their contents.

To use a specialized database usually requires the assistance of a librarian, who will ask you to fill out a form listing the keywords or descriptors that you will need for your search. Keywords are usually by subject, but sometimes include authors and titles. In most cases, the descriptors will be the same ones used in the *Library of Congress Subject Heading* catalogue; however, in some cases they will differ, so consult the thesaurus of keywords that is usually located near the particular database you are using. In many libraries there is a time limitation and a charge for conducting these searches.

SEARCHING ON-LINE

The most current sources of information are likely found on the Internet. Once you have an E-mail account, on-line services such as CompuServe, Prodigy, American On-line, or a variety of campus networks allow you to search, download, and use these sources in writing research essays. The

Internet mailing list is a two-way street: you can retrieve information from knowledgeable people on particular topics; they, in turn, can receive information from you. Learning your way around the Internet will take time and a good degree of trial and error. The easiest way to begin finding Internet resources is for someone already experienced to get you started; however, if you're on your own, the following introduction will be a good first step.

To begin searching the Internet, you may want to subscribe to the *computer-assisted reporting and research list* or *carr-1*. To subscribe to the list in digest form, send E-mail to *listserve@ulkyvm.bitnet* and type these words on the subject line:

subscribe carr-1 [your full real name]

Once subscribed, you will be notified how to locate information on whatever topic interests you as well as how to post information to others who subscribe to the list.

The most common Internet tools for finding and retrieving information are already installed on most library computers as well as being readily available through the on-line services mentioned above. Try the following and see where they lead:

telnet allows you to log on to a remote computer (host) so that your computer acts like a terminal attached to this remote system, allowing you to read directories and copy files.

Archie searches file archives such as file transfer protocol (ftp) sites looking for filenames that match keywords that you specify. Type the file topic name and let Archie do the walking. (To use Archie, you need to telnet to a specific site such as *archie.internet.net*.)

Gopher finds and sorts files from different internet sites so you can easily browse through them. Once you identify a file that you want, gopher (go for) handles the details of fetching and displaying it for you to read. Most colleges and universities have local gophers to help navigate their own information data bases.

Veronica (friend of comic strip character Archie) helps search gopher menus by using keywords and the Boolian logic of *and, or,* and *not.* For example, you can ask Veronica to find *mammals* and *endangered* but not *Asia* and the program will return references to endangered mammals on all continents except Asia.

World Wide Web is a network of visual and textual *pages* (called *Web pages*) that allow you to see and download pictures and graphic designs along with text. Each web page is linked to other pages via a technique called *hypertext* that allows you to find cross-referenced information; for example, if the italicized words in this paragraph were hypertext links, clicking on each with your mouse would take you to a related page. In order to read Web pages, you need a *browser* program such as *Netscape, Mosaic, or Microsoft Internet Explorer,* one of which will be installed on your campus computers or may have come already loaded on your personal computer. One of the best known and most frequently updated lists of Internet resources available on the World Wide Web is *Yanoff's List,* maintained by Internet consultant Scott Yanoff (http://www.edu/Mirror/inet.serv-ices.html).

When incorporating any online information in your papers, plan to cite it as you do field and library sources so that others who want to read further can easily find it; keep the standard documentation needs in mind and you won't be too far off: *Who* said *what, where* and *when*? (See Chapter Eleven, "Documenting Research," for instructions and examples on how to do this using specific documentation systems.)

EVALUATING SOURCES

How do you know when a resource is good? Its being in the library is no guarantee that the assertions contained therein are responsible, fair, useful, or relevant to your purposes. The card catalogue won't examine the author's biases, divulge how easy or difficult a book is to read, or offer what experts in the field think about it. For that, you need to check elsewhere—for instance, in the *Book Review Digest* (1905–date) for the year in which the book was published. In it, you can find a brief overview of what critics thought of the book when it was published and where more complete reviews are located. Indexes such as the *Reader's Guide* also will point to places where the book was reviewed originally.

Criteria for Evaluation

What do you do when you want to evaluate a text but can't find a review of it? Or perhaps the review you find is itself suspect because of that author's extreme bias. The following are some questions to ask of sources new to you:

1. Who is the author? Have you heard of him or her? If so, in what context? Could you find the author's name in another index or encyclopedia?
2. What clues does the title contain about the author's bias or point of view?
3. When was the book or periodical published? If the topic is one

on which new information is being rapidly generated, how old can the source be and still be trustworthy?

4. If a book, who published it: A university press? A popular publisher? A specialty publisher? Fly By Night Inc.? Will credibility here be a problem?

5. If an article, where was it published? Do you recognize the periodical? Does it make a difference for credibility if it's in *Reader's Digest, Psychology Today,* or *Psychology Abstracts*? How so and to whom?

6. If a book, what can you learn from skimming the table of contents about scope? thesis? direction? strength of authority?

7. Check the reference list or *Works Cited* list at the end of the article, chapters, or volume. Look for names of authors, books, or periodicals that you recognize as respected. If you find none, did you expect to? What does that tell you?

8. Look for signs of use: Has the book been checked out often? Or has it never been checked out? What might that tell you?

9. How long is the piece, chapter, or book? Is length an indication of depth of treatment?

10. Read the first page: What do the words and sentences tell you about tone? Point of view? What does the vocabulary level and sentence length tell you about the audience the author is aiming at?

11. Skim read. Does the author define terms and provide a glossary? Or do you encounter a highly specialized vocabulary and professional jargon unexplained?

12. Look for evidence of evidence. Does the author support assertions with examples? Do you find frequent and substantial documentation?

GUIDELINES FOR CONDUCTING LIBRARY RESEARCH

1. Start a research log. Dedicate a small notebook or a portion of your class journal to your current research project. Write here to find researchable topics and ask and answer research questions. Document where you look for what and when, whether in the library or at a computer terminal. Keep track of dead as well as living ends so you don't retrace steps already taken.

2. Learn to navigate both library and Internet space. Learn the catalogues and indexes that lead to more information, regardless of venue. Learn that reference librarians and computer specialists can answer questions you alone cannot.

3. Research from general to particular. When a research subject is unfamiliar, start with context-providing general searches of

dictionaries, encyclopedias, and indexes at the library and with broad topical key words when you search a Web browser.

4. Conduct key word searches. Whether in the library or on-line, use key word searches to cover the most ground in the shortest amount of time. To start a computerized key word search, write down all possible synonyms (using a thesaurus will help here).

5. Don't rely on first-found or single sources. Let the depth of the library or the breadth of the World Wide Web provide you with a range of sources to examine and evaluate.

6. Use note and bibliographic cards. While computers are great record keepers, sometimes nothing beats a small stack of 3 × 5 cards for catching and arranging notes wherever you may be; keep some in your book bag as well as next to your computer.

7. Write to research. Compose as much as you can while you research to allow questions to emerge as you try to make your topic make sense. If you wait to write until you think you have enough information, your writing may tell you that you don't— and it may then be too late.

8. Catalogue Internet sources. For resources printed from the Internet, keep an indexed folder, with like items clipped together, in alphabetical order, each folder with its own table of contents. Make appropriate bibliographic and note cards to interleave with your other paper notes.

9. Make bookmarks for Web sites. The World Wide Web allows you to make easily identifiable *bookmarks* that allow you to return rapidly to a once-visited and useful Web site. Use these not only for speed, but to document your search record.

10. Add field research. Papers on many topics profit from personal interview information as well as descriptive site visits. In the midst of dazzling high tech resources, don't overlook the value of shoe leather, pencils, and steno pads.

APPENDIX

SUGGESTIONS FOR JOURNAL WRITING

1. Make a list of library or Internet services you want to learn more about. Ask a librarian or media expert to help you; record what you learn.

2. Inventory your dorm room, building, apartment, and home and list the reference sources already contained therein. Were you surprised by what you found (or didn't)? How so?

3. Select a book at random from your roommate's bookshelf, one you

haven't read, and see how much you can learn about it by using the Criteria for Evaluation guidelines in this chapter.

SUGGESTIONS FOR WRITING RESEARCH ESSAYS

1. INDIVIDUAL: To any of the research ideas suggested in the last few chapters, add a substantial amount of library research: Can you use some of the reference works listed here? Can you include current periodicals as well as books? Will you make sure to look at more than one source? Plan to include at least three Internet sources.

2. COLLABORATIVE: Select a historical subject to research that all members of your group agree upon. Divide up research tasks so that each of you brings back to the group a one- to two-page review of a book and an article to share with the others. Invent an interesting form in which to report the results of your investigation.

Chapter Eleven

WRITING WITH SOURCES

Documenting research papers is easier than sometimes made out. You just answer the question *who* said *what, where,* and *when.* But don't be surprised if English teachers want you to answer it one way and history teachers another—but the information you need is exactly the same.

—Brian

Research writing can be only as convincing as the authority which informs it. Remember that every paper you write is an attempt to create belief, to convince your readers that you know what you are talking about, and that what you say is true. Though good personal writing often uses researched information (journal entries, letters, on-site descriptions), its primary means of persuasion derives from recreating the images, impressions, and language of your own experience and speculation. In research and report writing, however, persuasive authority is based on information outside the writer's self, by citing other people's ideas, knowledge, demonstrations, and proofs.

Citing authority includes *paraphrasing, summarizing,* and *directly quoting* other sources, and working these intelligently, logically, smoothly, and grammatically into your text. Regardless of which method you use, you will need to cite the sources in which you found the information using the documentation conventions appropriate to the discipline for which the paper is being written.

DIFFERENCES FROM DISCIPLINE TO DISCIPLINE

Each subject area in the curriculum has developed its own system for documenting sources in research-based papers. Each system does essentially the same thing, yet the conventions for citing and documenting sources within the text vary slightly. A student in English or a foreign language uses the system preferred by the Modern Language Association, or MLA, while a student in the social sciences (psychology, sociology, political science, etc.) uses the American Psychological Association, or APA. These two are the most commonly used across the curriculum; however, disciplines such as history, biology, chemistry, and mathematics each has its own documentation system. If you learn the basics of any one system, such as MLA, which is featured in this book, you can learn any of the others quite easily. If you are not sure which system to use in writing an academic paper, ask your instructor which he or she prefers; if you want to know which system to use when you write a paper for publication in a professional journal (e.g., *Change, College English,* or *The Journal of Chemical Education*), study the system used in that journal.

The guidelines for documenting sources outlined in this chapter are brief but basic, and should stand you in good stead for writing most undergraduate papers using MLA conventions. If you are required to write using the conventions of the APA—the other most common system across the curriculum—the end of this chapter explains the major ways in which it differs from the MLA system. If you undertake to write a thesis-length work in any discipline, consult your thesis director for the appropriate manual to follow.

If you keep in mind the reason for documenting in the first place, the process won't seem so mysterious or complicated. The reason is simply this: Whenever you solve a problem, answer a question, develop a case, or substantiate an idea, you need to tell your readers where you got that information. *Who* provided it? *What* did they say? *When* did they say it? *Where* can I look it up? The reason you include citations, references, footnotes, and such in research papers is, essentially, to answer this query: *Who said what when and where?*

The remainder of this chapter will describe the best ways to incorporate expert testimony from texts, interviews, and the Internet into your text as well as how to document that testimony.

PARAPHRASE AND SUMMARY

When you repeat another author's ideas in your own words to simplify or clarify it, you are *paraphrasing*. When you condense an author's idea, you are *summarizing* it. Notice in the following example how a direct quotation is changed first to a paraphrase, then to a summary:

> Henry David Thoreau writes in *Walden,* "Most of the luxuries, and many of the so called comforts of life, are not only not indispensable, but positive hindrances to the elevation of mankind" (115).

A paraphrase of this same passage might go something like this:

> Henry David Thoreau claims that many of the luxuries that people believe are necessary for living a comfortable life actually get in the way of living a spiritual life (115).

A summary of the same passage might go like this:

> Thoreau argues in *Walden* that material possessions interfere with spiritual thought (115).

Notice that the paraphrase is not much shorter—twenty-nine vs thirty-two words—but uses simpler more conversational language. The summary, however, is significantly shorter—eleven words—but, like the paraphrase, it remains faithful to the original idea.

Whether you quote, paraphrase, or summarize depends on your purpose in using the reference. For example, if you want to feature especially colorful, precise, or otherwise well-written passage from a text, quote it directly. The Thoreau passage above is well written and might well be quoted directly. However, if you sense the original might confuse your audience, then you want to simplify or clarify the passage, so you paraphrase it. Finally, if you are short on space and wish only to capture the essence of the idea, you summarize it. In one sense, paraphrase and summary are weaker than direct quotation, since readers are viewing material filtered through your perspective, not reading the expert's own formulation. However, paraphrasing is the better choice for dense or jargon-filled language, just as summary saves you space and helps get to your own point more rapidly.

DIRECT QUOTATION

Quoting authors directly brings the full authority of their voices into your text. When used carefully, a direct quotation both substantiates and enlivens your ideas. I use direct quotations when the language of the quote is especially strong—better than I could paraphrase—or when it is important for my argument that the reader see *exactly* what the expert said.

Some people are experts by reputation or fame: "According to Albert Einstein (or Virginia Woolf, or Tony Morrison, or Mick Jagger)." Other people become experts because of labels or titles: "According to President Smith (or Secretary Jones, or Captain Bob, or poet Joy Harju)." Citing the precise language of respected authorities allows readers to check your sources' and see that, yes, Einstein, Woolf, Morrison, or Jagger really did say that. You and your argument each gain strength by association.

At the same time, control your sources; don't let them control you. When you write a research essay it is *your* paper and not your sources. A good research essay is not a string of expert citations held together by your introduction and transitions; instead, it's your idea supported carefully and judiciously by others whose opinions matter to your audience.

The following guidelines for incorporating direct quotations into your papers apply to whatever documentation system you select:

1. Introduce each quotation with a lead that makes it clear who is speaking: *According to Arthur Miller, "The play failed."* If there is any doubt about the speaker's identity, add that information briefly: *According to playwright Arthur Miller. . . .*
2. Quote only as much of your source as you need to make your point so that readers know exactly why you are quoting. Insert an especially careful or colorful phrase, then paraphrase the rest: *In* Fate of the Earth, *Jonathan Shell argues that "knowledge is the deterrent" to nuclear war.*
3. Work each quoted passage into your text smoothly and grammatically:
   - Use a *comma* to introduce most quotations, such as the first quotation (above).
   - Use a *colon* to introduce quotations that are *examples* (often a long indented quote), *explanations, or elaborations of the previous sentence,* or *lists of items.*
   - Use no punctuation to introduce quoted language that, without the quotation marks, does not need punctuation (see number two above).
4. Include commas and periods within quotation marks: *"The play failed."* Put all other punctuation outside quotation marks, unless it is part of the quoted material itself: *Arthur Miller asked, "What is drama?"*
5. If you make changes in punctuation or capitalization in order to integrate quotations smoothly into your sentences, enclose the changes in brackets.
6. If you make changes in words or verb tense to integrate quota-

tions smoothly into your sentences, you must put the changed word(s) in brackets: *Before the end of the Cold War, Jonathan Shell argued that "knowledge [was] the deterrent" to nuclear war.*

7. If you add language in the middle of a quotation, include the additions in brackets: *Arthur Miller asked, "What is [American] drama?"*

8. If you delete material from within a quotation, indicate the omitted material with a three dot ellipsis: *"If you delete material, . . . indicate . . . with [an] ellipsis.* If you delete material at the end of a sentence, add a period to the ellipsis, making four dots. . . . If you omit words at the beginning of a sentence, make sure the quote is grammatical, but do not use an ellipsis.

9. After including a quotation that is complex or capable of being interpreted in more than one way, be sure to explain your reason for including it, the meaning you intend, or the value you believe it has.

THE MLA DOCUMENTATION SYSTEM

The following discussion of MLA documentation conventions is derived from the *MLA Handbook for Writers of Research Papers,* fourth edition (1995). MLA style incorporates brief parenthetical citations in the text that refer to complete citations on a "Works Cited" page at the end of the paper.

Guidelines for In-text Citation

The logic of the MLA format is to identify author and page number in the body of your text as briefly as possible, including only as much information as a reader needs in order to locate the complete source, alphabetically, on the final "Works Cited" page. Footnotes or endnotes are used only for additional comments not appropriate for the text body itself.

Author Not Named In Your Text   Identify the author so that readers can look up the full source at the end of your paper. Place author's last name in parentheses at the end of the sentence (*outside* the quotation marks, but *inside* the ending punctuation) followed by the page number:

> "In Arthur Miller's 1953 play, *The Crucible,* the witchcraft trials that took place in Salem, Massachusetts, in 1692, are presented as an open-and-shut case of social injustice" (Rafferty 119).

Author Named In Your Text   If you introduce the quote or paraphrase with the author's name so that it is apparent who is speaking, include only the page number in parentheses:

> Mark Twain reveals Huckleberry Finn's moral growth after the storm when Huck blurts out, "All right, then, I'll go to hell" (123).

Two Or Three Authors   For works with two or three authors, include each author's last name (Goswami and Stillman). For works with four or more authors, include only the first author followed by *et al.* (Spiller, et al. 917)

More Than Three Authors   If two or more authors are cited in the same sentence, identify each next to the relevant material:

> While one critic contends the major influence on Twin was Lincoln's view of democracy (DeVoto), others claim the enduring influence was Calvinism (Spiller, et al. 917).

Multiple Works, Same Author   When you cite more than one work by the same author, include a shortened version of the title of the book or article following the author's name in parentheses:

> Twain's voice is both innocent and ironic when he writes, "Animals talk to each other, of course. There can be no question about that, but I suppose there are very few people who can understand them" (*Tramp* 43).

Unsigned Work   If no author is listed in a book or article, identify by short title in the text and alphabetize on Works Cited page by the first word omitting A, An, and The.

A Source Referred To By Another Source   Make a shorthand notation that your source is not from a full original text, using *qtd. in* for *quoted in:*

> The anthropologist Robert Brain calls romantic love "a lunatic relic of medieval passions" (qtd. in Gray 203).

Long Quotations   If you quote five or more lines, indent the material *ten spaces* and omit quotation marks (the act of indenting tells the reader the passage is a quotation). Place title and page numbers in parentheses *outside* the end punctuation. Indented passages are double-spaced. Introduce all quoted material so that readers know what it is and why it's there, and punctuate correctly. For example:

> Author and columnist Diane Johnson describes the difficulty in writing neutrally about rape:

No other subject, it seems, is regarded so differently by men and women as rape. Women deeply dread and resent it to an extent that men apparently cannot recognize; it is perhaps the ultimate and essential complaint that women have to make against men. Of course men may recognize that it is wrong to use physical force against another person, and that rape laws are not prosecuted fairly, and so on, but at a certain point they are apt to say, "But what was she doing there at that hour anyway?" or "Luckily he didn't really hurt her," and serious discussion ceases. ("Rape" 296)

Electronic Source   If an electronic source uses no page numbers, identify by paragraph number (Smith, par. 5). If the source uses no paragraphs, identify as you would a whole book (Smith).

Footnote Or Endnote   Supplement in-text citations with notes only when you need to:

1. provide useful information that does not fit easily into the main body of your text
2. comment on a source (*There is no confirmation that Twain ever said this*)
3. cite several sources at once

Identify each note by a small raised number in your text where appropriate, then type the same number and the note either at the bottom of the page (footnote) or end of the text (endnote), preceding the "Works Cited" page:

(Four recent cookbooks contain the same salsa recipe[1]).

Guidelines for Works Cited Page

At the end of the paper, type "Works Cited" at the top of a separate page, centered, and list all the textual source referred to in the paper, following these general guidelines:

1. Alphabetize the list, by author's last name, then first name. If author's name is not given, alphabetize the source by the first main word in the title (exclude A, An, and The).
2. If there are multiple authors, after the first name, list the others in normal order (first name, last name), separating each with a comma.
3. Provide full titles, capitalizing all important words. (For periodicals, omit A, An, or The.) Underline the titles of books and

periodicals. Place titles of chapters, poems, and periodical articles in quotation marks.

4. Provide volume and edition number (if relevant) after title.
5. Provide publication information after the title. For books, give city of publication (add state abbreviation if city is small), the name of the publisher (short name only), and date. For periodical articles, give volume or issue number, the date (in parentheses), and the page numbers.
6. Double space each entry and between entries. Indent all lines after the first line, five spaces (1/2 inch).

Documenting Books

SINGLE AUTHOR

O'Brien, Tim. *The Things They Carried.* New York: Penguin, 1990.

TWO BOOKS BY ONE AUTHOR

Elbow, Peter. *Writing Without Teachers.* New York: Oxford UP, 1973.
———. *Writing With Power.* New York: Oxford UP, 1981.

TWO OR THREE AUTHORS

Strunk, William, Jr., and E. B. White. *The Elements of Style.* 3rd ed. New York: Macmillan, 1979.

MORE THAN THREE AUTHORS

Barr, Mary, et al., *What's Going On? Language/Learning Episodes in British and American Classrooms, Grades 4-13.* Montclair NJ: Boynton/Cook, 1982.

ANONYMOUS AUTHOR

American Heritage Dictionary. Second College Edition. Boston: Houghton Mifflin, 1982.

AN EDITOR OR EDITORS

Ellmann, Richard, and Robert O'Clair, eds. *Modern Poems: An Introduction to Poetry.* New York: Norton, 1976.

MORE THAN TWO VOLUMES

Parrington, Vernon L. *Main Currents in American Thought.* 2 vols. New York: Harcourt, 1927.

Parrington, Vernon L. *Main Currents in American Thought.* Vol. 1. New York: Harcourt, 1927.

A LATER EDITION

Aaron, Jane. *The Little Brown Essential Handbook for Writers.* 2nd ed. New York: Longman, 1997.

A TRANSLATION

Camus, Albert. *The Stranger.* Trans. Stuart Gilbert. New York: Random House, 1946.

A CHAPTER IN AN ANTHOLOGY

Britton, James. "The Composing Processes and the Functions of Writing." *Research on Composing.* Eds. Charles R. Cooper and Lee Odell. Urbana, IL: National Council of Teachers of English, 1978.

AN INTRODUCTION, PREFACE, FOREWORD, OR AFTERWORD

Graff, Gerald. Afterword. *When Writing Teachers Teach Literature.* Eds. Art Young and Toby Fulwiler. Portsmouth, NH: Boynton/Cook, 1995.

AN UNSIGNED ARTICLE IN A REFERENCE BOOK

"Style Manual." *The American Heritage Dictionary.* 2nd College Edition. Boston: Houghton Mifflin, 1982.

Documenting Periodicals

A SIGNED ARTICLE IN JOURNAL

Ohmann, Richard. "Reflections on Chaos and Language." *College English* 44 (1982): 1-17.

A SIGNED ARTICLE IN MONTHLY OR BIMONTHLY MAGAZINE

Mayersohn, Norman. "Rad Wheels." *Popular Mechanics* May, 1987: 84-87.

A SIGNED ARTICLE IN A WEEKLY OR BIWEEKLY MAGAZINE

Hoffman, Michael. "Hardly Cricket." *New Yorker* 2 Dec. 1996: 113-114.

DAILY NEWSPAPER

"Ex-Officials See Lobbyists' View." *The Burlington Free Press* 12 April 1987, sec. 2: 1.

Documenting Electronic Sources

Portable Databases

CD-ROM's and diskettes are cited the same as books and periodical entries; the word CD-ROM or diskette is inserted following the title and before place and date of publication.

> Virginia Woolf. *The 1995 Grolier Multimedia Encyclopedia.* CD-ROM. Danbury: Grolier, 1995

Internet Sources

To identify a **World Wide Web** or other **Internet** source, include all the relevant items in the following order, each followed by a period, except date of access.

- *Author (or editor, compiler, or translator).* If known, full name, last name first.
- *Title.* In quotation marks or underlined, as appropriate, followed by Online posting.
- *Editor, compiler or translator.* Include name, followed by Ed., Com., or Tran.
- *Print source information.* Same as printed citation.
- *Title of scholarly project, database, personal, or professional site* (underlined); if no title include description such as Home page.
- *Identifying number.* For a journal include volume and issue number.
- *Date of electronic publication.*
- *Discussion list information.* Include full name or title of list or forum.
- *Page, paragraph, or section numbers.*
- *Sponsorship or affiliation.* Include name of any organization that sponsors this site.
- *Date of access.* Include date you visited this site.
- *Address in angle brackets.* Include within angle brackets < >. Selected examples follow (Also see MLA Web site, *<http://www.mla.org>*).

PROFESSIONAL SITE OR PERSONAL SITE

> Fulwiler, Anna. Home page. 1 Feb. 1998 *<http://www.uvm.edu/~afulwile>*. Yellow Wall-Paper Site. U. Texas. 1995. 4 Mar. 1998<http://www.cwrl.utexas.edu/~daniel/amlit/wallpaper/wallpaper.html>.

ARTICLE IN A JOURNAL

> Erkkila, Betsy. "The Emily Dickinson Wars." *Emily Dickinson Journal* 5.2 (1996) 14 pars. 2 Feb. 1998 <http://www.colorado.edu/

POEM OR STORY

Poe, Edgar Alan. "The Raven." *American Review,* 1845. *Poetry Archives.* 4 Mar. 1998: <http://tqd.advanced.org/3247/cgi-bin/dispgi?poet=poe. Edgar&poem=10.html&frame=none>.

ARTICLE IN REFERENCE DATABASE

"Jupiter." *Britannica Online.* Vers. 97.1.1 Mar. 1997. *Encyclopedia Britannica.* 29 Mar. 1998 <*http://www.eb.come:180*>.

POSTING TO A DISCUSSION LIST

"New Virginia Woolf Discussion List." Online posting. 22 Feb. 1996. Virginia Woolf Society, Ohio State U. 4 Mar. 1998 <gopher://dept.english.upenn.edu:70/oro-1858-?lists/20th/woolf>.

E-MAIL, LISTSERV, OR NEWSGROUP (USENET) MESSAGE

Fulwiler, Toby. <*tfulwile@zoo.uvm.edu*> *"A question about electronic sources." Jan. 23, 1998. 24 Jan. 1998. Personal e-mail. 23 Jan. 1998.*
Note: You must get permission before including a personal address on the Works Cited page.

FILE TRANSFER PROTOCOL (FTP), TELNET, OR GOPHER SITE

King, Jr., Martin Luther. *"I Have a Dream Speech." 28 Aug. 1963. 30 Jan. 1996* <*Telnet ukanaix.cc.ukans.edu*>.
Substitute abbreviation ftp, telnet, or gopher for http before the site address.

SYNCHRONOUS COMMUNICATIONS (MUD, MOO, IRC)

StoneHenger. *The Glass Dragon MOO. 6 Feb. 1995. 6 Feb. 1995 Personal Interview* <*telnet://surf.tstc.edu*>.
After posting date, include type of discussion (e.g./personal interview, group discussion), followed by a period.

Documenting Other Sources

AN UNPUBLISHED DISSERTATION

Smith, Peter. "Literacy Reconsidered." Diss. U of Vermont, 1994.

RECORD

Springsteen, Bruce. *Nebraska.* Columbia, TC38358, 1982.

TELEVISION/RADIO

Rather, Dan. *CBS Evening News.* 13 April 1987.

PERSONAL INTERVIEW

Strauss, Michael. Telephone interview. Burlington, VT: 12 May 1985.

For an example of a complete paper written in MLA format, see Chapter Twelve.

THE APA DOCUMENTATION SYSTEM

The system used by most of the social science and professional disciplines, including psychology, sociology, political science, anthropology, education, and business is called APA, taking its name from the Publication Manual of the American Psychological Association, fourth edition (1994). The most obvious difference between MLA and APA is the stress on the date for in-text citations. The following provides brief descriptions of the chief differences between APA and MLA, with a sample Reference page attached.

In-text Citation

When you use the APA format, follow these conventions when citing sources in the text of your paper:

1. When you refer to an author or authors in your text, include the date of publication immediately following the name: *According to Smith (1986) and Jones (1974) the system is at fault.*
2. When you quote directly, but do not mention the author's name, include all necessary information immediately following the quotation: *"All that glittered was not gold" (Smith, 1986, p. 12).*
    Note: In APA put commas between the name, date, and page numbers; include *p.* for page numbers.
3. When you quote an author, put the date reference immediately following her name, and the page reference following the quotation: *According to Smith (1986), "All that glittered was not gold" (p. 23).*
4. When you quote three to five authors, mention each in the first reference: *According to Smith, Jones, Miller, and Wilson (1996).* . . . . Use only the first name followed by et al. for subsequent references: *Furthermore, Smith et al. (1996) argue.* . . .
    Note: When you quote six or more authors, include only the first name followed by et al. for all references.
5. If no author is listed, mention the title followed by the date: *One article ("Gold Found in New Mexico," 1994) claimed a new gold rush had begun.*
6. When you cite more than one source in a single year by a single

author, differentiate by adding a, b, c, etc., to the date according to alphabetical order of titles: *Smith (1987a) found no evidence of gold anywhere.*

7. When you refer to a source in another source, explain in parentheses where it can be found: *This researcher's findings contradict the Smith (cited in Miller, 1990) study in every significant way.*

8. When an author comments on a source or chooses to include explanatory information not directly relevant to a given paragraph, footnotes—not endnotes—are used.

Reference Page

At the end of your APA style paper attach a separate page entitled "References" listing all works alphabetically as follows.

1. In alphabetical order, list the first author of each entry flush with the left margin, last name first, followed by initials: *Smith, L. H.* Double space within and between entries and indent subsequent lines in same reference 5 spaces.

2. If more than one author, list all authors last name first followed by initials; separate last author from previous authors with an ampersand: *Smith, L. H., Miller, J. O. & Ruger, B. G.*

3. Include the date immediately following the author(s) and period: *Smith, T. E. and Jones, S. F. (1995).* For periodicals, include month and day *(1995, March 21).*

4. If no author, list title's first main word, then date: *Gold found in New Mexico (1994).*

5. In titles of books and articles, only the first word, first word of subtitle, and proper nouns are capitalized: *College writing: A personal approach to academic writing in America.* For journal titles, capitalize all significant words: *College Composition and Communication.*

6. Underline the titles of books and periodicals, along with any comma or period following. Also underline volume numbers in journals. Do not underline or use quotation marks around the titles of periodical articles or book chapters: *Rinaldi, J. (1996, November). Rhetoric and healing. College English 58 (7), 820–834.*

7. Follow place of publication with full names of university presses (Cambridge, MA: *Harvard University Press*) and associations acting as publishers *(American Mathematics Association).* Give brief names for other publishers, omitting first names: *Wiley.*

8. Use *p. or pp.* before page numbers in books and newspapers, but not in other periodicals; separate from publication information with a comma.

9. Separate the parts of each reference (author/date, title, publication information with a period and one space.
10. Document personal communications (letter, interview, email messages) in-text following quotation, but do not include on Reference page:*John Clarke explained how the process worked (Personal interview, 1993, July 26).*
11. For Internet sources, follow guidelines for print sources, but add the type of source following the title, the date source was accessed, and electronic address with no end publication. (*Williams, S. Back to school with the quilt. AIDS memorial quilt Website. N.d:n.pag. [Online]. Available from the World Wide Web: http//www.aidsquilt.org/newsletter/stories/backto.html*)

APA Sample Reference Page

References

American heritage dictionary: Second college edition (1982). Boston: Houghton Mifflin.

Camus, A. (1946). *The stranger.* (Stuart Gilbert, Trans.) New York: Random.

Elbow, P. (1973). *Writing without teachers.* New York: Oxford University Press.

Elbow, P. (1990). Democracy through language (pp. 31–48). *What is English.* New York: Modern Language Association.

Ex-officials see lobbyists' view. (1987, April 12). *The Burlington free press,* p. B1.

Hoffman, M. (1996, December 2). Hardly cricket. *New Yorker,* pp. 113–114.

O'Brien, T. (1990) *The things they carried.* New York: Penguin.

Parrington, V. L. (1927). *Main currents in American thought.* (Vols. 1–2). New York: Harcourt.

Rinaldi, J. (1996, November). Rhetoric and healing: Revising narratives about disability. *College English,* 58 (7), 820–834.

Strunk, W., Jr. & White, E. B. (1979). *The Elements of Style.* (3rd ed.). New York: Macmillan.

Williams, S. Back to school with the quilt. *AIDS memorial quilt Website.* N.d: n. pag. [On-line]. Available from WWW:http//www.aidsquilt.org/newsletter/stories/backto.html

(For electronic address, omit any punctuation not part of the Internet address, including final period.)

APPENDIX

SUGGESTIONS FOR JOURNAL WRITING

1. Find the passage in this chapter that taught you something you didn't already know. Copy it in your journal. Then write a paraphrase and a summary of it.

2. Compare your experience investigating electronic sources with investigating library or living resources. Which do you prefer? Why?

SUGGESTIONS FOR WRITING RESEARCH ESSAYS

1. INDIVIDUAL: After you have written and documented an academic research paper for any of your courses, recast it in a different form for a different, more popular audience. Consider these options: as a feature story for a local or school paper; as a script for *60 Minutes;* as a report to a class of sixth graders; or as anything else you may imagine.

2. COLLABORATIVE: At the beginning of a research assignment, pair with a classmate and arrange to exchange drafts outside of class before each is handed in. Act as editors for each other, and check each other's use of sources according to the guidelines presented in this chapter: Is each quotation properly introduced, documented, and explained in the text? Does each reference appear correctly on the "Works Cited" or "Reference" page? Does the writer consistently follow MLA or APA conventions? On the final draft, sign off on the paper as the editor.

Chapter Twelve

WRITING RESEARCH ESSAYS

I liked writing this paper more than any other paper I've ever done. I think it was because we worked as a team when we toured the factory and later, when we wrote each of the three different drafts of this paper. Everybody pitched in, nobody slacked, we had a really good time, and we even learned how to make ice cream!

—Sandy

Writing based on research need be neither dry nor dull. This chapter features a single research essay written in response to an assignment to investigate any issue or institution using both library and field research. To research and/or write the essay in collaboration with others in the class was an option selected by approximately half the class.

The following research essay examines Ben & Jerry's Homemade Ice Cream Company as an institution concerned with issues of both local and national importance. It was researched and written by the team of Michelle Anderson, Pamela Jurentkuff, Sandy Martin, Heather Mulcahy, and Jennifer Stanislaw. The essay gains authority by using both local and electronic library research, in addition to personal interviews and site visits. They also composed the essay with a lively, first-person plural voice (we) to which they added other voices they encountered along the way.

The essay is not included here as a model for you to follow. Instead, read it as one possibility for combining formal academic research and the MLA style with a lively personal voice.

161

BEN & JERRY'S HOMEMADE ICE CREAM COMPANY:
CARING CAPITALISM AT WORK

Ben and Jerry's Homemade Ice Cream Company has developed an international reputation for making "the world's best ice cream" while, at the same time, setting a new standard for socially responsibility. Numerous trips to the local scoop shop had already convinced our research team—Pam, Sandy, Heather, Michelle, and Jennifer—that Ben and Jerry's ice cream was good; now we wanted to find out the rest of the scoop.

THE SCOOP (SHOP)

When you enter the front door of Ben and Jerry's Homemade Ice Cream Shop in downtown Burlington, Vermont, you find yourself standing on a clean, tiled, black-and-white checkered floor. To the left are three dark-red booths with white tables, just big enough for four people to look out onto the street while eating their ice cream. The opposite wall is covered with eight black-and-white spotted cows standing in a lush, green field, probably somewhere in Vermont. The sky above them is a bright blue with several white, puffy clouds.

Just around the corner are five black steps that lead to the upstairs where the ice cream is sold. At the top of the stairs, next to a white metal wastebasket, is a blue plastic sign that says, "We are now recycling spoons!"

On the right wall is the white, chest high ice cream counter. Behind it a colorful, wooden sign reads, "Today's Euphoric Flavors," listing twenty-nine flavors, including Cherry Garcia, Chocolate Chip Cookie Dough, Chunky Monkey, Heathbar Crunch, Coffee Heathbar Crunch, New York Super Fudge Chunk, and Rainforest Crunch. To the left of the flavors, is a white sign with black writing that tells the prices—$1.44 for a small, $1.84 for a medium, $2.60 for a large.

Sitting on the counter, in glass containers, are waffle cones, almonds, walnuts, Jimmies, M&Ms, and Reese's Pieces. At the end of the counter sits a freezer with factory-second pints, chocolate chip ice-cream sandwiches, and Peace Pops—in case you want to take some home with you, which most people, including us, want to do.

One of the reasons we chose to investigate Ben and Jerry's was to find out more about the delicious ice cream that we love to eat. We asked the person behind the counter, "How do you get the names of the flavors for the ice cream?"

"Most of them are pretty basic. Well, like Cherry Garcia was thought up by a Grateful Dead fan in Maine. Some lady in New Hampshire wrote in with the idea of Chunkey Monkey. They gave her a lifetime supply of the ice cream and it turns out she doesn't even like it" (Martin).

The three workers behind the counter all seem to be having fun while scooping ice cream and joking with the steady line of customers. They are all wearing Ben & Jerry's T-shirts, but different hats—a blue beret, a baseball cap, a beanie. We asked the nearest scooper, a young woman named Susan, "Why do you all wear hats?"

"Actually, it's a health regulation. We have to keep our hair back. In the factory they have to wear elastic caps and all-white sanitary outfits. Here we're encouraged to have fun with it. We wear all different types. I'm known for my Viking hat that I often wear. I wear my hair braided, they all nickname me Helga."

Another scooper adds: "There are some limitations. Like they wouldn't let me wear a hat made out of a pair of jeans or one out of a paper bag. But I have a great hat planned for Christmas. It's a secret though."

It was clear from our visit to Ben and Jerry's main scoop shop in downtown Burlington, that both eating and serving ice cream could be fun. How, we wondered, did such a funky business get started?

IN THE BEGINNING

Ben and Jerry's Homemade Ice Cream company began when two old friends from Long Island, Ben Cohen and Jerry Greenfield, decided to honor a childhood pact that one day they would go into business together and "do something more fun" (Hubbard 57). At the time, Ben was working with emotionally unstable children in New York, and Jerry was a lab technician in North Carolina. They selected Burlington, Vermont, as just the right sized rural college town for a small food business—a food and ice cream emporium, as they first envisioned it ("Solid"). However, neither Ben nor Jerry had any experience in making ice cream, so in 1977 they took a five-dollar correspondence course in ice cream making from Penn State. In 1978 they received a four thousand dollar loan which, combined with eight thousand dollars in savings, was enough to establish the first Ben and Jerry's scoop shop—an old run-down gas station on the corner of St. Paul and College Street, which opened on May 5, 1978.

At first Ben and Jerry tried to sell both bagels and ice cream. As Jerry tells it, "At first it was almost like a race to see who would sell the most, would it be Ben with his bagels covered with marinated artichoke hearts, mushrooms, and sliced cucumber? Or Jerry with his Sweet Cream Oreo ice cream?" (Greene). They saw the handwriting on the wall when everybody bought the ice cream and nobody bought the bagels. So at the end of 1979, Ben gave up the bagels and joined Jerry in the ice cream business.

The ice cream succeeded because it was hand made in an old fashioned rock salt ice cream maker; the flavors were original and fun; and they claimed to use only Vermont dairy products and strictly natural ingredients. They also double-flavored their ice cream, making it with twice as much flavor as a recipe normally called for. How did they know how much flavoring was enough? "Well when we first started, I made the ice cream and Ben tasted it. If Ben couldn't tell what flavor the ice cream was with his eyes closed, he would tell me it needed more flavoring" (Greene).

After a year in business, Ben and Jerry celebrated by offering free ice cream cones to all their customers. "We always told ourselves that if we were still open after the end of the first year, we'd give away free cones on or about our anniversary" (Smith). The demand for their ice cream became so great that often their daily supply was not enough, forcing them to introduce the International No Ice Cream Sign, a cone with a red slash through it symbolizing that there is no ice cream left for the day.

However, it took time and practice to perfect their recipes. Jerry remembers, "I once made a batch of Rum Raisin that stretched and bounced" (Hubbard 57). By 1981, however, through the process of trial and error, they were noted in *Time* magazine for making "The best ice cream in the world" ("They").

By 1983, the small shop in downtown Burlington could not generate enough ice cream to keep up with the streams of customers that poured in each day, so they relocated their main store to Cherry Street and their production facilities to the outskirts of town. By 1986, when they launched a nationwide campaign, distributing free ice cream around the country from a black and white "Cowmobile," they needed an even larger plant, so they reestablished their headquarters in Waterbury, Vermont, some forty miles east of Burlington, where they continue to produce the majority of their ice cream.

MAKING THE "WORLD'S BEST ICE CREAM"

Our research team toured the Ben and Jerry's Ice Cream Plant in Waterbury to see how the ice cream is actually made. The main lobby smelled like peppermint and was packed with people holding ice cream cones in one hand and T-shirts, sweatshirts, bumper stickers, boxer shorts, cow socks, and hats in the other. We were surprised to find so many people there in the middle of the week in the middle of a Vermont winter.

We arrived just in time to take the noon tour. We joined a dozen other people and slowly followed our tour guide, Rick, into a long corridor with light green trees, pale yellow flowers, and bright pink birds painted on the walls. A tape recording of toucans and other tropical birds played in the background—"Vermont's only tropical rain forest," Rick laughed.

From the rain forest we entered another long hallway with a large window that looked down over the production room where the ice cream is made. The number 44,560 was painted in big, black, bold numbers on the wall. This is their record pint production for a seventeen hour period, enough ice cream for an individual to eat a pint a day for one hundred ninety-six years. You might think that this is a lot of ice cream, but every employee takes home three pints a day. "It's a wonderful benefit," Rick explained, "but not too good for the waistline, which is why Ben & Jerry's also offers a free health club membership to everyone that works there."

The ice cream begins in the Blend Tank, a two hundred forty lb. stainless steel tank that combines Vermont milk, cream, egg yolks, unrefined sugar, and the flavor of the day. From there, the mix is sent in big vats to the thirty-six degree Tank Room, where it sits for four to eight hours before it receives further flavoring.

The plant has two production lines. On this day, one was making Coffee Heath Bar Crunch and the other Mint Oreo, which are good sellers, but not their top sellers. The current top five flavors are Heath Bar Crunch, New York Super Fudge Chunk, Cherry Garcia, Rainforest Crunch, and Chunkey Monkey, flavors that have proved popular year in and year out in all parts of the country.

From the Tank Room, the mix moves to into four, three hundred gallon Flavor Vats, so they can put in the peppermint extract for the Mint Oreo and the coffee extract for the Coffee Heath Bar Crunch. From the Flavor Vat, the mix goes to the Fruit Feeder, where they mix in big chunks of Oreos or Heath Bar or whatever chunks they need for the ice cream they are producing on that day.

After all the ingredients are put into the mix, the mix is sent through a freezer made to hold seven hundred fifty gallons of ice cream, turned by a crank which adds air to the ice cream. Companies are allowed up to a 100% over-run—for every one gallon of mix, two gallons of ice cream should come out. However, Rick told us that "Ben & Jerry's has a twenty percent overrun, making it much thicker than standard commercial ice cream found in supermarkets."

The automatic filler fills the pints, sometimes in the wrong container. When this happens, the pint becomes a "factory second" and is sold in local stores in Vermont at a lower price. Vermonters are used to finding the "seconds" freezers full, but according to Rick, only two percent of their pints become factory seconds. Mistakes are identified in the Quality Control Room, where every hour four pints are taken and tested for color, taste, texture, and consistency.

The packaged ice cream is then sent to the Spiral Hardening Tunnel to be frozen solid at thirty-five degrees below zero. A life size doll, called "Freezer Fred," sits in a snowsuit watching the ice cream as it passes through the tunnel. We poked our noses into the tunnel, but did not stay long. After that, the packages are sent to shipping for distribution throughout the country.

We enjoyed the thirty-minute tour, but felt a little self-conscious because we were the only ones taking notes. One man in the production room picked up a pad of paper and started taking notes to mimic us. At one point, Rick said over the loud speaker, "Looks like we have a lot of people

taking notes here today, doesn't it?" Our faces turned red
and we all started laughing. But in the end, Rick gave us
free ice cream to take home, which is exactly what we
hoped for. (For more information about Ben & Jerry's factory tours, see their site on the World Wide Web: http:/ben-
jerry.com/tourinfo.html).

The tour impressed us, and the cleanliness and
efficiency of the whole operation made it clear that the
workers enjoy their jobs. But we still wondered where the
Ben & Jerry's reputation as a "socially responsible company" came from, so we continued our investigation.

"CARING CAPITALISM AND SOCIAL ACTIVISM"

According to a story in *People* magazine, by 1984 Ben realized that, "We're no longer ice cream men, but businessmen" (Hubbard 58). Since their opening in 1978, their
profits increased annually. Being businessmen instead of ice-
cream men, however, made the two old friends nervous. As
Ben said in a *Washington Post* interview, "We were sitting
at desks, and we were people's bosses and giving orders.
Growing up in the 60s, being a businessman wasn't a cool
thing to do. I started feeling we were a cog in the economic
machine" (Kurtz). How much of a cog you wonder? Their
most recent net sales for the quarter ending April 1, 1995,
were $34,205,000, up from $32,191,000 for the same time
the previous year ("Ben & Jerry's First").

However, Ben and Jerry also realized that just because they were successful businessmen who made money,
they didn't have to change what they believed in. In fact,
their substantial annual income allows them to make a
profit *and* give to their community at the same time. Jerry
explained, "Early on, we knew that if we stayed in the business, it was because of the support of a lot of people, so it
seemed natural to want to return that support" (Hubbard
55). They began to sell public stocks to Vermonters to keep
their center of operations within the state.

Ben and Jerry believe in a concept called "Caring Capitalism and Social Activism," which means giving a percent
of the profits back to the community. Every day seven-and-
a-half percent of the company's profits go to a worthy
nonprofitable organization and to preserving the environment. They developed a *Statement of Mission,* which

explains the product mission, the social mission, and the economic mission:

> *Product Mission*—To make, distribute, and sell the finest quality, all natural ice cream and related products in a wide variety of innovative flavors made from Vermont dairy products.
>
> *Social Mission*—To operate the company in a way that actively recognizes the central role that business plays in the structure of society by initiating innovative ways to improve the quality of life of a broad community—local, national, and international.
>
> *Economic Mission*—To operate the company on a sound financial basis of profitable growth, increasing value for our shareholders, and creating career opportunities and financial rewards for our employees.

Underlying the mission of Ben and Jerry's is the determination to seek new and creative ways of addressing all three parts, while holding a deep respect for the individuals, inside and outside the company, and for the communities of which they are a part. (*About* 5)

> Part of their social mission is evident in the program called "One Percent for Peace," a campaign that advocates redirecting one percent of the United States defense budget to a global effort "to solve world problems of hunger, disease, the environment, poverty, and human rights" (Kurtz). Whenever you buy a Peace Pop, chocolate covered ice cream on a stick, you help promote this campaign.
>
> In addition to promoting peace, Ben and Jerry's promotes helping people. According to *Ben and Jerry's Annual Report*, Greyston Bakery, based in Yonkers, New York, supplies Ben and Jerry's with brownies for use in their Brownie Bars and their Chocolate Fudge Brownie Ice Cream. The bakery employees are people who are unemployed and without homes who are trying to better themselves and improve their lifestyles. Greyston donates the majority of its profits to programs that "assists such disadvantages citizens in becoming economic and social contributors to the community" (Severence 7).
>
> The company's social concerns include consumer health issues. Recently, Ben & Jerry's has taken a stand against using dairy products from cows injected with bovine growth hormones (BGH) that are meant to increase milk production. They argue that artificially injected hormones may affect the quality of the milk as well as pose health

risks for consumers. Consequently, though the Food and Drug Administration does not require it, they label their packaged ice cream as BGH free ("Ben & Jerry's Position").

Ben & Jerry's also promotes environmental issues, such as saving the rain forests in Brazil by directing a percent of the profits from Rainforest Crunch ice cream and Rain Forest buttercrunch candy, which is manufactured by Community Products Inc. of Montpelier, VT, a company founded in 1989 and directed by Ben Cohen. Both the ice cream and candy contain Brazil and cashew nuts purchased from Cultural Survival, a human rights organization, which is using the profits to set up Brazil nut processing plants owned and operated by natives of Brazil. They provide a market for rainforest products which helps to decrease the destruction of the forests.

Closer to home, Ben and Jerry's does all it can to contribute to the safety of the environment. Remember that sign about recycling spoons when you first entered the Burlington scoop shop? At every Ben and Jerry's scoop shop there are big buckets for depositing used plastic spoons. On every table the napkin dispensers have a sign saying, "Save a tree, please take only one napkin." Presently, they are recycling approximately sixty percent of their paper supply products either to outside recyclers or for internal use as note paper. The company is now looking for an alternative material for their pint containers, because they are made from paperboard and covered with a plastic coating for moisture resistance. "As a result of this and other recycling efforts, we have reduced our solid waste volume by about 30 percent this year" (Severence 6).

Ben and Jerry's is a growing enterprise which shows continued signs of world-wide expansion, not only because they make and market an excellent product, but because they care about the future of the planet. Their socially-responsible and profitable business practices have gained the partners the support of both environmentalists and the business community. The wonderful tastes of their Heath Bar Crunch and Chunky Monkey have gained them our support as well.

Works Cited

About Ben & Jerry. Pamphlet. Burlington, VT 1.

"Ben & Jerry's Homemade, Inc. Announces 1995 First Quarter Results."

http:/www.benjerry.com/library/quarterly-statements/1st-qtr-1995.html 25 November 1996.

"Ben & Jerry's Position on rBGH." http:/www.benjerry.com/bj-position-bgh.html 25 November 1996.

"Ben and Jerry's Sells Boston Franchises." *The Burlington Free Press* 5 June 1984: B1.

Greene, Robert. Personal interview. 30 October 1984.

Hubbard, Kim. "For New Age Ice Cream Moguls Ben and Jerry, Making 'Cherry Garcia' and 'Chunkey Monkey' Is A Labor of Love." *People* 1990, 55–58.

Kurtz, Howard. "Ben and Jerry: Premium Ice Cream Sprinkled with Liberal Ideology." *Washington Post* 4, Oct. 1989: A3.

Martin, Sandy. Personal interview. 12 October 1990.

Severance, Lyn. *Ben & Jerry's Annual Report.* Boston: Daniels Printing 1995.

Smith, James L. "Ben and Jerry's Homemade Meltdown of Total Pleasure." *Rutland Herald,* 23, Feb 1981: 2.

"Their Ice Cream Takes the Cake." *Sunday Times Union* 26 Sep. 1982: C1.

"They All Scream For It." *Time* 10 Aug. 1981: 42.

APPENDIX

SUGGESTIONS FOR JOURNAL WRITING

1. Mark the passages in the Ben & Jerry's research essay that you most enjoy. Mark those that seem dull or tedious. Explain the difference.

2. Name an institution in your community that would lend itself to both an on-site investigation as well as library research. Imagine at least two different approaches or angles you might take if you investigated this institution.

SUGGESTIONS FOR WRITING RESEARCH ESSAYS

1. INDIVIDUAL: Select an institution that exists within a one mile radius of where you live. Visit that institution, interview employees and customers and, if possible, take a guided tour. Then collect any artifacts and, photograph or photocopy any printed material put out by this place. Finally, look up its history by checking local records, libraries, or newspapers. Write a first-person story—a personal research essay—detailing the process and results of your research.

2. COLLABORATIVE: Do assignment number one by selecting a team of classmates to help you. Either select an institution and recruit coresearchers or team up and together select an institution to study.

Section Four

WRITING WELL

Chapter Thirteen

OPTIONS FOR REVISION

> This class has finally taught me that rewriting isn't just about correcting and proofreading, but about expanding my ideas, trying experiments, and taking risks. Why did it take me so long to learn this? And why don't I do it on all my papers?!
>
> —Rachel

Yes, Rachel, rewriting is about expanding ideas, trying experiments, and taking risks. It's also chancy, unpredictable, laborious, frustrating—and impossible to do if you don't make time for it. But in every way, it makes your writing better. There are no guarantees, no formulas, no shortcuts. How and when then, does one learn to rewrite? I do it all the time, yet I'm not always sure what I'm doing. Often when I rewrite, I don't know exactly what I'm doing or looking for, but recognize the need for change when I see it. I doubt I ever rewrite the same way twice, sometimes starting here, sometimes there, but I always do rewrite, and because I do, my writing always gets at least a little better than it was before.

Revising differs from editing. Revision is conceptual work, where I reread, rethink, and reconstruct my thoughts on paper until they match those in my mind. Revising is reseeing my approach, topic, argument, evidence, organization, and conclusion, and experimenting with change. Editing is stylistic work, changing language more than ideas. I usually edit *after* I know what to say, testing each word or phrase to see if it is necessary, accurate, and correct. The last stage of editing is proofreading, checking spelling, punctuation, capitalization, and the like. (See Chapter Fourteen, "Options for Editing").

As a rule, review before you edit; attend to conceptual matters first, then fine tune your sentences. But don't be worried if sometimes the rule doesn't work, if you revise and edit simultaneously. In my own case, there are times when I can't develop an idea further until I get a certain sentence or paragraph just right, where the revising and editing simply blur. As a writer, what I've learned above all else is "There ain't no rules" that apply to every situation—only good suggestions that sometimes work better than other times.

PRELIMINARIES

Much that has to do with writing is a matter of habit and time. To change writing habits or find more time, remind yourself that all writing by all writers gets better when returned to, reviewed, and revised. If you want to improve your writing, from now on, *plan* for revision. Plan to make more time.

Start Today

If an essay, report, or story is due next week, start this week, no matter if you have all your information and ideas or not, no matter how otherwise busy you are. Beginning to write, even for ten minutes, will start the incubation process in your own mind, and you'll actually be working on the paper in your subconscious as you go about your daily business. You cannot revise if you haven't first written. Start your papers *before* the night before they are due.

Set Deadlines

All writers are deadline writers. Learn that deadlines are friends, not enemies. Use the external deadlines set by the assignment, then create your own internal ones to get it done on time. Plan at the outset to finish on time. And plan for at least three drafts—one rough, one revised, one edited—or more. I always do more.

Keep a Revision Notebook

Make a point of writing about revision in your journal or class notebook. Record notes about books, authors, and articles related to your project. Capture ideas about theme, direction, and purpose. Writing informally about your revision plans will almost certainly advance the project in useful and surprising ways.

Compose With a Computer

If you have access to a computer, use it. Computers make rewriting almost easy. Save early drafts by relabeling files, that way you always have early copy to restore in case you change your mind. If you don't have access to a computer, try to make at least one typed draft before the final one: Typed words give you greater distance from your own ideas and invite more possibilities for change. For early drafts, start a new file each time and see what else your paper can become. You can always merge files later on and synthesize your several insights. (And *always* make back up files [copies] of every paper on separate disks, in case a disk or drive goes bad!)

Prepare to Let Go

Treat first drafts as language experiments, meant to be changed, even discarded. No matter how much you like the draft as you write and just after you finish, know that you will like it less the next day, even less the day after. And that's okay! First drafts are first drafts, meant to be let go of to make room for seconds and thirds. (Sometimes there are exceptions, and your first language will stand the test of time; that will be wonderful, but don't plan on it happening.)

PRACTICES

Some of the following specific practices may help you revise.

Revise for Ideas

Focus on what you want and need to say, try to get that out, and worry later about how it looks. Keep rereading and keep asking yourself: What is my story? What else should be included? What's no longer necessary? At this stage, don't worry too much about sentence structure, word choice, spelling, or punctuation. (It's not an efficient use of your time to carefully edit a paragraph which you later delete because the gist of your paper changed.)

Establish Distance

Let your draft sit overnight. When you return to it the next day, you'll see more clearly what works well, what doesn't, and where it can be improved. Do the same for each draft, returning later to see freshly.

Believe and Doubt

Read your first draft, trying to believe everything you've written; put check marks next to the passages that are most convincing. Read your draft again, this time trying to find places that don't convince you; put an *X* next to each such passage. Revise accordingly.

Ask, So What?

Writing should teach readers something. Reread your paper and, at the end, ask what have you learned. If you're not sure, it's time to revise.

Evaluate Evidence

To convince readers that your claims or assertions are good ones, double check your facts and examples, and ask: What evidence supports my thesis or advances my theme? What objections can be raised about this evidence? What additional evidence will answer these objections?

Find the Center

Gloss each paragraph by writing in the margins about its central idea. If there is more than one idea, should there be more than one paragraph? Use the margin notes to reassess the arrangement of your paragraphs: Are related paragraphs kept together? Does a different arrangement suggest itself? Is the beginning, middle, and end as you want it?

Limit and Focus Close

When you're describing a personal experience, write a second draft that tells what happened during one small moment of that experience—an important day or hour of the story. Focus close on the details of setting, character, and action. When you're writing a paper based on research, write the second draft about one small part of your story. In either case, ask detail questions: What time of day? Where did this happen? Who else was there? What words were said? What color, size, and shape was it? What ran through your mind? This limited draft does not need to be your final version of the story, but the careful details here may suggest how to add similar details to other parts of your story, or what to emphasize and what not to emphasize in you final draft.

Add Research Information

Finding supporting information in texts on your bookshelves or in the library will always make your case stronger. In addition, wherever appropriate, interview experts in the field the paper is about; quoting people adds both useful support and liveliness to your writing. And where appropriate, visit places and carry that information back into your paper by your own careful observation and note taking. Remember, personal narratives as well as research essays will benefit from conveying accurately recalled information, and such information is often most accurately recalled by returning to the site of the experience.

Switch Positions and Points Of View

Sometimes, when your writing seems especially dull, stuck, or blocked, consider switching perspectives. Consider adopting another point of view: If you've been telling your story from the first-person point of view, switch to third person. Or write a draft from your opponent's perspective—seeing the other side lets you answer questions before someone thinks to ask them. Likewise, if you've been writing in past tense, try a draft in the present tense. Any of these seemingly mechanical changes actually cause interesting conceptual shifts and add new life to old ideas.

Let Form Follow Content

Writing can be, do, and look like anything you want it to. There are, of course, certain conventions, and following these usually helps readers understand you. For example, stories of personal experience usually start with the earlier events and end with later events. However, some writers use flashbacks, starting later, then moving backward in time. In other words, don't be afraid to experiment with form: Is your story best told as a report? Would it make sense as an exchange of letters? As recreated journal entries? As drama? Does it need to be logical? Chronological? See what happens to your ideas in these alternate forms: They may continue to metamorphose and enter still newer territory.

Reconsider Everything

When you return to your draft, reconsider the whole text. If you change the information on one page, it may change ideas on another. If a classmate or instructor suggests improvements on some pages, don't assume the others are perfect.

Start Over

Even when you return to a draft that you think just needs a conclusion, reread the whole thing all over, from start to finish, with an eye toward still other possible changes. Every time you read your own paper you create yet another dialogue with it, from which could emerge still a better idea. The conclusion may be all the old paper needed when last you read it, but don't stand pat: Keep looking for what else could happen to the story you are telling.

Play With Titles, Introductions, and Conclusions

Beginnings and endings are emphatic, highly visible points in any paper. Provocative titles catch readers' attention. Good introductions keep readers going. Powerful conclusions leave strong memories in readers' minds. But these same elements work on the writer as well as the reader, as a good title, introduction, or conclusion can suggest changes for what follows (or precedes). Sometimes these elements come first—as controlling ideas—sometimes later, but in any case they can capture (or recapture) the essence of your paper, telling you what to keep and what to cut.

Rewrite to Your Audience

Keep your teacher or several skeptical classmates in mind as you write and especially as you reread. Of course your writing is clear to you, but ask: What information do *they* need to know that I already take for granted? Then put it in because they'll understand you better.

Seek Response

As soon as you have enough copy in reasonable shape, read it or show it to someone you trust and get their reaction. Another person can often see what you cannot. Most good writers ask others to read and react to their work *before* the final copy is due. Listen, don't be defensive, and take good notes, but you needn't feel obligated to take all the suggestions you're given.

Listen for Your Voice

Finally, read your paper out loud and see if it sounds like you—your ideas, your commitments, your style. If it doesn't, revise so that it does.

ONE EXPERIMENT WITH REVISION

Let me share one personal essay—an imaginatively treated factual essay—
that went through several of the revision moves discussed above, eventually combining authentic personal experience with a fictive form. In writing a personal narrative, Joan, a twenty-year-old first-year student, chose to
write about the year after she graduated from high school, when she
worked as a waitress at a Dunkin' Donuts coffee shop. Her first draft was
lively and in the form of a conventional narrative.

> I was a Dunkin' Donuts girl. Just another face behind a
> pink hat and a grease-stained uniform. The job could have
> been degrading if I ever let it get under my skin. To get
> the job I had to be able to count out a dollar's worth of
> change and read.

While this opening was especially lively, the rest of the piece was not, so
Joan decided to play with her format, and revised it as if it were a letter
home to her mom:

> Dear Mom,
>   If you could see me now . . . I'm a Dunkin' Donuts
> girl. I was so tired of job hunting day after day that when
> I found work here I couldn't say no. I was kind of sur-
> prised that I was hired right off the street, without any
> questions about my work experience or character, but I'm
> not complaining. It will put food on the table and gas in
> the car.

Here Joan is trying to imitate a real letter home. However, the form seemed
limited unless she fashioned a series of letters to show her involvement over time, and then she figured she'd have to write some from her
mother as well, so she continued to ask herself: "What's the story I want
to tell?"

Narrative writing usually gains by close focus and concrete detail.
Joan wanted to focus close enough to show us her daily life in the donut
shop, by showing her behind-the-counter perspective ("Each customer got
only one napkin because they cost three and a half cents apiece.") But
the real story Joan wanted to tell involved both her feelings in the shop
itself, and her progressive disillusionment working there over several
months. In fact, this latter was her actual theme, so her problem became
one of form: Which form would best contain both the nitty-gritty, everyday
detail and yet cover a time span of three months?

Joan kept experimenting with format, voice, time, and tense, until she found one in which she could tell her story—a daily diary. While fictive (Joan had not kept a diary during those months) the diary format solved problems of detail, time, and psychological involvement nicely: Here she could convincingly portray time passing, keep her piece rich in detail, and avoid sweeping generalizations. Her diary starts with this entry:

> Oct. 28 I've driven into Augusta everyday looking for work, but no one's hiring. Today for the twenty-fifth time I asked "Who would I talk to about applying for a job here?" And for the twenty-fifth time I was told "I'm sorry, but we're not hiring right now. But if you'd care to fill out an application anyway . . ." It takes every bit of strength I've got to walk out the door with my head up.

Joan is taking personal-experience writing an imaginative step further. She's making up a format, inventing dates, recreating dialogue, and re-imagining details to carry the truth she wants to tell, which is essentially what great imaginative writers do. And she's finding room for this in her composition class, where format is wide open. Her diary continues:

> Oct. 29 My work outfit is a khaki dress, garnished with an orange apron and a pink jockey hat. The clothes are old and worn, grease-stained and mended by hand with many colors of thread.
> I tried the uniform on, adding a pair of old white nurse's shoes from the depth of my closet, and went to admire myself in the mirror. My reflection took me by surprise—I looked just like every Dunkin' Donuts girl I've ever seen! The only part of me left was my face.
> Tomorrow is my first day. Already I'm nervous, wondering if I'll do a good job.

Joan's writing solution allows her to describe her experiences with purposeful immediacy, yet keep the reader suspensefully in the present, with Joan herself quite close. We can *see* her as a Dunkin' Donut girl because she has real facts and colors there, but had she forgotten the details of the uniform, she could have either invented them or, more likely, made a coffee stop at another Dunkin' Donuts to recapture what she'd forgotten. In the following entry, Joan imagines concretely a dimly remembered piece of conversation to add credibility to her narrative:

> Nov. 23 I almost quit my job today, and I'm not sure why I didn't. Mr. Stacy brought me face to face with his temper,

and it lives up to its reputation. He went wild, yelling and swearing at me because I only had two pots of coffee made and he thought there should be more. He shouted, "Customers equal money, see? And we can't have customers without coffee, can we? You have to watch these things!"

Unlike informational or argumentative essays, narratives seldom start with a strong thesis stated right up front: "Dear Reader, let me tell you about how I became disillusioned with my job as a fast-food worker and how I decided to attend college instead." Notice how Joan's implied thesis approach lets the reader see the more subtle process of disillusionment as it actually occurred over a period of several months. Here is Joan's last entry:

Dec. 7 I wonder how much longer I'll be at Dunkin' Donuts. There's no room here to move up or get a raise. I can't imagine doing this job for another ten or fifteen years, like some of these people I work with. The turnover is high and the names on the schedule change every week. . . . Starting to look at "Help Wanted" ads again—or did I ever stop?

Joan's final draft diary totaled seven entries which together completed her five-page personal essay. There were many other more conventional ways she might have told the same tale—as a narrative focusing on highlights, as a series of flashbacks from her present college life, as part of a larger essay on work, etc. For Joan, writing the narrative assignment in an alternate form brought it to life in a way both she as writer and I as reader thoroughly enjoyed.

EXPERIMENTS IN REVISION

Revision is a good time to experiment with theme, voice, tense, point of view, style, and genre. Such experiments often create texts that recreate your thinking about a subject, and sometimes the changes are more superficial or cosmetic. The problem is, you can't tell unless you do the writing and see what it does to your thinking. The following are some ideas for reseeing and reinventing assignments—instructor willing.

Role Play

Assume the perspective of someone else and attempt to write as consistently as possible from that perspective, seeing the situation as that person is constrained to see it. For example, describing life in the pre-Civil War South from the point of view of slave Frederick Douglass, or from the point of view of his white Christian master or mistress. A good format for such an assignment might be an exchange of letters, a dramatic scenario, or an imaginary interview on a late night talk show; in other words, in addition to recreating each character's voice accurately, I would hold my piece together in a format in which these characters would actually speak their opinion—imagined yet authentic.

Invent Dialogue

Ask in what circumstances would these two characters be likely to meet and talk? If, for example, you were to recreate a conversation between Edgar Allen Poe and Walt Whitman, it might be set in either a bar or an open field—depending on whose turf you wished to dwell.

Imitate

Write in the style of the work you are studying. For example, you might be explaining or interpreting a passage of James Joyce and you run your sentences together as he does in the style usually called *stream of consciousness*. Or you might attempt to mimic the prose or poetry of a favorite writer. Or you might recreate the political speech of a president or the patter of a game show hostess. It helps to imitate a stylistic extremist, someone whose writing is clearly distinctive. In any case, to do this effectively, you need a thorough knowledge of the style, which you might gain by practicing it in your journal before you tackle it on the assignment itself.

Imagine

Invent new endings for classic works, such as a new ending for the Shakespeare play *Hamlet*. First figure out what thematic difference it made that *X* now happened rather than *Y*, then recreate the act/scene/line format of the original play, paying attention to the small details, such as stage directions.

Pose Hypothetical Situations

You are a vice-president in charge of developing new uses for the bricks your company manufactures. Your task is to write a report explaining some of these new options to the company board of directors and recommend a marketing plan. Here you must stick close to the style and format of a real company report: I would be sure to use a formal title page, lots of subheadings, and include graphs and charts. You have fun—and prove you know a hell of a lot about bricks, corporate development, and report writing all at once!

Parody

Write a spoof or satire about something serious. Parody is a well respected genre in its own right. Think of Jonathan Swift's "A Modest Proposal" or *Mad Magazine* or *National Lampoon*. A parody is a possible response to any serious content, especially if the writer wishes to make a point at the expense of some of that content. Before tackling parody, lest people think you are taking an easy way out, know well the object of your parody; be consistent in the voice, theme, and format, and write carefully!

APPENDIX

SUGGESTIONS FOR JOURNAL WRITING

1. Describe your own revision habits. How do they compare with some of the suggestions in this chapter? Which ideas here seem especially useful? Which do not?

2. When you read the passages about imitation, imagination, and parody in this chapter, what author or work came first to mind? What element of this author or work would you choose to imitate, recreate, or parody?

SUGGESTIONS FOR ESSAY WRITING

1. Select one assignment for a course you are now taking and revise it according to some of the ideas in this chapter. (If you intend to hand it in for a different course, hand it in to that instructor first, then to your writing instructor.)

2. Select one paper already written for this (or another) course and rewrite it in an alternate form, keeping in tact the essential ideas of the original piece.

SUGGESTIONS FOR RESEARCH

1. INDIVIDUAL: Research the literature of revision and see if you can discover what well-known writers have to say about the subject. See for example, the several volumes of interviews published by the *Paris Review;* also search the *New York Times Book Review* and biographies or autobiographies of your favorite fiction or nonfiction writers.

2. COLLABORATIVE. Each student in the class can interview a selected professor from a group who is known to publish frequently— one who writes textbooks, has books displayed in the bookstore, or

shows up in authorial searches in the library. Ask these publishing professors about their revision habits: When and where do they revise? How often? With what specific intentions? Do they have any samples to share? Do they have any advice for student writers? Write up in summary or interview form the results of these investigations, select class editors, and compile the results of these interviews in a class written *guidebook to revision* (see *Postscript Three*).

Chapter Fourteen

OPTIONS FOR EDITING

How do you know when your writing is done? Me, I'm
never sure when it's done, when it's good enough. I mean,
if it says basically what I want it to say, who cares how
pretty it is?

—Tom

I agree with Tom that writing need not be "pretty," but I wouldn't be
satisfied with writing that "says basically what I want it to say." I want
my writing to say *exactly* what I want it to say—which is where editing
comes in.

Editing is finishing. Editing is making a text convey precisely what
you intend in the clearest way possible. Editing is sentence-level work,
attended to after a text's ideas are in order. Editing is polishing to make
the paragraphs, the sentences, and the individual words communicate
carefully, accurately, and correctly with clarity, style, and grace. Edit first
for clarity, to make sure your purpose is clear to your audience. Edit also
for a style appropriate for the occasion. Finally, edit for grace—some sense
that this text is not only *clearly* and *appropriately* written, but that it is
enjoyable, moving, and even memorable. At the same time, remember that
editing is more a matter of making choices than following rules.

EDITING SUGGESTIONS

Sentences are written in relation to other sentences, seldom by themselves.
Attention so far has been with the larger more conceptual concerns in
composing. This chapter focuses on the elements that make sentences

strong. First, look at particular words within sentences, especially nouns, verbs, and modifiers. Second, consider the importance of rhythm and emphasis in whole sentences. And finally, identify and avoid the common problems of wordiness, cliches, jargon, passive constructions, and biased language. The following suggestions will help.

1. **Edit for concrete nouns.** Nouns label or identify persons (man, Gregory), animals (dog, retriever), places (city, Boston), things (book, *Ulysses*), or ideas (conservation, Greater Yellowstone Coalition). Abstract nouns stand for general classes or categories of things (man, dog, city), while concrete nouns refer to specific particular things (Gregory, retriever, Boston). Notice that concrete nouns let you see specific images (not just any dog, but a retriever), which in turn appeal more strongly to a reader's senses (I can see the dog!) than abstract nouns, and create a more vivid and lively reading experience.

2. **Edit for action verbs.** Action verbs *do* something in your sentences; they make something happen. Action verbs walk, stride, run, jump, fly, hum, sing, sail, swim, lean, fall, stop, look, listen, sit, state, decide, choose, and conclude—all these words and hundreds more are active verbs. But static verbs are words that simply appear to describe how something is, like the verbs are, appear, and is in this sentence. Action verbs, like concrete nouns, appeal to the senses, letting us see, hear, touch, taste, or smell something. Thus they too create more vivid images for readers, drawing them more deeply into our story.

   Sometimes we write noun phrases as substitutes for action. In the sentence, *We need to reach a decision,* the phrase *reach a decision* substitutes for the simpler, stronger verb *decide.* Whenever you find yourself writing with noun phrases, consider how to make them more active:

reach a decision	decide
make a choice	choose
hold a meeting	meet
formulate a plan	plan
arrive at a conclusion	conclude
have a discussion	discuss

3. **Edit to modify carefully and selectively.** Well-chosen modifiers can individualize both nouns and verbs, making them more detailed, concrete, and more appealing to the senses. Modifiers which amplify nouns are called adjectives (*yellow* car); those that amplify verbs are called adverbs (listen *closely*). Modifiers convey useful clarifying information and help us see situations more vividly and realistically.

It is possible, however, to add so many modifiers that they distract from, rather than enhance, the paragraph's central purpose. To describe a car as *really ugly, dull, rusted, chipped,* and *pale yellow* calls extra attention to the car; you'll need to decide whether that suits your purpose or creates a distraction. In other words, you can edit *out* modifiers as well as edit them *in.* But that's what editing is all about: looking carefully, trying out new things, settling for the effect that pleases you the most.

Finally, not all modifiers are created equal: Specific modifiers which add descriptive information about size, shape, color, texture, speed, and so on, appeal to your senses and usually make your writing more realistic and vivid. But more general modifiers such as the adjectives pretty, beautiful, good, bad, ugly, young, or old can actually weaken sentences by adding extra words that do not convey specific or vital information. And the adverbs very, really, and truly can have the same weakening effect because these words are so commonly overused that they provide no additional clarifying information.

4. **Edit for pleasing rhythms.** Rhythm is the sound sentences make when you hear them out loud. Some rhythms sound natural, like a real person in a conversation. Such sentences are easy to follow and understand, and are usually pleasing to the ear. Others sound awkward and forced; they make comprehension difficult and offend the ear. In most cases of college writing, it pays to read your sentences out loud and see if they sound like a real human being talking. To make sentence clusters sound better, try increasing *sentence variety* and making *parallel constructions.*

Varied sentence patterns make sentence clusters more clear and enjoyable for readers. In the following example, the first long sentence is followed by a short one, creating an easily understood and pleasing rhythm:

> We looked at the old yellow Pontiac, noticing its dented doors, rusty bumpers, and oil leak, and realized we could afford to fix them all. We bought it on the spot.

Parallel constructions repeat an identical grammatical pattern within the same sentence, which has the effect of reinforcing a comparison or contrast. Parallelism creates symmetry and balance, makes an idea easier to remember, and more pleasing to the ear.

> A battle is being waged between environmental conservationists *who support* the reintroduction of wolves, and sheep and cattle farmers and western hunters *who oppose* it.

The parallelism is established by the repetition of the word *who*. The effect is to clearly separate these opposing forces into two distinct opponents, those *who* are for it and those *who* are against it.

5. **Edit for emphasis.** As with paragraphs, so with sentences, *the most emphatic place is last*. When you end-weight a sentence, you place the information that is older, less essential, contextual, or introductory earlier in the sentence, so that the sentence ends with the idea you most want your reader to remember. Notice the difference in emphasis in the following version of the same idea:

1. If you want to buy the yellow car, act now.
2. Act now if you want to buy the yellow car.

Either is correct, but you would choose the first to emphasize the need to act, the second to emphasize the car itself. Which one you choose will depend upon the effect you want to convey.

6. **Edit wordy sentences.** Cut out words that do not pull their weight or add meaning, rhythm, or emphasis. Look, for example, at this set of sentences, each of which says essentially the same thing:

1. In almost every situation that I can think of, with few exceptions, it will make good sense for you to look for as many places as possible to cut out needless, redundant, and repetitive words from the papers and reports, paragraphs, and sentences you write for college assignments. [forty-eight words]
2. In most situations it makes good sense to cut out needless words from your college papers. [sixteen words]
3. Whenever possible, omit needless words from your writing. [eight words]
4. Omit needless words. [three words]

In the forty-eight-word sentence you can almost watch the writer finding his or her way as she writes. By simply eliminating repetitious or awkward words, the same idea condenses to the sixteen-word sentence, saying much the same thing with one-third the number of words. Only the end is recast: "from the papers and reports, paragraphs, and sentences you write for college assignments" to "from your college papers."

Careful rephrasing reduces the sixteen-word sentence by half, resulting in a good strong eight-word sentence. If an even briefer imperative is called for, you write this three-word sentence, "Omit needless words." While the first sentence is wordy by any standard, each of the next three might serve well in different situations. When you edit to make language more concise, you need to think about the overall effect you intend to create. Sometimes the briefest construction is not the best construction for all purposes.

The best test of whether words are pulling their own weight, as well as whether they are rhythmic, balanced, and emphatic, is to read the passage out loud and let your ear tell you what's sharp and clear and what could be sharper and clearer.

7. **Edit out clichés.** Clichés have been heard so often that they lose their power to convey an original thought. The test to apply is whether you write the phrase you remember hearing in the same exact words as before, especially more than once. If so, look for a fresher construction that is your own. Common clichés to avoid would include the following:

> the last straw
> better late than never
> without further ado
> the handwriting on the wall
> tried and true
> last but not least
> lay the cards on the table
> jump starting the economy

Each of these phrases once captured attention because it was new and fresh (usually a new metaphor or a pleasant alliteration); however, each has since been overused so that now we listen right through it, perhaps even noting that the writer is not very thoughtful or original.

8. **Edit passive constructions.** A construction is passive when something is done to the *subject* of the sentence rather than the subject doing something: *John wrote the letter,* is an active sentence, with the subject *John* doing the action in the sentence; however, *The letter was written by John* is passive. Not only is the second sentence needlessly longer by two words, it takes a second or two longer to understand since it seems an unnatural way to make that assertion. Passive constructions are indirect, tiresome, and risk putting readers to sleep.

9. **Edit biased language.** Writing should not hurt people. Review your drafts to make sure your language doesn't discriminate against categories of people based on gender, race, ethnicity, or social class—issues about which most of your college instructors will be sensitive.

10. **Eliminate sexism.** Sexist language is biased for or against one gender. The most common occurrence of sexist language is the use of the words *man* or *men* to stand for human beings or people, which seems to omit *women* from participation in the

species. Since the 1970s, Americans have been sensitized to the not-so-subtle bias against woman embedded in our historical use of the English language. Texts written in earlier decades took masculine sexist pronouns for granted, using the words *man, men, he, him,* and *his* to stand for all members of the human race. Consider Thomas Jefferson: "All men are created equal," or Tom Paine: "These are the times that try men's souls."

Texts written from the 1980s on usually try to avoid this gender bias, so that today we would prefer "All people are created equal" or "These are the times that try our souls," two of several possible fixes for this form of gender nearsightedness.

Eliminating sexism in current English is made more difficult because the language does not have a gender-neutral singular pronoun (he/she, him/her, his/hers) to match the gender-neutral plural pronouns (they, their, them). For example in the sentence "Everybody has his own opinion," the collective singular noun "everybody" needs a singular pronoun to match. So while it is grammatically correct to say "Everybody has his own opinion," the sentence is biased. It is grammatically incorrect to write: "Everybody has their own opinion," but it is gender neutral. To fix these problems, consider the following:

- Make the subject plural: People have their own opinions.
- Include both pronouns: Everybody has his or her own opinion.
- Eliminate the pronoun: Everybody has an opinion.
- Alternate masculine/feminine pronouns throughout your sentences or paragraphs.

11. **Avoid stereotypes:** Stereotypes prejudge individuals by lumping them into overly-simplified and usually negative categories based on race, ethnicity, class, gender, sexual preference, religion, or age: "Get out of the way, old man" or "Don't behave like a baby." I am willing to repeat these examples here since we've all been babies and we're all growing older. But most other examples are too offensive to reproduce.

12. **Proofread.** The last editing act is proofreading to make sure your manuscript is correct. Proofread for typing and spelling errors by using the spell check feature on your computer. Be aware that computers will not catch all errors, so proofread the old fashioned way by reading slowly, line-by-line with a ruler.

    Proofread for punctuation and paragraphing by reading your text out loud and looking for pauses, full stops, questions, and exclamations.

    Proofread for each other. We all see mistakes in others' writing more easily than we do in our own. Proofread as a whole class by taping final drafts on the wall and roam the class with pencils, reading each other's final drafts for both pleasure and correctness.

APPENDIX

SUGGESTIONS FOR EDITING

1. Replace vague abstract nouns with specific concrete nouns.

2. Replace static verbs with action verbs.

3. Add modifiers for detail, but delete them if they distract from your main point.

4. Write in the rhythm of natural speech unless you have a good reason for doing otherwise. (To check, read aloud.)

5. Begin sentences with old information, end with new. This strategy makes the end of your sentences stronger.

6. Make sure all words in your sentences contribute to the meaning you intend; if not, delete them.

7. Eliminate all cliches.

8. Make passive constructions active.

9. Delete or rephrase all stereotypes.

10. Proofread by computer spell check and also line-by-line with your intelligent eye.

Chapter Fifteen

WRITING ALTERNATE STYLE

Why is academic writing so cut and dried, so dull? Why can't it be more fun to read and write?

—Christine

Contemporary nonfiction writing is not dull. At least, it doesn't have to be, as the pages of the prestigious *New Yorker,* the trendy *Rolling Stone,* and the popular *Sports Illustrated* will attest. Read these and dozens of other current periodicals, and you'll see a variety of lively, entertaining, and informative prose styles. While the modern revolution in nonfiction writing, often called "literary journalism," has been slow to find its way from the popular periodicals to academic textbooks, professional journals, and student writing assignments, I believe it's coming.

Current nonfiction writers commonly borrow stylistic and formal techniques from the fast-paced, visual narratives of film and television and from the innovative language of poetry, fiction, and drama. These influences encourage a multifaceted, multi-dimensional prose style to keep pace with the multifaceted and multi-dimensional world in which we live. In short, many current nonfiction prose writers find the traditions of continuity, order, consistency, and unity associated with conventional prose insufficient to convey the chaotic truths of the postmodern world. This chapter examines some of the writing strategies associated with alternative or experimental prose and suggests appropriate venues within the academic curriculum in which such prose strategies could be useful.

LISTS

Lists can break up and augment prose texts in useful, credible, and surprising ways. Lists of names, words, and numbers add variety, speed, depth, and humor to texts. And lists are everywhere we look. In the following excerpt from "Marrying Absurd,"* Joan Didion uses lists to illustrate that Las Vegas weddings are big business.

> There are nineteen such wedding chapels in Las Vegas, intensely competitive, each offering better, faster, and, by implication, more sincere services than the next: Our Photos Best Anywhere, Your Wedding on a Phonograph Record, Candlelight with Your Ceremony, Honeymoon Accommodations, Free Transportation from Your Motel to Courthouse to Chapel and Return to Motel, Religious or Civil Ceremonies, Dressing Rooms, Flowers, Rings, Announcements, Witnesses Available, and Ample Parking.

Didion's list of competitive wedding services convinces us she's observed carefully—she's not making this stuff up. While Joan does not specifically name it, we see some level of absurdity in the way this town promotes marriage.

Lists need not be clever so much as purposeful. That is, you include a list of names, items, quotations, and so on to show readers that you know your stuff. You've done your homework, read widely or observed carefully, taken good notes, and made sense of what you've found. Lists deepen a text by providing illustrations or examples. And they add credibility by saying, in effect, look at all this evidence that supports my point.

In her well-known "Bryn Mawr Commencement Address,"** Ursula K. LeGuin urges graduating women to speak with strong voices when they enter the world:

> Now this is what I want: I want to hear your judgments. I am sick of the silence of women. I want to hear you speaking all the languages, offering your experience as your truth, as human truth, talking about working, about making, about unmaking, about eating, about cooking, about feeding, about taking in seed and giving out life, about killing, about feeling, about thinking; about what women do; about what men do; about war, about peace, about who presses the buttons and what buttons get pressed and whether pressing buttons is in the long run a fit occupation for human beings. There's a lot of things I want to hear you talk about.

*(New York: Simon and Schuster, 1968, p. 81)
**From *Dancing at the Edge of the World*, New York: Grovel Atlantic Inc., 1986.

Unlike Didion's list, which focuses close on a single subject, LeGuin's list opens things up, suggesting the many possibilities for speaking out on subjects that matter. Note that LeGuin's repetition of *about* before each topic on her list adds an easy-to-remember rhythm; after all, these words were written to be read aloud, and repetition helps readers listen and remember.

On the printed page, sometimes lists are presented simply as lists, not embedded in prose paragraphs. Such is the case when William Least Heat Moon overhears people describing the desert as full of "nothing" in *Blue Highways: A Journey into America:**

> Driving through miles of nothing, I decided to test the hypothesis and stopped somewhere in western Crockett County on the top of a broad mesa, just off Texas 29. . . . I made a list of nothing in particular:
> 1. mockingbird
> 2. mourning dove
> 3. enigma bird (heard not saw)
> 4. gray flies
> 5. blue bumblebee
> 6. two circling buzzards (not yet boys)
> 7. orange ants
> 8. black ants
> 9. orange-black ants (what's been going on?)
> 10. three species of spiders
> 11. opossum skull
> 12. jackrabbit (chewed on cactus)
> 13. deer (left scat)
> 14. coyote (left tracks)
>
> Heat Moon's list continues through thirty items, ending this way:
> 28. earth
> 29. sky
> 30. wind (always)

Itemized lists such as this change the visual shape of prose and call extra attention to the items listed; in this case, Heat Moon is being mildly humorous by using a list to prove there is always something, even in nothing.

When Craig, a student in my advanced writing class, examined sexist stereotypes in children's toys, he made the following list of dolls on a single shelf at a local Woolworth's store:

> To my left is a shelf of Barbie: Animal Lovin' Barbie, Wet
> 'n Wild Barbie, Barbie Feelin' Pretty Fashions, Barbie

---

*New York: Houghton Mifflin, 1982, 149–150

Special Expressions (Woolworth Special Limited Edition), Super Star Barbie Movietime Prop Shop, Step 'n Style Boutique, My First Barbie (Prettiest Princess Ever), Action Accents Barbie Sewing Machine, Barbie Cool Times Fashion, Barbie and the All-Stars, Style Magic Barbie, a Barbie Ferrari, and tucked away in a corner, slightly damaged and dusty, Super Star Ken.

This list simply documents by name the products on the toy shelf, actually adding a dimension of authenticity and believability to the writer's case that the Barbie image and influence on children is considerable.

Creating an extended list is a bold, even audacious move, breaking up prose sentences, surprising readers and therefore picking up their interest, engagement, involvement. The purposeful use of lists may make readers pause to note the change in the form of words on the page; at the same time, lists allow readers to pick up speed—reading lists is fast.

However, lists that are quick to read may not be quick to write; an effective list that appears to be written by free association may, in fact, have been laboriously constructed as the writer ransacked his memory or her thesaurus for words, then arranged and rearranged them to create the right sound or sense effect.

SNAPSHOTS

Writing prose snapshots is analogous to constructing and arranging a photo album composed of many separate visual images. Photo albums, when carefully assembled from informative snapshots, tell stories with clear beginnings, middles, and endings, but with lots of white spaces between one picture and the next, with few transitions explaining how the photographer got from one scene to the next. In other words, while photo albums tell stories, they do so piecemeal, causing the viewer to fill in or imagine what happened between shots. You can also think of snapshots as individual slides in slide shows or as pictures in an exhibition— each piece of the work by the same maker, each with a different view, each by some logic connected, the whole forming a story.

Prose snapshots function the same way as visual snapshots, each connected to the other by white space and requiring leaps of logic and faith by the reader, with the whole making a self-explanatory story structure. You might imagine written snapshots as a series of complete and independent paragraphs, each a whole thought, without obvious connections or careful transitions to the paragraph before or after.

Sometimes individual snapshots are numbered to suggest deliberate connectedness; other times each is titled, to suggest an ability to stand alone, such as chapters within books. Sometimes they appear on a page as block paragraphs without transitions, making it necessary for active reader interpretation. As such, they are satisfying for fast readers. Each contains a small story unto itself, while the whole is a larger story, in part of the readers' making.

Margaret Atwood wrote snapshots to emphasize the dangers of men's bodies in the following passage from her essay "Alien Territory"*

> The history of war is a history of killed bodies. That's what war is: bodies killing other bodies, bodies being killed.
>
> Some of the killed bodies are those of women and children, as a side effect you might say. Fallout, shrapnel, napalm, rape and skewering, anti-personnel devices. But most of the killed bodies are men. So are most of those doing the killing.
>
> Why do men want to kill the bodies of other men? Women don't want to kill the bodies of other women. By and large. As far as we know.
>
> Here are some traditional reasons: Loot. Territory. Lust for power. Hormones. Adrenaline high. Rage. God. Flag. Honor. Righteous anger. Revenge. Oppression. Slavery. Starvation. Defense of one's life. Love; or, a desire to protect the men and women. From what? From the bodies of other men.
>
> What men are most afraid of is not lions, not snakes, not the dark, not women. What men are most afraid of is the body of another man.
>
> Men's bodies are the most dangerous things on earth.

Note how the white space between one snapshot and another gives readers breathing space, time out, time to digest one thought before supping at the next. The white space between snapshots actually exercises readers' imaginations as they participate in constructing some logic that makes the text make sense—the readers themselves must supply the connectives, construct the best meaning, which, nevertheless, will be very close to what skillful authors intend.

Aldo Leopold wrote snapshots in *Sand County Almanac* (1948), using the "topical" almanac form for essay purposes. Norman Mailer wrote snapshots in *The Executioner's Song* (1979), each a passage or impression from 16,000 pages of interview transcripts with convicted killer Gary Gilmore. Joan Didion wrote snapshots in "Slouching Toward Bethlehem" from the book of the same name (1961). Annie Dillard wrote snapshots in "An Expedition to the Pole" (1982). Gloria Steinam wrote them to

*From *Good Bones and Simple Murders,* New York: O.W. Todd Ltd., 1992

portray Marilyn Monroe as more person than sex goddess in *Marilyn: Norma Jean* (1986). And Douglass Coupland wrote snapshots to portray postmodern confusion in *Generation X* (1991).

The following four-snapshot sample is taken from Sonya's eight-shot snapshot essay explaining her search for an undergraduate major:

1. What I care about is the environment, and what I want to do is teach younger children to care about it too. That's what brings me to college, and to this English class, writing about what I want to be when I grow up.

2. My first teaching was this past summer on the Caribbean Island of South Caicos. In the classroom one morning, I tried to teach local teenagers about the fragility of their island environment, but they did not seem to hear me or attend to my lesson, and I left class very frustrated. Later on, we went to the beach, and they taught me back my morning lessons, and I felt so much better. I thought then I wanted to be a teacher.

3. The School of Education scares me. A lady named Roberta and professor named Merton gave me a list of classes I would need in order to major in education. "Environmental education is not a real field, yet," the professor said. I realized it would take four years and many courses and still I wouldn't be studying the environment or be sure of ever teaching about it in public schools.

4. The School of Natural Resources excites me. Professor Erickson is my advisor, and in one afternoon, she helped me plan a major in "Terrestrial Ecology." I now know, for the first time, exactly what I'm doing in college. I need to study natural resources first, later on decide, whether I want to teach, work in the field or what.

These excerpts reveal telling scenes from her first-semester search for a major, revealing her basis for choosing one major over another without editorializing. By showing us snapshots of the highlights and skipping most of the complaining that characterized earlier drafts, we experience more directly her reasons for majoring in natural resources rather than in education.

Becky, a college senior, wrote a twenty-snapshot self-profile to convey a lot of information in a brief amount of space. Following are seven snapshots that examine the part of her that is highly religious:

- My mother grew up in Darien, Connecticut, a Presbyterian. When she was little, she gave the Children's Sermon at her church. My father grew up in Cleveland, Ohio, a Jew. When I went away to college, he gave me the Hebrew Bible he received at his Bar Mitzvah.

- The only similarity between my parents' families is freckles. They both have them, which means I get a double dose. Lucky me. My mother once told me that freckles are "angels kisses." Lucky me.

- I am a Protestant. I have attended First Presbyterian Church of Boulder, Colorado, for most of my life. When I was baptized, Reverend Allen said: "Becky is being baptized here today, brought by their believing mother and their unbelieving—but supportive—father."

- When I was little, I was terrified of the darkness. Sometimes, I would wake up in the night and scream. It was my mother who came in to comfort me, smoothing my hair, telling me to think of butterflies and angels.

- When I am in Vermont, I attend North Avenue Alliance Church. I chose it because it is big, like my church at home. The last two Sundays I have sung solos. The first time, I sang "Amazing Grace." The second time, I sang "El Shaddai," which is partly in Hebrew.

- I have always said my prayers before going to bed. Lying silently in the dark, talking to God. Like the disciples in the Garden of Gethsemane, I have been known to fall asleep while praying. Now I pray on my knees, it is harder to doze off that way.

- I wear a cross around my neck. It is nothing spectacular to look at, but I love it because I bought it at the Vatican. Even though I am not a Catholic, I am glad I bought it at the Pope's home town. Sometimes, when I sit in Hebrew class, I wonder if people wonder, "What religion is she, anyway?"

These shapshots portray Becky's mixed religious heritage, strong commitment to Protestantism, and current participation in Christian rituals. Each focuses on a single small event—a cross necklace, prayer, a church, and so on. Note how each actually tells a small story, complete with a beginning, middle, and punch line. At the same time, the cumulative effect of these seven snapshots reveals Becky's broad tolerance, education, and interest in a spirituality that goes well beyond separate religious creeds. This theme emerges as one experience is juxtaposed against another, past tense against present tense, without editorializing, allowing readers to supply the connective tissue by filling in the white spaces for themselves.

Snapshots allow busy writers to compose in chunks, in five- and ten-minute blocks between appointments, schedules, classes, or coffee breaks. And, as we've seen, five or ten or twenty chunks—reconsidered, rearranged, revised—can tell whole stories.

While it's fun to write fast, random, and loose, the real secret to a successful snapshot essay is putting them together in the right order—some right order—some pattern that, by the end, conveys your theme as surely as if you had written straight narration or exposition. Writing snapshots on a computer is especially fun, since you can order and reorder indefinitely until you arrive at a satisfying arrangement. Composing snapshot essays on three-by-five-inch cards also works. In either case, assemble and arrange the snapshots as you would arrange pictures in a photo album, playfully and seriously. Begin at the beginning, alternate themes, begin *in media res,* alternate time, begin with flashbacks, alternate voices, consider frames, alternate fonts, reinforce rhythms, experiment with openings and closings, type, and titles.

PLAYFUL SENTENCES

No matter what your form or style, sentences are your main units of composition, explaining the world in terms of subjects, actions, and objects, suggesting that the world operates causally: some force (a subject) does something (acts) that causes something else to happen (an object). English prose is built around complete and predictable sentences such as those in which this paragraph and most of this book is written. Sometimes, however, writers use sentences in less predictable, more playful ways, which we will explore here.

Fragment sentences suggest fragmented stories. Stories different from the stories told by conventional subject–verb-object sentences. Fragmented information. Fragment sentences, of course, can be used judiciously in conventional writing—even academic writing, so long as the purpose is crystal clear and your fragment is not mistaken for fragmentary grammatical knowledge. However, alternate style writers use fragments audaciously and sometimes with abandon to create the special effects they want. A flash of movement. A bit of a story. A frozen scene. Fragments force quick reading, ask for impressionistic understanding, suggest parts rather than wholes. Like snapshots, fragments invite strong reader participation to stitch together, to move toward clear meaning.

Fragment sentences suggest, too, that things are moving fast. Very fast. Hold on. Remember the snapshot passage from Margaret Atwood's "Alien Territory"? Note that she used fragments to emphasize the sharp dangers of men's bodies:

> Some of the killed bodies are those of women and children, as a side effect you might say. Fallout, shrapnel, napalm, rape and skewering, anti-personnel

devices. But most of the killed bodies are men. So are most of those doing the killing.

Why do men want to kill the bodies of other men? Women don't want to kill the bodies of other women. By and large. As far as we know.

Atwood's fragments make the reader notice sharply the brutal and jarring truths she is writing about; in this example, the lack of conventional connections between words mirrors the disconnectedness she sees in her subject: men, violence, and war. Notice, too, that some of her fragments illustrate another use of lists.

Write fragments so your reader knows they are not mistakes. Not ignorance. Not sloppiness or printer error or carelessness. Purposeful fragments can be powerful. Deliberate. Intentional. Careful. Functional. And brief.

Labyrinthine sentences tell stories differently from either conventional or fragment sentences. In fact, a labyrinthine sentence is quite the opposite of the fragment sentence because it seems never to end; it won't quit, and goes on and on, using all sorts of punctuational and grammatical tricks to create compound sentences (you know, two or more independent clauses joined by a comma and a conjunction such as *and* or *but*) and complex sentences (you know these, too; one independent clause with one or more dependent clauses) and is written to suggest, perhaps, that things are running together and are hard to separate—also to suggest the "stream of consciousness" of the human mind, where thoughts and impressions and feelings and images are run together without the easy separation into full sentences or paragraphs complete with topic sentences—the power (and sometimes confusion) of which you know if you have read James Joyce or Virginia Woolf or William Faulkner or Toni Morrison.

Or James Agee, who in the following passage imaginatively enters the thoughts of the people he is profiling in *Let Us Now Praise Famous Men,** the poor Alabama tenant farmers:

But *I* am young; and I am young and strong and in good
health; and I am young and pretty to look at; and I am too
young to worry; and so am I for my mother is kind to me;
and we run in the bright air like animals, and our bare
feet like plants in the wholesome earth: the natural world
is around us like a lake and a wide smile and we are growing: one by one we are becoming stronger, and one by one
in the terrible emptiness and the leisure we shall burn and

*New York: Houghton Mifflin, 1941, pp. 80–81

> tremble and shake with lust, and one by one we shall
> loosen ourselves from this place, and shall be married, and
> it will be different from what we see, for we will be happy
> and love each other, and keep the house clean, and a good
> garden, and buy a cultivator, and use a high grade of fertil-
> izer, and we will know how to do things right; it will be
> very different:) (?:)

Agee's long connected sentence creates the run-together, wishful, worried, desperate internal dream of his subjects in a way a conventional paragraph could not. Notice, too, that punctuation and grammar are conventional and correct—even in the end, where they are used in unexpected ways to suggest something of the confusion and uncertainty these people live with daily.

You may also write run-on or fused sentences—where punctuation does not function in expected ways the missing period before this sentences is an example of that. However, such writing more often suggests error and mistake than experiment so be careful. I use both fragments and labyrinthine sentences to create certain effects, since each conveys its information in an unmistakable way; but I never, deliberately, write with run-on sentences, and when I encounter them as a reader, they make me suspicious.

REPETITION

repeat: v. to say again in the same words.

Writers repeat words, phrases, or sentences for emphasis. They repeat words to remind us to think hard about the word or phrase repeated; they repeat words to ask us to attend and not take for granted. They repeat words to suggest continuity of idea and theme. They repeat words to hold paragraphs and essays together. And, sometimes, they repeat words to create rhythms that are simply pleasing to the ear.

The following paragraph opens Ian Frazier's book-length study, *The Great Plains:*

> Away to the Great Plains of America, to that immense Western shortgrass
> prairie now mostly plowed under! Away to the still empty land beyond
> newsstands and malls and velvet restaurant ropes! Away to the headwaters
> of the Missouri, now quelled by many impoundment dams, and to the
> headwaters of the Platte, and to the almost invisible headwaters of the
> slurped up Arkansas! Away to the land where TV used to set its most popular
> dramas, but not anymore! Away to the land beyond the hundredth meridian
> of longitude, where sometimes it rains and sometimes it doesn't, where
> agriculture stops and does a double take! Away to the skies of the sparrow

hawks sitting on telephone wires, thinking of mice and flaring their tail feathers suddenly, like a card trick! Away to the airshaft of the continent, where weather fronts from two hemispheres meet and the wind blows almost all the time! Away to the fields of wheat and milo and Sudan grass and flax and alfalfa and nothing! Away to parts of Montana and North Dakota and South Dakota and Wyoming and Nebraska and Kansas and Colorado and New Mexico and Oklahoma and Texas! Away to the high plains rolling in waves to the rising final chord of the Rocky Mountains!

Frazier's singing chant invites us, in one sweeping passage, to think about the great plains as geography, biology, history, and culture. Along the way he uses fragments and lists and a plentitude of exclamation marks to invite readers to consider this arid and often overlooked part of America.

DOUBLE VOICE

Good nonfiction writing usually (I'd like to say always but don't dare) expresses something of the writer's voice. But all writers are capable of speaking with more than one voice (how many more?), or maybe with a single voice that has a wide range, varied registers, multiple tones, and different pitches. No matter how you view it, writers project more than one voice from piece to piece of writing, and sometimes within the same piece.

In any given essay, writers may try to say two things at the same time; sometimes they want to say one thing that means two things; sometimes to express contradictions, paradoxes, or conundrums; sometimes to say one thing out loud and think another silently to themselves. (It's clear to me what I mean by this, but I'd better find some examples.)

Double voices in a text may be indicated by parentheses, the equivalent of an actor speaking an aside on the stage or in films, where the internal monologue of a character is revealed as voice-over or through printed subtitles while another action is happening on screen (I hate subtitles on small screen television sets—I can't see them). It can also be shown in text by changes in font or type face: a switch to italics, boldface, or capital letters, equals a switch in the writer's voice. Or the double voice may occur without distinguishing markers at all, or be indicated by simple paragraph breaks, as in the following selection from D.H. Lawrence in his critical essay on Herman Melville's *Moby Dick* from *Studies in Classic American Literature:*

Doom.
Doom! Doom! Doom! Something seems to whisper it in the very dark trees of America.
Doom of what?

Doom of our white day. We are doomed, doomed. And the doom is in America. The doom of our white day.

Ah, well, if my day is doomed, and I am doomed with my day, it is something greater than I which dooms me, so I accept my doom as a sign of the greatness which is more than I am.

Melville knew. He knew his race was doomed. His white soul, doomed. His great white epoch, doomed. Himself doomed. The idealist, doomed. The spirit, doomed.

Here, Lawrence critiques Melville by carrying on a mock dialogue with himself, alternating his caricature of Melville's voice with his own whimsical acceptance of Melville's gloomy prophesy. Lawrence's essay seems written to provoke readers into reassessing their interpretations of literary classics, and so he provokes not only through the questions he raises but through his style as well. Note his poetic use of repetition and sentence fragments that contribute to his double-voice effect.

COLLAGE

A collage is an artistic composition of various materials and objects pasted together in incongruous relationships for their symbolic or suggestive effect. Collages are more often associated with visual than verbal art, but, again, alternate-style writers borrow freely from other media. In some ways, my own journal has elements of a collage when I use it as a scrapbook, taping in photos or clippings wherever I find white space, thus creating sometimes strange juxtapositions. However, collage writing has been used to more deliberate effect in the novels of John Dos Passos—a technique since borrowed by both Tom Wolfe and Hunter S. Thompson, in their New Journalistic essays. Dos Passos began his essay, "The Death of James Dean"* with quotations taken from newspaper headlines:

TEENAGE DANCES SEEM THREATENED BY PARENTS FAILURE TO
COOPERATE
MOST OFFENDERS EMULATE ADULTS

James Dean is three years dead but the sinister adolescent still holds the headlines.

James Dean is three years dead; but when they file out of the close darkness and breathed out air of the second-run motion picture theatres where they've been seeing James Dean's old films

they still line up;

the boys in the jackboots and the leather jackets, the boys in the skintight jeans, the boys in broad motorbike belts,

Esquire, December 1959

     before mirrors in the restroom
     to look at themselves
     and see
     James Dean;

Note, too, the unconventional prose lines in this essay, more like poetry than prose, as well as the repetition of the opening line.

    Collage techniques can be used in similar ways in nonfiction essays to provide background for an essay to follow. Or an entire essay may be crafted collage-style by the skillful juxtaposition of textual fragments— possibly with the addition of photos, newspaper clippings, or other two-dimensional items taped, photocopied, or scanned into the text. One of my students wrote a self profile by inserting photocopies of quotations, photos, and posters throughout her paper, suggesting that who she was contained these outside as well as inside sources.

A CAUTION ABOUT ALTERNATE STYLE

Wise writers will master both grammars, conventional and unconventional, using each as occasion and audience demand. Proficiency in one is a poor excuse for sloppiness or neglect of the other. Alternate-style techniques, used carefully and judiciously on selected writing tasks, are fun to write, and enjoyable to read. Overused, they become predictable, routine, and dull, losing the surprise and freshness that made them effective in the first place. Check with your instructor before handing in an unconventional paper in response to a conventional assignment.

APPENDIX

SUGGESTIONS FOR JOURNAL WRITING

1. Describe any experiences you have had reading or writing alternative-style texts.

2. For the next week, when writing in your journal, try different alternative-style techniques. Which are most effective for you and why?

SUGGESTIONS FOR ESSAY WRITING

1. Select one or more of the following techniques to compose your next essay: lists, snapshots, fragmented sentences, labyrinthine sentences, repetition, double voice, and collage.

2. Recast an essay previously written in one or more of the alternative-

style techniques above. Compare and contrast the effects created by each version.

3. As a class, compose a collaborative collage profile of your class, piecing together writing from each classmate in one thematically-consistent text.

SUGGESTIONS FOR RESEARCH PROJECTS

1. Read the works of one of the authors listed in this chapter and write a review essay on the intersection of theme with style.

2. Write a conventional research paper in traditional academic style (see Section III); write an additional draft in alternate style.

Chapter Sixteen

FINDING YOUR VOICE

> If you feel that you can never write as well as John Stein-
> beck [or] Charles Dickens . . . you may be right. But you
> can write well . . . if you find a voice that rings true to
> you and you can learn to record the surprises of the world
> faithfully.
>
> —Ken Macrorie*

Early in this book, we looked at the several purposes that cause people
to write in the first place: to learn something better, to question, to share,
and to present. Later, we looked at the audiences for whom writers write,
including teachers, friends, the public, and oneself. In this final chapter, I'd
like to reflect on the writer's *voice* and to consider how it develops.

In a book such as this, a discussion of voice in writing belongs either
first because it's so important, or last because it's so slippery. I have saved
it for last because, ultimately, voice is something that develops uncon-
sciously or intuitively and largely apart from the more conscious techniques we have studied.

The concept that each speaker or writer has a unique voice, one
that's indisputably his or hers, is perhaps the most difficult idea in this
book. I'd like to think that with each sentence and paragraph in these
chapters you can hear *me* speaking—that you can imagine the same
person speaking, page after page, without ever having met me, the author.
I'd like to think you can, for that is the best illustration of voice that I can
think of. However, I cannot speak for you.

*Telling Writing, Portsmouth, NH: Boynton/Cook, 1985.

But what really constitutes a writer's voice? The type and length of words, sentences, and paragraphs? The ideas expressed in the paragraphs? The arrangement of the ideas into a whole? The values embedded in the ideas? Some unidentifiable quality best described as mystical? Or, as some would argue, do we each have many voices, which vary according to one's purpose and audience? It will be the business of this chapter to explore where voice lies and what control, if any, writers have over it.

THE STYLE OF VOICE

Think a little bit about Cicero's definition of rhetoric: "The good man speaking well." (Changed to nonsexist language—"the good person speaking well"—the rhythm is less, but the content is more.) What I enjoy about this simple definition is the implied attention to the character of the whole speaker: What he or she stands for. What he or she believes. The quality of his or her words. The truth of those words. And the embedded notion that these words are, in fact, his or her own.

When we consider written instead of oral speech, the concept of voice becomes even more difficult to pin down. In writing, we can't, of course, hear the timbre of the voice or see the expressions on the face. Instead, we hear the voice through our reading, perhaps gleaning our first clues about the writer from the particular combination of words, punctuation, sentences, and paragraphs that we call *style*.

If I look for a moment at my own style, as evidenced in this chapter, a few things become obvious:

1. I use lots of first-person pronouns ("I") to let you know that these are *my* truths, not somebody else's. Other books about college writing assert things quite different from those found here.
2. I frequently use contractions to make my voice more conversational and less formal. In fact, I'd like this book to read like conversations between you and me about writing, only I have to imagine your concerns and questions.
3. As much as possible, I eschew large or pretentious words (like *eschew*, which simply means *avoid*) because that's how I speak with my family, friends, and students.
4. And I use a fair number of qualifiers *(fair, well, rather, perhaps, of course)*. I want to suggest that my assertions are not absolute, to give the reader time to chew on the assertions, and to help readers hear the tone of my informal speaking voice.

Of course, there are more observations we could make about my style— about clause length, fragments, figures of speech, active versus passive verbs, punctuation patterns, sentence rhythms, and the like, but this will do. Style is a matter of choices—some conscious and some not—about the language impression you leave behind.

To the extent that we control our style, we control our voice. We modify our language—sometimes consciously, sometimes not—to suit our several purposes and audiences. Especially at the editing stage, after we have worked out our central ideas, we have the luxury of going back over our draft and selecting just the right word or phrase to convey an idea: to select the word *large* rather than *big, huge, enormous,* or *humongous.* At this level of construction, we choose words to represent our ideas in one way rather than in another. But we don't have time to edit everything that comes out, nor do we want to, and so we probably make more unconscious than conscious choices.

THE CONTENT OF VOICE

The voice you find in a piece of writing is much more than a matter of style; otherwise, this chapter would be nearly over. When someone reads my writing and tells me that they could hear my *voice,* I take that as different from telling me they liked my style. Voice implies for me a deeper, more permanent resonance; *style* implies surface elements that are readily manipulated to produce various effects.

In addition to style, there is something that I stand for, some set of beliefs and ideas that characterize me as distinct from you—that, too, is a part of voice. There are some sentences that I could not utter, so foreign are they to my particular way of thinking and living. (At least I'd like to think that's true.) I'd like to think that the words of a Hitler, Stalin, a Ku Klux Klansman, or a terrorist could not appear among my utterances, nor those of the beer commercials on television, nor those of some colleagues down the hall. *My* voice not only permeates my words, but reflects my thoughts and values as well.

THE ARRANGEMENT OF VOICE

My voice also arranges, organizes, and focuses whatever material comes before it. In other words, voice is also a matter of the patterns through which we see and express the world. From even this chapter you will see the degree to which I am governed by logic or emotion, am inductive rather than deductive, am linear or circular, am probing or casual. Do I begin a piece of writing with an anecdote or a proposition? Do I provide examples for all of my generalizations?

Arranging ideas is easier in writing than in speaking because we can see our thoughts. In writing, we have the leisure to develop a thought carefully, to work from an outline, and to review and revise until we are satisfied that the order of presentation is as strong as we can make it.

THE EVOLUTION OF VOICE

Ultimately, when we communicate in writing, *style, content,* and *arrangement* are all working together simultaneously, somehow combining to represent us. Although we modify elements of our voices from time to time, person to person, situation to situation, we are more likely to play variations on a theme than to make radical departures from some fundamental expression that has come to represent us. Yes, I can write like an impartial, dispassionate, passive-voiced scientist if called upon to do so. Yes, I can write free-association, stream-of-consciousness mind play if I'm in certain moods. But these are not the me you'll usually find when you read what I write most often: my journal, letters, memos, articles, and books.

Your voice is something you may create consciously as you do a research paper or a poem. But more often it's what spills out whenever you talk candidly to your friends and when you write in your journal or to your mother, a classmate, or a teacher. Your voice evolves over time as you do. What I write today is basically the same as I would have written five years ago, but a little different, because I'm a little different at fifty-four than I was at thirty-eight or twenty-five or twelve. You are who you are, and when you speak or write it is reasonable to expect that your language represents you. If not your language, what does?

HOW MANY VOICES?

I *do* have more than one voice. I *can* become other people when I choose. I am even capable (sometimes) of uttering thoughts in which I do not believe. In short, whenever I write, to some extent I am putting on an act, the meaning of which changes as my purpose does. In this view, each of us is also a collection of several voices, none more genuine than another.

Whether we each believe we have one or many voices may simply depend upon how we define the word *voice*. When I asked the students in my advanced writing class how many voices they had, their answers differed in interesting ways. For example, Jen insisted that she had only one:

> My voice always maintains, if not screeches, an egocentric notion of who I am.

Carter insisted that all writers have only one:

> Good writers or bad, we cannot change our voice from one moment to the next. We can disguise it with style, but our own voices will ring true.

However, Bobby and Lisa both believed they each had three distinct voices, though each described these differently:

> BOBBY: I think I have three different writing voices: one academic, one personal, and one which lies somewhere in between. The ones I use most are the two extremes.
>
> LISA: I have three voices: the first is a writing-for-the-teacher voice, the second is a letter-writing voice, the last is a train-of-thought voice. . . . I am more comfortable with the last two—they are both like a real person speaking.

And Kim believed she had many:

> The writing home voice, the chemistry-lab voice, the writing-to-boyfriend voice, the writing-to-best-friend voice, the freshman English voice, the journal voice. Each one requires me to author it, but my actual presence in the piece will be stronger or lighter depending on the topic.

What may be most important in this discussion is not whether you actually have one, three, six, or more voices, but your awareness that your readers hear one whether you like it or not.

To college writers, I usually put it this way: We each have some bundle of beliefs, values, and behaviors that constitutes who we are (including our own perception of who we are). When we write, we represent some part of that self-concept on paper, unless, for certain purposes, we choose to modify it—at which time the shape of our voice becomes more problematic, less clearly *us,* more possibly some single quality exaggerated: the scientific me, the poetic me.

As a writer, you will be most versatile to the extent that you can assume a variety of voices, some less comfortable than others, perhaps, but possible. Learn, then, to view your voice as a powerful personal tool that you can shape as the occasion demands, recognizing that some shapes can become gross distortions of that for which you generally stand.

HEARING THE VOICE

In one of my first-year writing classes, Stephany chose to write about her summer job on an egg farm. I watched her write several drafts, her voice getting stronger and more assertive as she wrote. If we look at the first paragraphs of three of her drafts, we will see Stephany's voice in various stages of development.

DRAFT ONE: 9/6

This last summer my father said I had to get a job. I got a
job at a girls' camp, but I didn't dig the idea and hoped
that something better would come up. Much to my distaste,
I applied for a job at a nearby egg farm. I wasn't all that
thrilled with the prospects of spending the summer picking
eggs, but it would mean more money, so I said "what the
hell" and applied.

Stephany moves in this opening paragraph from her father to the girls'
camp to the egg farm in a rambling, informal adolescent voice. Yes, I hear
someone talking—complaining, actually—but despite the profanity, I do
not find Stephany's voice to be especially distinctive here: she tells us what
she doesn't like, but nothing of what she does.

In her next draft, Stephany concentrated on the job at the egg farm
from her opening and dropped the indecisive period leading up to it.

DRAFT TWO: 9/7

My summer job was at Arnold's Egg Farms in Lakeview,
Maine. I was the candler for Complex 70s, a series of ten
barns. I worked six days a week, Thursday through Tuesday.

Here Stephany has the tight focus, but has lost most of the verbal cues
that told us something about her personality. I would describe the voice
here as fairly objective and cautious, with no boldly distinctive qualities
to make us know much of the writer herself.

Her last draft started like this:

DRAFT THREE: 9/16

T.G.I.T. Thank God It's Tuesday. I always look forward to
Tuesdays. They mean two things: Tomorrow is my day off
and today is my boss's day off, so I won't be asked to pick
eggs. I really hate picking eggs—I get all covered with dust,
eggs, and grain. By the end of the day, I'm so tired that I
just want to sack out. When I was hired, my boss told me
I'd only have to pick eggs once in a while, but this week I
had to pick three times. It really gets me, because my real
job is candling eggs.

Stephany has changed more than her style here: she now starts fast, with
a little riddle; she includes good details; she writes with new rhythm. But

I would argue that the real gain in this draft is in the totality of her voice. In place of an aimless, complaining teenager or a technical report writer, we find a whole, self-assertive, mildly cocky, genuinely humorous person. After she found the story she really wanted to tell, her voice got stronger and her overall writing much better.

FINDING YOUR VOICE

It's an interesting exercise to try to discover the origins and nature of your own voice. In the last assignment of the semester, I asked my first-year writing students to do just that—to reconstruct, by examining past writing, how their writing voices developed, and to locate the features that presently characterize them. Some students, such as Amy, went all the way back to their elementary school writing:

> One of the earliest things I can remember writing is a story called "Bill and Frank." It was about a hot dog (Frank) who could sing and play the banjo. Bill was the hot dog vendor who discovered his talent and became his manager. I wrote this story somewhere around third grade. It was very short, simple and to the point.
>
> As the school years passed, assignments got more and more complex. Short, simple and to the point was no longer a plausible style. Of course, page requirements often went along with these assignments also causing a change in style.

She also remembered major influences on the development of her voice:

> My first taste of truly more complex writing was in my ninth-grade European history class. Mr. Page taught me how to write an essay. He taught me about making a thesis, supporting this thesis with evidence (from documented sources), and writing a conclusion.

Other students found truly negative influences on their development as writers. Here Steve remembers Mr. Higgins with some anger.

> Mr. Higgins was always on our case about grammar. I don't blame him for it, but he taught it totally wrong. He forced it upon you. It is harder when you have to learn all those picky rules all at once. I think you can learn much easier by just plain writing. The more you write the more you use

words. By the continuous use of sentences the learning becomes natural.

And Karen remembers not so much a single influence as her own attitude
towards writing, which was well developed by the time she was a high
school senior:

> As I look back and review my writing habits I discover a
> pattern: name, date, title, one draft, spell check, done!! I
> handed it in and never looked at it again. My senior thesis,
> I sat down at the computer, typed out a draft, and as soon
> as the page numbers reached ten I wrote a conclusion, ran
> it through spell check, and handed it in. I never proofread
> it. I was content it didn't have any spelling errors. So, why
> did I get a *D* on it? I couldn't figure it out.

In completing this assignment to analyze their own writing voices, many
college writers reported a new awareness of themselves as writers, of their
voices as distinctly their own. Colleen, for example, for the first time
believes she is a writer:

> The important part of my growth as a writer is the fact
> that I have grown into a writer rather than grown as a
> writer. I never used to consider myself a writer and per-
> haps now I am being too bold by saying that I have become
> one. I used to be afraid of writing. I despised anything that
> resembled a diary. It was hard for me to get the idea into
> my head that writing was for your personal use. That's
> what I think writing is all about.

Gavin reports major growth in selecting certain topics:

> My major development as a writer has occurred in the top-
> ics that I write on. Through the years I have focused on
> continually more powerful subjects. From violence in chil-
> dren's literature to the destruction of tropical rain forests
> to gang violence to my work this year on nursing homes
> and the homeless.

Wendy views her changes as a writer as closely akin to her changes as a
person:

> Changing one's personal voice is sort of like changing one's
> personality. . . . I see that as I grew older, my writing

matured, became more open, and developed in the same ways I did as a person.

DEVELOPING YOUR WRITING VOICE

Voice is difficult to isolate and analyze. I've chosen to write about it last because, to a large extent, voice is determined by other skills and beliefs. However, there are some things you can do that will have a positive impact on your writing voice. None will be as important as living, learning, working, loving, raising families, and growing older, but each will help the process along.

1. *Speak when you are afraid.* You grow fastest when you take the most risks, slowest when you remain safe. For me as an undergraduate, speaking out loud in class was as risky as anything I had ever done, but until I tested my voice and my beliefs in the arena of the class, I really didn't know who I was, what I stood for, or what I *could* stand for. The more you test your oral voice, literally, the more your written voice will develop.

2. *Keep a log or journal.* These are safer places in which to take risks than classrooms, so take advantage of that as often as you can. The more you explore who you are in your journal, the more easily you will be able to assert that identity both out loud and in your more formal writing. Use your journal to rehearse your public self.

3. *Share your writing with others.* Sharing is another form of risk taking, of being willing to see how others perceive you. Asking friends, roommates, classmates, and teachers to respond to your writing in general, to your voice in particular, helps you see how your voice affects others, which in turn allows you to tinker with it for this or that effect. If you hear good things back about your writing, you will be most likely to do more writing; if you hear bad things, you won't write. Pick your sharing audience carefully!

4. *Notice other people's voices.* One of the best means of growing in every direction at once is simply reading. The more you read, the more other voices you learn about. Read and notice how others convey this or that impression. Take reading notes in your journal to capture what you found. Notice the writers who make you keep reading and notice those who put you to sleep, and try to determine why.

5. *Practice other people's voices.* One of the best of the old-fashioned composition exercises was copying, word for word, the style of someone else. One day you copy a passage from Virginia Woolf, the next day you try Thomas Wolfe, then Tom Wolfe, then

you try to determine which is which and why. These exercises also help you notice what features characterize your own writing.

6. *Show, don't editorialize, generalize, or summarize.* Practice projecting your voice without telling your reader that's what you're doing. Work so hard at noticing and describing and recreating that you don't need to explain in any obvious way what you think, believe, and value. Place your observations, overhearings, and discoveries so judiciously in your text that they make your point and project your voice in tacit rather than explicit ways.

OBSERVATION

As I've presented it here, the matter of voice is fairly complex. I've suggested that, on the one hand, we each have a voice that is ours; yet I've also suggested that we have more than one voice. I've also suggested that voice is something that develops over time—over one's lifetime, actually—but I've also shown a sample of voice developing itself over a several-week draft. As I said at the outset, the concept of voice is both important and slippery: others perceive us as our language represents us. Some of this we don't control, at least not yet, and some we never will.

APPENDIX

SUGGESTIONS FOR JOURNAL WRITING

1. Explain your understanding of voice in writing. How would you describe your own?

2. What influences have determined your current writing voice(s)? That is, can you think of particular teachers or a parent or an incident that influenced how you write today?

3. Describe how you vary or change your voice according to whom you are writing.

SUGGESTIONS FOR ESSAY WRITING

1. Write an analysis of your current writing voice. Collect as much of your recent (during the past year) writing as you can in a single folder. Consider writing you did in previous schools (for example, high school, if that was recent), in other college courses, earlier in this course, copies of letters, personal diaries, or journals. Arrange these samples one of several ways: for example, according to subject, type, or audience. Then examine each specimen and identify

the features that seem to characterize your own voice—those that appear from piece to piece: style? attitude? arrangement? word choice? subject? Write a report describing that voice, using your analyzed data as evidence. (You could report the results of this study in either first or third person—try a passage of each to appreciate the difference.)

2. Describe the development of your current writing voice. Follow the procedures described above, but go back as far as you are able (middle school? elementary school?) and arrange your samples chronologically. Look from sample to sample and see if you can determine any pattern or see any evolution in the development of this voice. Write an essay describing and speculating about your personal evolution as a writer, using both samples and memories of particular influences to help you.

SUGGESTIONS FOR RESEARCH WRITING

1. INDIVIDUAL: Research the concept of voice in the library. Start with authors such as Irving Goffman, Walker Gibson, and Loren Eiseley. Write a paper in which you examine the degree to which a writer's voices are determined by particular social influences (neighborhood, school, religion, family, friends, etc.) acting upon them.

2. COLLABORATIVE: Write a voice profile. Pair up with somebody else. Interview each other about the nature of your writing and speaking voices. In addition, you might ask to see samples of each other's writing. Write a profile describing each other's voices, using interview and written material as data to support you. Conclude each report with a response by the person interviewed: How accurately have you portrayed his or her voice?

Postscript One

GUIDELINES FOR WRITING GROUPS

Writing gets better by reading, practice, and response. The first two you can do for yourself by selecting books that stimulate your interest and show you interesting prose styles, and by writing regularly in a journal or on a computer and not settling for drafts that don't please you. But at some point, to get really better, you need to hear other people respond to your words and ideas. If you are using this book in a class, chances are that your teacher confers with you individually about your work, and chances are that you meet every week or so with your classmates in a writing group where you take turns receiving and giving responses. During the last several years my students and I worked together to develop guidelines to help writing groups work even more smoothly.

TO THE CLASS

1. Writing groups work best in classrooms where there is a sense of community and trust. All members of a given class share the responsibility for making this happen.
2. Permanent writing groups of three to five work best in most classes. Fewer than three makes a weaker dynamic—though twos are fast and work well for ad hoc situations where you have only fifteen or twenty minutes. More than five becomes cumbersome for time and equal participation—though larger groups work very well outside of class where time is less restricted. So I shoot for groups of about four and plan for these to stay together for the duration of a given assignment, meeting preferably once a week

for a series of weeks. For new assignments, I suggest forming new groups.

3. The length of a given paper determines what happens to it in a group. It's possible for three papers of four or five pages each to be read and commented on in their entirety in a fifty-minute class. With longer papers, or larger groups writers need to read selections from their paper or take turns being featured. (I use a rule of thumb that it takes two minutes to read a page of typed double-spaced writing.)

4. Groups work best when they become habit. Keep the groups meeting regularly and keep the group meeting time sacred. Jettison other things before you jettison group time in class. What does the teacher do while you all meet in groups? I stay out of all groups for the first few meetings, then participate in a group if invited.

5. It's helpful to distribute papers before class so that readers have had a chance to make private comments. However, in most classrooms, early distribution is very difficult. The following suggestions are made on the assumption that people show up in class, on time, with fresh papers to be talked about.

TO THE WRITER

1. Plan to read your paper *out loud* to the others in your group. Hearing a paper read by the author adds a special dimension to the writing—for the reader as well as the listening audience. There's no substitute for a little rehearsal reading aloud before class—you'll be surprised at how much you notice, both positive and negative, about your writing when you hear yourself read it.

2. Prepare enough copies of your paper for each person in the group. If finances are short, two could look at one copy together, following you while you read aloud. Without duplicate copies it's difficult for your audience to remember all the language they would like to comment on. (If you cannot make extra copies, plan to read your paper—or portions of it—out loud twice.)

3. Direct your listeners' response: Sometimes ask for general reactions: "How does it sound?" "Is it believable?" "What do you like best?" "Where does it need more work?" "What questions do you have?" "What do you expect next?"

4. Sometimes ask for more focused responses about the parts of the paper that you most want to hear about: "Does my introduction work? Why?" "Which evidence for my argument is most convincing?" "How would you describe my tone?" "Am I too

colloquial? too formal? inconsistent?" "Does my conclusion conclude?" "Does it sound like me talking?" (You will notice that you get more mileage if you are able to phrase questions that can't simply be answered "Yes" or "No.")

5. Sometimes ask for assignment-specific responses: "Where is my interpretation most convincing?" "What holes do you see in my analysis?" "Where do you think I show versus summarize?" "Does effect clearly follow cause? If not, why not?" "What details tell you that I was really there?"

6. Try some response exercises, such as those Peter Elbow describes in *Writing with Power* (Oxford, 1981): Ask people to tell you the "movies of their mind" as they listened to you—what impressions the language created, emotional or otherwise, as you read. Or ask for metaphors stimulated by the writing. Or ask them to summarize your paper back to you. Each of these exercises gives you a different kind of information to help you rewrite.

7. Listen more than talk. The writing group is your chance to hear others' reactions unaided by your own biases. Listen to your groupmates, say as little as possible, and try not to get defensive. Instead, take good notes and plan to use your verbal energy revising for next time. (It's very nice to hear nice things about your work and very hard to hear criticism, but both are very instructive.)

8. Keep track of time or have a timekeeper do so for you. You each want your fair share and it's a good idea to allocate it evenly at the start: If you've got three papers in fifty minutes, stick pretty close to fifteen minutes apiece.

9. At the end of your time, collect copies from people who have written responses to you and say some kind of thank you.

10. It's your paper. Revise based on your own best judgment, not necessarily what the group told you. This is especially true if you hear contradictory responses. But to ignore the group suggestions altogether may also be a mistake, especially if you find more than one group member making the same comment. And remember that if you have a chance to read to the same group again, they will be especially attuned to whether or not you took any of their suggestions.

TO THE AUDIENCE

1. Look for what the writer asks. Follow along silently as the paper is read and try to focus on the kind of response the writer wants, at least at first.

2. Mark small things such as typos and errors in spelling or punctuation, but do not spend group time on such comments. Plan to return your copy to the writer at the end of the session with such items marked or corrected, preferably in pencil, never in red ink.

3. Say something nice about the writer's work. In spite of the value of critical comments, we grow as much by comments which confirm that we are doing something right. People are much more willing to listen to critical comments once they feel confident that much of their work is good.

4. Ask questions. If you find problems with the paper, the most effective comment is often a question to the writer about the spot or intent or language or format or whatever: "What did you mean here?" "What would happen if you told this story in the present tense?" "What were some examples that might support you here?" Questions point to problems but do not dictate solutions.

5. Share emotional as well as intellectual responses. Sometimes it's good for a writer simply to know how you felt about something.

6. Be specific. Try to identify the word, sentence, paragraph, or page where you had this or that response. That way a writer has something concrete to react to.

7. Don't overwhelm the writer by commenting on absolutely everything you found bothersome about her paper. Try to mention the most important issues out loud in the group and let others go.

8. Share your response time equitably among group members. One good way to do this is for each of you in turn to say one quick thing, asking the writer to remain quiet while you do. This guarantees that you all participate at some level. The discussion will naturally go on from there.

9. Be honest. If you really find nothing you like, don't invent things that are not true. But in thirty years of teaching, I've never found a paper about which something positive could not be said (and I don't mean inane things such as "Nice spelling!" or "Deft use of commas"). So maybe the best advice here is "be honest, gently."

10. Stick to the paper. While it's fun and sometimes fruitful to digress into related but peripheral issues, keep in mind that your time—if you're critiquing in class—is brief. And keep your comments focused on the writing, not the writer—that helps keep egos and personalities out of the work at hand, which is writing good papers.

Postscript Two

GUIDELINES FOR WRITING PORTFOLIOS

In simplest terms, a writing portfolio is a folder containing a collection of your writing. A *comprehensive portfolio* prepared for a writing class usually presents a cumulative record of all of your work over a semester and is commonly used to assign a grade. An alternate form of class portfolio is the *story portfolio,* which presents selections from your semester's papers described and discussed in narrative form.

PREPARING A COMPREHENSIVE PORTFOLIO

The most common portfolio assigned in a writing class is the comprehensive or cumulative portfolio, containing all your writing for the term; it usually includes a cover letter in which you explain the nature and value of the portfolio contents. The following suggestions may help you in preparing a cumulative portfolio.

1. **Make your portfolio speak for you.** A clean, complete, and carefully organized portfolio presents you one way; a unique, colorful, creative, and imaginative portfolio presents you another way; and a messy, incomplete, and haphazard portfolio still another. Before turning in your final portfolio, consider if it presents you the way you want to be presented.
2. **Include exactly what is asked for.** If an instructor wants three finished papers and a dozen sample journal entries, that's what your portfolio should contain. If an instructor wants five samples of different kinds of writing, be sure to include those five samples. You may include more than is asked for, but never include less.

3. **Add supplemental material judiciously.** Portfolios are among the most flexible means of presenting yourself. It is usually your option to include samples of journals, letters, sketches, or diagrams when they suggest other useful dimensions of your thinking. But include extra samples only in *addition* to the required material (and be sure to explain why it's there in a note or letter to the instructor).

4. **Include careful final drafts.** Show that your own standard for finished work is high. Final drafts should be double-spaced on one side only of high quality paper; they should be titled, dated, corrected, and follow the language conventions appropriate to the task—unless otherwise requested.

5. **Demonstrate evolution and growth.** Portfolios, unlike most other instruments of assessment, allow you to show your reader how a finished product came into being. Consequently, instructors commonly ask that early drafts of each paper be attached to final drafts, with the most recent on top—an order that shows how a paper developed: It shows how you followed revision suggestions, how hard you have worked, how many drafts you wrote, and how often you experimented. To create such a record of your work, date all drafts and keep them in a safe place.

6. **Demonstrate work in progress.** Portfolios allow writers to present partially finished work to suggest future direction and intention. Instructors may find such preliminary drafts or outlines as valuable as some of your finished work. When you include such tentative drafts, be sure to attach a note explaining why it's there and where it's going next.

7. **Attach a table of contents.** For portfolios containing many papers, attach a separate table of contents. For those containing only a few papers, embed your table of contents in the cover letter.

8. **Attend to the mechanics of the portfolio.** Make sure the folder containing your writing is the kind specified and that it is clean and attractive. In the absence of such specification, use a two-pocket folder or three-ring loose leaf binder, inexpensive ways to keep the contents organized and secure. Put your name and address on the outside cover. Organize the material inside as requested. And turn it in on time.

9 **Include a cover letter.** For many instructors, the cover letter will be a key part of your portfolio since it represents your latest assessment of your work. A cover letter serves as an introduction describing and explaining the portfolio's contents and organization (what's there as well as what's not) and your own assessment of the work, from earliest to latest draft of each

paper, and from earliest to latest work over the course of the semester. The following is Chris's informal letter of self assessment:

> As I look back through all the papers I've written this semester, I see how far my writing has come. At first I thought it was stupid to write so many different drafts of the same paper, like I would beat the topic to death. But now I realize that all these different papers on the same topic all went in different directions. This happened to some degree in the first paper, but I especially remember in my research project, when I interviewed the director of the Ronald McDonald House, I really got excited about the work they did there, and I really got involved in the other drafts of that paper.
>
> I have learned to shorten my papers by editing and cutting out needless words. I use more descriptive adjectives now when I'm describing a setting and try to find action verbs instead of "to be" verbs in all of my papers. I am writing more consciously now—I think that's the most important thing I learned this semester.

PREPARING A STORY PORTFOLIO

A story portfolio is a shorter but more carefully edited and crafted summary of your work. Instead of writing a cover letter and including all papers and drafts written during the term, a story portfolio *narrates* the evolution of your work and thought. In a story portfolio, you include excerpts of your papers to illustrate points in your own development as a writer. In addition, you include excerpts of whatever other written records you may have accumulated at different times during the semester that help tell your story: early paper drafts, journal entries, relevant class notes, in-class writing, letter writing, and instructor and classmate comments on your papers.

In other words, to write a story portfolio, you conduct something like an archaeological dig through the written remains of your work in the class, usually assembling it in chronological order, choosing the most telling snippets and excerpts from these various documents. Then you write the story that explains, amplifies, or interprets the documents you include or quote. The best story portfolios commonly reveal a theme or set of issues that run from week to week, and/or work to work throughout the semester. In truth, a story portfolio is actually a small research paper, featuring claims about your evolution as a writer supported with evidence from texts you've written.

You may choose to write your story portfolios in an informal voice (like a journal or letter) or in a more formal voice (like a report). Or you may prefer to write in the third person, analyzing the semester's work as if you do not know the writer and are making inferences strictly from the texts themselves. Experiment with form: Is it better to present your work as a series of snapshots or as a more fluid essay? Following are a few pages from Karen's ten-page story portfolio:

> When I entered English One, I was not a confident writer and only felt comfortable writing factual reports for school assignments. Those were pretty straight forward, and your personal opinion was not involved. But over the course of the semester I've learned that I enjoy including my own voice in my writing. The first day of class I wrote this in my journal:
>
>> 8/31 Writing has always been hard for me. I don't have a lot of experience writing papers except for straight forward things like science reports. I never did very well in English classes, usually getting Bs and Cs on my papers.
>
> But I began to feel a little more comfortable when we read and discussed the first chapter of the book—a lot of other students besides me felt the same way, pretty scared to be taking English in college.
>
> I decided to write about our basketball season last year, especially the last game that we lost. Here is a paragraph from my first draft:
>
>> *We* lost badly to Walpole in what turned out to be *our* final game. *I* sat on the bench most of the time.
>
> As I see now, that draft was all telling and summary—I didn't show anything happening that was interesting or alive. But in a later draft I used dialogue and wrote from the announcer's point of view and the result was fun to write and my group said it was fun to read:
>
>> "Well folks, it looks as if Belmont has given up. The coach is preparing to send in his subs. It has been a rough game for Belmont. They stayed in it during the first quarter, but Walpole has ran away with it since then. Down by twenty with only six minutes left, Belmont's first sub is now approaching the table."
>
> You were excited about this draft too, and your comment helped me know where to go next. You wrote:
>
>> Great draft, Karen! You really sound like a play-by-play announcer—you've either been one or listened closely to lots of basketball games. What would happen if in your next draft you alternated between your own voice and the announcer's voice. Want to try it?

The following suggestions will help in preparing a story portfolio:

1. **Assemble all of your collected writing.** Arrange both formal and informal writing, in chronological order, from beginning to end of the semester.
2. **Reread all your *formal* work.** Examine typed final papers, drafts with instructor comments, and highlight brief passages that illustrate your development as a writer. Note particular passages that have evolved or disappeared over several drafts in the same paper—what was going on?
3. **Reread all your *informal* work.** Examine journals, letters, and instructor and student comments, and highlight brief passages that further amplify your work at that time.
4. **Arrange highlighted passages in a sensible order.** Write the story that shows how one passage connects to another, as well as explaining the significance of each passage. (Indent passages ten spaces for ease of reading.)
5. **Identify common themes, ideas, or questions.** Focus your portfolio so that it tells a coherent story. Include an *Introduction* aimed at someone unfamiliar with this class. Tell your main *Story,* and conclude with a section called *Reflections.*
6. **Append all drafts in chronological order.** Date and label each as d/1, d/2, etc., with teacher comments as an appendix to the main story portfolio. Include the story portfolio in one side of the pocket folder, the appendix in the other side.

Postscript Three

GUIDELINES FOR PUBLISHING CLASS BOOKS

Publishing a class book is a natural end to a writing class. A class book is an edited, bound collection of student writing, usually featuring some work from each student in the class. Compiling and editing such a book is commonly assigned to class volunteers, who are given significant authority in designing and producing the book. It is a good idea for these editors to discuss book guidelines with the whole class so that consensus guidelines emerge. Editor duties usually include the following:

1. Setting a **deadline** for collecting final manuscripts. This is usually set so published copies can be delivered on the last class day or next-to-last-class day (this latter allowing for reading and discussing the book on the last class day).
2. Defining the **editorial mission:** Usually students ask for camera-ready copy from classmates to simplify and speed the publishing process. However, editors may want to see near-final drafts and return with comments; or they may wish to set up class editorial boards to preview or screen near-final drafts; or they may wish to leave this role with the instructor.
3. Setting **page-length limits.** For example, each student may be allowed a certain number of single or double spaced pages. Since printing charges are usually made on a per-page basis, page length discussion is related to final publication cost.
4. Getting **cost estimates.** Editors explore with local print shops such as Kinko's, Staples, or the college print shop the cost of producing a certain number of copies of class books (e.g., sixty pages @ .05 ea., plus color cover $1.00 ea., plus binding .50 ea

= $4.50 per book). Alternatively, editors may ask the class to assemble the book—each student bringing in twenty copies of his or her essay to be collated and bound with the rest.

5. Posing **manuscript guidelines** for what each submitted paper should look like. Class editors should ask for camera-ready copy to speed production and decrease their own work load. Other guidelines may include:
   - typing double- or single-spaced
   - type face
   - font size
   - margins: top/bottom, right/left
   - justified or not
   - centered title
   - position of author name

6. **Arranging** collected essays according to some ordering principle. This may depend upon how many and what kind of writing was done during the term. For example, students may have written personal profiles, feature stories, and reflective essays: Should there be a separate section for each? How should the essays be arranged within each section?

7. Writing an **Introduction** and preparing a **Table of Contents (TOC).** The most significant editorial work is writing an introduction to contextualize the class book, explain its development, and describe the contents. Introductions vary in length from a paragraph to several pages. TOCs are routine but helpful.

8. Asking the instructor to write a brief **Afterword** or **Preface** describing the class, the assignment objectives, or any other instructor perspective that seems relevant to the book.

9. Collecting student-writer **Biographies.** Most class books conclude with short (fifty to one hundred word) biographies of the student writers, which may be serious, semiserious, or comical depending on class wishes.

10. Designing a **cover.** The editors may commission a classmate or one of themselves to design a suitable cover for the book. Covers can be graphic or printed, black-and-white or color.

11. Dividing up **editorial responsibilities.** Class books are best done by editorial teams consisting of two or more students who arrange among themselves the various duties described above.

The final responsibility of class editors is usually **leading a last-class discussion** on the theme, format, and voice as represented by the class book or its various sections. Class responsibilities here include both a careful reading of their own book and bringing cookies and cider to share along with the discussion.

Since editors do a significant amount of work in compiling their classmate's writing, I usually excuse them from making oral reports or leading class discussions—which the rest of the students do during the term.

Finally, when I assign editors to design and publish a class book, I make it clear that the act of publishing in the book is the final draft of that particular paper; when reading student portfolios at term's end, it is in the class book that I find the final drafts of one or more essays.

Postscript Four

GUIDELINES FOR WRITING ESSAY EXAMINATIONS

Instructors assign essay exams instead of objective tests (multiple choice, matching, true/false) because they want students to go beyond identifying facts and to demonstrate a mastery of the concepts covered in the course.

The best preparation for taking an essay exam is a thorough knowledge of the course subject matter. If you have attended all the classes, done all the assignments, read all the texts, you should be in good shape for such writing. If you have also kept journals, annotated textbooks, discussed the course material with other students, and posed possible essay exam questions, you should be in even better shape for such writing.

Equally important is your strategic thinking about the course and its syllabus. If the course has been divided into different topics or themes, anticipate a general question on each one covered; if it has been arranged chronologically, expect questions focusing on comparisons or cause and effect relations within a particular period or across periods. Consider, too, the amount of class time spent on each topic or work, and pay proportionately greater attention to emphasized areas. The following suggestions may help in writing essay examinations:

1. **Read the whole examination.** Before answering a single question, read over the whole exam to assess its scope and focus. Answering three of four questions in fifty minutes requires a different approach than answering, say, five of eight questions in the same amount of time. If you have a choice, answer those questions that provide a good demonstration of your knowledge of the whole course, rather than two or more that might result in repetitive writing. Finally, decide which questions you are best

prepared to answer, and respond to those first (budgeting your time to allow you to deal fully with the others later).

2. **Attend to direction words.** Analyze each one before you begin to write. Focus close on the particular question before you. Read it several times. Underline and understand the direction words that identify the task you are to carry out, and be sure to follow this direction:

Define or identify asks for the distinguishing traits of a term, subject, or event, but does not require an interpretation or judgment. Use appropriate terminology learned in the course. For example, "Define John Locke's concept of tabula rasa" is best answered using some of Locke's terminology along with your own.

Describe may ask for a physical description ("Describe a typical performance in ancient Greek theater") or to request an explanation of a process, phenomenon, or event ("Describe the culture and practices of the mound builders"). Such questions generally do not ask for interpretation or judgment, but require abundant details and examples.

Summarize asks for an overview or a synthesis of the main points. Keep in mind that "Summarize the impact of the Battle of Gettysburg on the future conduct of the war" asks only that you hit the highlights; avoid getting bogged down in too much detail.

Compare and contrast suggests that you point out both similarities and differences, generally between two subjects but sometimes among three or more. Note that questions using other direction words may also ask for comparison or contrast: "Describe the differences between the works of Monet and Manet."

Analyze asks that you write about a subject in terms of its component parts. The subject may be concrete ("Analyze the typical seating plan of a symphony orchestra") or abstract ("Analyze the ethical ramifications of Kant's categorical imperative"). In general, your response should look at one part at a time.

Interpret asks for a definition or analysis of a subject based on internal evidence and your own particular viewpoint: "Interpret Flannery O'Connor's short story 'Revelation' in terms of your understanding of her central religious and moral themes."

Explain asks what causes something, or how something operates. Such questions may ask for an interpretation and an evaluation. "Explain the function of color in the work of Picasso," for example, clearly asks for interpretation of the artist's use of color; although it does not explicitly ask for a judgment, some judgment might be appropriate.

Evaluate or critique asks for a judgment based on clearly articulated analysis and reasoning. "Evaluate Plato's concept of the ideal state" and "Critique the methodology of this experiment," for example, ask for your opinions on these topics. Be analytical as you lead up to your judgmental verdict, and don't feel that your verdict must be completely one-sided. In many cases, you will want to cite more experienced judgments to back up your own.

Discuss or comment on is a general request, which allows considerable latitude. Your answers to questions such as "Discuss the effects of monetarist economic theories on current third world development" often let you demonstrate what you know especially well. Use terms and ideas as they have been discussed during the course, and add your own insights with care and thoughtfulness.

3. **Plan and outline.** Take one or two minutes per question to make a quick potential outline of your answer. If asked, for example, to compare and contrast three impressionist painters, decide in advance which three you will write about and in which order. While other ideas will come as you start writing, starting with a plan allows you to write more effectively. If you create a quick outline in the margins of your paper or even just hold it in your head, you will include more information and in a logical order.

4. **Lead with a thesis.** The surest way to receive full credit when writing an essay examination is to answer the question briefly in your first sentence. In other words, state your answer as a thesis which the rest of your essay will explain, support, and defend.

5. **Write with specific detail, examples, and illustrations.** Remember, most good writing contains specific information that lets readers see for themselves the evidence for your position. Use as many supportive specifics as you can; memorize names, works, dates, and ideas as you prepare for the exam so they can be recalled accurately as needed. Individual statistics alone may not be worth much, but when embedded as evidence in an essay that also contains strong reasoning, these specifics make the difference between good and mediocre answers.

6. **Provide context.** In answering a question posed by an instructor who is an expert in the field, it is sometimes tempting to assume your instructor does not need a full explanation and to answer too briefly. However, in a test situation you are being asked to demonstrate how much *you* understand. Briefly explain any concepts or terms that are central to your answer. Take the time to fit any details into the larger scheme of the subject. View each question as an opportunity to show how much you know about the subject.

7. **Use the technical terminology of the discipline.** Be careful not to drop in names or terms gratuitously, but if names and terms have been an integral part of the course, use them in your answer. Make sure you define them, use them appropriately, and spell

them correctly. Essay exams also test your facility with the language and concepts peculiar to a particular discipline.

8. **Stay focused.** Answer what the question asks. Attend to all parts of an answer, cover those parts and, once you have done that, do not digress or add extraneous information. While it may be interesting to some instructors to hear your other ideas on the subject at hand, for other instructors, your digressive ideas may actually divert attention away from your more focused answers.

9. **Write strategically.** The following technical tips will make your exam answers easier to read:

    1. Start each new answer at the top of a new page by repeating the number and *part* of the question. (1. The Civil War was caused by . . .)

    2. Paragraph for each new point to make sure your fast-reading instructor sees each distinctive point you make.

    3. Memorize and include short, accurate quotes of exceptional power where relevant, and cite each by author, title, or date, as relevant.

    4. Outline the answers or the rest of answers if time runs out.

    5. Reread and proofread each answer during the last five minutes before handing in the finished exam; even this little distance from your first composing will allow you to spot errors and omissions.

Postscript Five

GUIDELINES FOR PUNCTUATION

Listed below are general explanations for punctuation. I have included the most common uses for the punctuation marks described. If you know the uses described here, you will be in good shape as a writer. However, be aware that numerous exceptions to all the punctuation rules also exist— exceptions that I have not attempted to cover here. To learn about these, consult the handbook appended to most dictionaries, Strunk and White's *The Elements of Style,* or one of the many writer's handbooks available in libraries, bookstores, or English teachers' offices.

APOSTROPHES [']

1. Indicate that somebody possesses or *owns* something. In single nouns or pronouns, place an 's at the end of the word: *John's sister; the girl's brother; the cat's pajamas.*

    For plural words, add the apostrophe, but omit the s: *the boys' books; the cats' pajamas* (meaning more than one boy or cat).

    Notable exception: it's, since the 's in this word indicates the contraction it is.

2. Indicate contraction. Use an apostrophe to indicate missing letters: *can't* for *cannot; it's* for *it is.*

BRACKETS [[ ]]

1. Indicate that the author has added additional or substitute words in a quotation: *"Then she [Susan Smith] voted again,"* or *"Then [Susan Smith] voted again."*
2. Indicate parentheses within parentheses: *(This is parenthetical [this even more so]).*

COLONS [:]

1. Indicate that an example follows: *This is an example of an example following a colon.*
2. Introduce lists of items: *The ark housed the following animals: cats, dogs, chickens, snakes, elephants, and goats.*
3. Introduce questions in your text. (MLA documentation recommends indenting material five spaces or more; when you indent quotes, the identification substitutes for quotation marks.) Example: *The first paragraph of the Declaration of Independence reads as follows:*
4. Introduce phrases or sentences that explain or illustrate previous ones: *The explanation was clear: the example made it work.*
5. Separate titles from subtitles: *College Writing: A Personal Approach to Academic Writing.*

COMMAS [,]

Note: misplaced or missing commas account for many of our punctuation errors. You may take some comfort in knowing that even experts disagree about some of these so-called rules. Journalists, for example, don't put commas after the next-to-last item in a series; professors most likely do: *The cat, the rabbit[,] and the bat.*

In general, commas indicate pauses within sentences. You can usually hear the pause when the sentence is read aloud. I often read aloud to myself to tell me where commas go. However, the following guidelines will remind you more specifically when and where to use commas:

1. Separate two main clauses (complete sentences) joined by and, but, or, for, nor: *I can run fast, but I can't run far.*
2. Separate words or phrases in a series: *His favorite sports included motorcycle riding, hockey, tennis, golf, fishing, and baseball.*
3. Set off a clause or long phrase that introduces a main clause (the major part of the sentence): *After we attend class, we'll eat lunch and take our afternoon naps.*

4. Set off transitional words from the rest of the sentence: *She asked, however, that she not be quoted. It is not true, for example, that squirrels fly. In other words, writing is easy.*
5. Set off extra, explanatory information not absolutely essential in the sentence: *Toby, a professor of mine, occasionally gives good lectures. That dog, the black one, ate the garbage.* (The same information could be set off in parentheses, which would indicate it was even less essential for an understanding of the sentence.)
6. Set off words that address or exclaim and people who say things:

   "How are you, Paul?" she said.
   "Oh, not so hot," he replied.

7. Introduce or conclude direct quotations: *According to the study by Smith and Rocket, "acid rain is the major cause of the decreasing trout population in Vermont."*

EM DASHES [—]

1. Mark abrupt changes or breaks in sentences: *It isn't true—or is it?*
2. Set off information not considered essential to the understanding of sentences: *The stock market crash—it was 1929—did my grandfather in.*
3. Summarize earlier items in a sentence: *The amount of unemployment, the price of gold, the availability of oil, the weather—all these influence the amount of taxes we pay.*
   Note: dashes can often be used to set off apparently digressive information in the manner of commas or parentheses; however, they imply that the information is, while slightly off track, essential. Note, too, that the use of dashes to connect loose thoughts (in place of periods or semicolons) is not considered a sign of good writing in the academic world, where one's thoughts are not supposed to be loose.

ELLIPSES [. . . .]

1. Three dots in a quoted passage indicate an omission of one or more words in a quotation: *John argued . . . that he should stay.*
2. Four dots in a quoted passage indicate the omission of one or more sentences, or missing words at the end of a sentence (the fourth dot being the missing period): *Remember Lincoln's opening words "Four score and seven years ago. . . ."*
3. Four dots indicate the writer's thoughts trailing off mid-stream: *a deliberate strategy to convey. . . .*

EXCLAMATION POINTS [!]

Indicate strong emotional statement, either positive or negative, on the part of the writer: *"Stop, you can't go in there!" Henry, I love you!*
Note: use these marks sparingly in academic writing as they imply over-statement—and academics are wary of overstatement. Also use them sparingly in personal writing as they give away too much emotion and *tell* the reader how to feel.

HYPHENS [-]

1. Divide a word of more than one syllable at the end of a line.
2. Connect some compound concepts: *brother-in-law, know-it-all.*
3. Connect some compound modifiers: *student-centered program, fast-sailing ship, four-cylinder engine.*
4. Connect prefixes to some words (emphasize the prefix): *post-op-erative, self-educated.*
5. Connect compound numbers between twenty-one and ninety-nine: *twenty-one, ninety-nine, one hundred thirty-five.*
   Note: like commas, there is some debate about when and what to hyphenate. Look up particular words in a current dictionary to be absolutely certain. Note too that a writer may hyphenate whenever she wishes to create a special emphasis in a word or phrase.

PARENTHESES [( )]

1. Set off explanatory material the author does not consider neces-sary to understand the basic meaning of the sentence: *In 1929 (the year the stock market crashed) he proposed to his first wife.* (The same information set off by commas would be considered more essential to the sentence.)
2. Allow an author to use a double voice and comment about her subject from a different perspective, often ironic: *Parentheses allow an author to comment on his text from an ironic per-spective (whatever that means).*
3. Enclose numbers and clarifying information about numbers and acronyms in a sentence: *forty-seven (47), NFL (National Football League).*

PERIODS [.]

1. End sentences. Bring readers to a full stop. Period. (Is used the same way with full sentences or deliberate sentence fragments.)

2. Indicate abbreviations in formal *(Dr., Jr.)* and informal *(abrv., esp.)* writing.

QUESTION MARKS [?]

1. Indicate that a question has been asked: *What do you want?*
2. Indicate an author's uncertainty: *(Sp?)*

QUOTATION MARKS [" "]

1. Enclose direct quotations: *"What's for dessert?" she asked.*
2. Enclose words or phrases borrowed from others: *It really was "the best of times," wasn't it?*
3. Enclose titles of poems, stories, articles, songs, chapters, TV programs: *Who wrote the poem, "To an Athlete Dying Young"? Faulkner's "Barn Burning" is ultimately a comic story. My favorite chapter in this book is "Finding Your Voice."*
   Note: to indicate a quotation within a quotation, use single marks (' ') instead of double: *"She said 'It really isn't necessary,' but that didn't stop him long."*

SEMICOLONS [;]

1. Can be used in place of a period when you want to imply a close relationship to the following sentence; *here that's what I want to imply.*
2. Replace commas in a series of phrases when the phrases include commas: *Considering the circumstances, it is dangerous to run, when you can walk; talk, when you can listen; and read, when you can write.*
   Note: semicolons are most frequently used in quite formal language; they are especially common in prose before the twentieth century; academics are fond of them since they imply formal relationships and make sentences long—and long sentences appear to be more intellectually rigorous; whether they are more rigorous or simply more ponderous is a question for you to decide.

ITALICS [UNDERLINING]

1. Indicate special emphasis in typed and handwritten papers: *He was very careful to underline all the examples, except this one.*
2. Indicate the titles of published works, including books, movies, albums/tapes/CDs, and collections of articles, stories, poems, and

essays: <u>*For Whom the Bell Tolls*</u> *is a novel by Ernest Hemingway.*
Only a few successful plays; such as <u>*The Sound of Music,*</u> *also*
become successful movies. My favorite tape is <u>*Bruce Live.*</u> *The*
story "Burning" can be found in <u>*The Portable Faulkner.*</u>

3. Indicate words and letters being referred to as words and letters:
   Is the correct word to indicate a struggle <u>*founder*</u> *or* <u>*flounder?*</u>
   The letter <u>*x*</u> *is the least used letter in the alphabet, isn't it?*

Index